Doubt and
Identity in
Romantic
Poetry

Doubt and Identity in Romantic Poetry

Andrew M. Cooper

Yale University Press

New Haven and London

A version of chapter 3 appeared in *Studies in Romanticism* 20 (1981):85–110 and is reproduced here courtesy of the Trustees of Boston University.
A portion of chapter 6 appeared in the *Keats-Shelley Journal* 32 (1983):63–80 and is reproduced here courtesy of the Keats-Shelley Association of America, Inc.

Designed by Jo Aerne and set in Sabon type by Keystone Typesetting, Orwigsburg, PA. Printed in the United States of America by Book Crafters, Inc., Chelsea, MI.

Library of Congress Cataloging-in-Publication Data
Cooper, Andrew M., 1953–
Doubt and identity in romantic poetry.
Includes index.
1. English poetry—19th century—History and criticism.   2. Romanticism—England.   3. Belief and doubt in literature.   4. Skepticism in literature.   5. Identity (Psychology) in literature.
6. Narrative poetry, English—History and criticism.   7. Philosophy in literature.   I. Title.
PR575.B44C66 1988   821'.7'09145
87–10651
ISBN 0–300–04004–0 (alk. paper)

The paper in this book meets the guidelines for permanence and durability of the Committee on Production Guidelines for Book Longevity of the Council on Library Resources.

10 9 8 7 6 5 4 3 2 1

To the memory of Jonathan Grandine

. . . for axioms in philosophy are not axioms until they are proved upon our pulses: We read fine things but never feel them to the full until we have gone the same steps as the Author.
—Keats, letter to Reynolds of
May 3, 1818

Contents

Acknowledgments

"But who shall parcel out / His intellect by geometric rules, / . . . / Who that shall point as with a wand and say / 'This portion of the river of my mind / Came from yon fountain?' " Poets know better, but critics must try to say—preferably briefly. My greatest debt is to Karl Kroeber, who directed my Ph.D. dissertation too long a time ago, and also Carl Woodring. This book, such as it is, would not have existed without their scholarship, enthusiasm, and example. I'm also grateful in various ways to Edward Tayler and Martin Elsky.

More recently, Kurt Heinzelman and Walt Reed shouldered the brunt of the first draft and suggested numerous revisions from the grammatical to the ideological. Thanks likewise to Joan Lidoff and Bill Worthen for advice and comments, and especially to Brad Mudge, to whom I am oxygen-indebted for much running commentary some six to ten miles in length. One simply could not wish for colleagues more generous and incisive than these. A version of chapter 3 appeared in *Studies in Romanticism*, and a large part of chapter 6 appeared in the *Keats-Shelley Journal*; my thanks to the editors of these journals for permission to reprint. The University of Texas at Austin gave me a Summer Research Award at a crucial juncture. I should also mention the anonymous reader for Yale University Press, who made several particularly probing, and probably still unanswered, criticisms of the manuscript (let them, too, remain anonymous). As editor, Ellen Graham has piloted the manuscript into print with much more efficiency than a procrastinator deserves.

Harder than all these to specify is the different sort of debt I owe my college History & Lit. tutor named in the dedication.

Introduction

The premise of this book is that eighteenth-century sensationalist psychology produced two quite different forms of doubt which it distinguished only imperfectly. My argument is that much Romantic poetry strives to explore and demonstrate in concrete human terms the final irrelevancy of the one and the urgent necessity of the other.

First, there is the philosophical suspension of belief in the existence of an external physical world. A prime feature of such material-object skepticism is its paradoxical nature. From Sextus Empiricus to Hume, its proponents have always admitted it is a sheerly intellectual doubt that cannot actually be "lived"[1] except at the cost of paralysis and ultimately, as Hume himself says, death from starvation and exposure. Then there is skepticism about the reality of other minds. Unlike the first, this kind of doubt cannot be dismissed on practical grounds, because in an intersubjective relationship it is impossible finally to separate what is immediate and needful—my love for you, say—from what is merely passive conjecture—my supposition that you are seeing another man. The supposition may be groundless, an empty abstract possibility, but the jealousy it generates can become just as compelling as the original love, perhaps more so. As Friedrich Schlegel sees, intersubjectivity subsumes external exigencies in an endless ironic regress. The reason for this is simply that, unlike inanimate objects, another person is capable of mirroring—or of seeming to mirror—one's own consciousness. Whatever doubts one has of the other, she is equally liable to have of oneself. Skepticism toward other minds therefore does really affect how we experience our lives. Let me put the contrast more simply. Whether I like it or not, my concern that you are dissimulating or lying to me becomes an inescapable part of our relationship. Even if I suppress any change in my outward behavior, my doubt is bound to affect my attitude toward you and hence, in some measure, yours of me; whereas only if I'm crazy will my inability to demonstrate the necessity of tomorrow's sunrise prevent me from setting the alarm clock tonight.

Indeed, craziness, the poets show—the craziness of solipsism—is the likely consequence of confusing together these two different doubts. To forgo all interpretive questioning of the physical and verbal expressions by which another person discloses her private thoughts and feelings denies not only *her* otherness but, if the relationship is still at all reciprocal, also one's own. The result is a deluded sense of omnipotence undercut by the paranoid suspicion that others can read, even control one's innermost secret thoughts. Thus the irony of such egotism is that it is accompanied by powerlessness and insensibility, a loss of self. Unable to acknowledge and repossess his self-projections, the solipsist views people, including himself, as objects and views objects animistically as extensions of himself. For the Romantics, the source of such errors is the intellectual's typical overvaluing of consciousness. In the words of Alfred North Whitehead, consciousness, "the supreme vividness of experience," is what makes us human— but it does not make us exist. Our struggle to reacknowledge the body's role in supplying the ground of consciousness, and indeed of all fully human relationships, is the common theme of the narratives I investigate.

Of course, there is nothing *inherently* redemptive about the body. It, too, can be the locus of pain and loss, as the merest glance at Coleridge's life shows. I have no wish to purvey the now-discredited intuitive connection between texts and what F. R. Leavis tended to call "felt experience" or "life as it is lived"—honorifics whose pleonastic form is now generally recognized to conceal a specific critical ideology—as if what I am terming "human relationship" and "concrete human life" were necessary imperatives to be drawn from a purely textual logic. But if the symbolist idea of an unmediated, transparent language is a fallacy, so is its opposite, the deconstructionist idea of a purely indeterminate, unmotivated language. (Indeed, now that it has become the new critical orthodoxy, "dissemination," the Derridean "free-play" of signifiers, at times looks disturbingly like the New Critical "ambiguity" it supplanted.)[2] The common assumption of the poems in question is not that physical experience is always exhilarating but that alienation from one's body—pains and all—and also from the realm of the bodily and from the processes of embodiment in general is always damaging. For what substantiates the Romantic imagination is the body's enhanced capacity for self-extension in the world. One way of achieving such self-extension is through a poem, where the relationship between form and content can be seen to parallel the relationship between the author's (and, less directly, the reader's) body and soul.[3]

In his exposé of contemporary criticism's absorption in a range of Romantic self-representations, Jerome McGann argues that "the poetic response to the age's severe political and social dislocations was to reach for solutions in the realm of ideas[,] . . . to define human problems in ideal and spiritual terms. To characterize the Romantic Period as one marked by an 'epistemological crisis' is to follow Romanticism's own definition of its historical problems."[4] Of course, as McGann himself stresses, neither the Romantic imagination nor the Romantic concept of Imagination was uniformly escapist. Indeed, Romantic skeptical idealism arises largely as an effort to grasp how epistemological doubts about the existence of the material world tend to emerge as a defensive displacement of personal doubts about the self. The Romantics seek to resolve self-doubt partly by emphasizing the speciousness of this displacement, so explaining it away, but mainly by demonstrating how the self is a synthetic construct that comes into existence through its relationship with a defining Other (thus reader and writer can be cocreators of each other). They then complete the demonstration by showing the contradictory nature of the attempt to conceive of the self in material-object terms as something fixed and external to one's own experience.

As I said, the Romantic resolution of doubt through moral-performative acts of love or imagination is in no sense prescribed by text or language, any more than is the Humean resolution of doubt by a naturalist argument of somatic-performative behavior. This is why the Romantic poet strives like Blake to repossess and internalize his poetic narrative through a culminating act of insight into its overall unity and that of the self expressed therein; or if his skepticism about the possibility of genuine self-expression makes this impossible, why like Shelley he sacrifices himself that the reader might become able to perform such a repossession. Admittedly, seeing *Alastor*, for example, as an allegory of the reader's possible redemption through love is not *entailed* by the text, nor do I offer this reading as a strict deduction that should replace the more familiar view of the poem as a parable of the inevitably negative end of narcissism. The poem accommodates both readings with no need to reconcile the contraries. Yet for this very reason, it forces us to confront why, both readings being equally valid, we would prefer the one tending to disempower rather than invigorate us. And this, I would point out, is a psychological and applicative, not a purely rhetorical question; as soon as we ask it, we begin to move off the page, relinquishing the shelter of the textual enclosure for the intractable world of contingency in separation from which all wars of intellect are merely academic.[5]

Thus, to reject the deconstructionist celebration of undecidability is not necessarily to embrace an even more insular Romantic ideology of the transcendent imagination. There exist a number of major Romantic narrative poems that actually dramatize the process of representation by which their epistemological crisis is brought before the reader. They do so by repeating a single basic plot line in a series of different, increasingly immediate narrative styles. The model for this process is the movement in *Paradise Lost* "from shadowy types to truth," whereby the more or less inconceivable supernatural events and characters of the opening books eventually give way to a demonstration of the Fall's direct relevance to the reader's life; but in case "immediacy" and "directness" appear to beg the epistemological question, let me point out that I use these terms to denote a context-determined poetic effect rather than any specific represented content or style of representation. So, for example, the shock of *Christabel*'s ending and the exultation of *Milton*'s are products of a mounting naturalism whereby themes hitherto presented in an overtly oblique and fictive manner are finally seen to pertain to one's own world; but conversely the pathos of *Alastor*'s ending and the horror that closes out the shipwreck episode in *Don Juan* spring from a gradual abandonment of naturalism for a phenomenalistic portrayal of events from the protagonists' more and more clearly subjective, even delirious viewpoints. The technique of repeating subnarratives elicits a mounting awareness of the poem's textuality which then works to counter the escapist tendencies of the Romantic imagination. The repetitions yield ironies, but of a sort associated with the native British tradition of empiricism rather than with the transcendental idealism of German theorists such as Schlegel. For the irony is always controlled by an urgent awareness of temporality and contingency; it belongs to what Mary Jacobus, following Paul de Man, has termed "the language of temporality, a means of structuring the self in time."[6]

For the poet, this awareness of temporality comprises, ultimately, a recognition of his own mortality, which is found to be not only ineluctable but inexpressible, inasmuch as its only authentic expression is, precisely, his own life. For the reader, it involves the parallel realization that since reading literally takes time, it is an experience not essentially different from the rest of life; so far from sanctioning escapism, the poems force one to reconfront the world through the retrospective discovery of the total form of their multiple subnarratives. Closure is not predetermined by the poet but results from a merely provisional act of totalization by the reader. In other words, the poems do not contain their own closure in objectified fashion; on the contrary, they achieve closure only through a progressive, self-subverting emphasis on the actual, temporal basis of their existence as fictions. One closes the poem by seeing how it threatens to usurp one's existence in a thoroughly nontextual world, the disclosure and enrichment of which is, finally, the poem's raison d'être. Of course, the narrative has been arranged to elicit this crisis and to do so at the very end, so there is a kind of symbiosis or preestablished harmony between it and the reader's experience. Yet this in no way diminishes the authenticity of that experience. Quite the reverse, the poets' point is that reading being a moral activity, one cannot interpret without taking responsibility; ultimately, therefore, it is up to the reader to validate his reading in what Wordsworth deems "the very world, which is the world / Of all of us,—the place where, in the end, / We find our happiness, or not at all!"[7]

As you may already suspect, I am much indebted to reader-response theory, and particularly Stanley Fish's *Self-Consuming Artifacts*. But whereas such criticism views reading as per se a logocentric activity whose ultimate aim is a full recovery of textual meaning, so that reader-response procedures ought to be applicable to any and all texts, my own claims are more periodized. The Romantic narrative poems I examine do not merely tolerate a reader-response approach the way most texts do—including those the Romantics were reacting against, such as Hume's *Treatise of Human Nature*—they positively demand it if they are to be grasped on even the simplest level as anything more than an incoherent sequence of discrete episodes. This study began with the perception that *Milton*, *Christabel*, and *Alastor* do not make narrative sense if approached any *other* way (*Don Juan* is a partial exception: the shipwreck and cannibalism of Canto II are depicted coherently, indeed graphically, but they don't make *moral* sense except via reader response).

This distinction explains why I apply reader-response methods to one form of writing, Romantic poetry, but not another, Humean philosophy. Might the opposition I see between them merely reflect my own inconsistency, derived from the specious assumption that poetry possesses a special "literariness" which distinguishes it absolutely from philosophy's essentially unliterary striving after a preverbal, perfectly transparent truth? The objection gains strength from John J. Richetti's recent *Philosophical Writing: Locke, Berkeley, Hume*, which persuasively extends a reader-response approach to these writers:

> All three make the philosophical text a special kind of event that calls attention to its own inadequacy and lack of transparency. . . . The relationship closest to hand for them as writers is that provided by their own text, that which obtains between ideas and words, between writer and writing, and between reader and writing. . . . What Derrida identifies as the secret duplicity of philosophy, these writers exploit as an inherent irony and a literary pleasure in empirical philosophizing.[8]

And yet Richetti acknowledges that "neither Locke nor Berkeley is interested in representing rather than signifying his thought, neither presents his books with the possibility that they are as much persuasive enactment as compelling argument. Rather, those tendencies are inevitable adjuncts of their writing" (p. 39). Hume, of course, discloses much greater rhetorical awareness, but Richetti specifically rejects the view that "the intellectual and moral melodrama" of Hume's thought reflects a " 'metaphysical agony.' " Such a view, he says, overlooks the comic, even theatrical aspects of Hume's irony, "where the reader's anticipation of actual solutions is never really an issue, where a supervising tone prepares us for what are actually mock surprises, and where the artificial disappointments of philosophical inquiry, as Hume stages it, are nothing less than moral-rhetorical consolations" (p. 195). I quite agree; but this means that the "extended passage through uncertainty" in Book I of the *Treatise* and Hume's "commitment to movement" generally (p. 200) are reader responsive only in the relatively passive way of most conventional representational narratives. Ensconced at a comfortable distance from the action, the reader spectates at the pratfalls and perplexities of the author's persona: "Unlike Kierkegaard's subversive ironist, Hume's persona in the *Treatise* is ready to protect himself and his audience with a literary manner that invokes as a consoling constant the intrinsic and absolute limitations of human understanding" (p. 196). By contrast, the reader's involvement in the Romantic narrative poems I examine is much more bewilderingly direct and constructive, precisely because there is no consoling awareness of a fixed and stable author manipulating his persona from behind the scenes. Even if you accept the premise of much reader-response criticism that the author who has arranged this bewilderment still exists "in" the text, my point remains that in these poems we are aware of him only as a confused presence whose identity is not preestablished but emerges in symbiosis with our own progressive journey through the narrative. The strong reciprocity I claim to find between Romantic poet and reader is, I would argue, a peculiarly Romantic phenomenon, not simply a way of reading any and all texts but a way certain texts ask to be read.

Two more remarks about my method. In several places I have relied, largely for descriptive rather than analytical purposes, on the pronouncements of Alfred North Whitehead, a figure not much in fashion these days. Not only is Whitehead's sensibility steeped in much the same Protestant dissenting tradition as were the poets, but his doctrines are intended to resolve the same inconsistencies in Locke and especially Hume as the Romantics were themselves struggling to work through. Second: if the pursuit of literature tends to seduce the writer from his sources of inspiration in immediate, particularized experience, as the Romantics often thought, then literary criticism should avoid the doubly insipid error of seducing the reader from its inspiration, literature. Thus much of the discussion that follows is close reading. If the poems discussed seem an exceedingly diverse group, this only underscores, mutatis mutandis, the basic similarity of their method, which leads cumulatively through doubtful confusion to a final crystallization of awareness, if not in the protagonist then at least in the reader. No doubt I've succeeded well enough in crafting the first of these effects. May my book yield the other one as well!

Repetition and Realization
in Locke, Hume, and Shelley

I think Poetry should surprise by a fine excess and not by
Singularity—it should strike the Reader as a wording of his
own highest thoughts, and appear almost a Remembrance.
                    Keats, letter to Taylor of February 27, 1818

David Hume's *Treatise of Human Nature* begins by contending that our knowledge of reality is limited entirely to private, hence unverifiable perceptions: "Let us fix our attention out of ourselves as much as possible: let us chace our imagination to the heavens, or to the utmost limits of the universe; we never really advance a step beyond ourselves, nor can conceive any kind of existence, but those perceptions, which have appear'd in that narrow compass."[1] For Milton, such self-confinement is tantamount to perdition: "Which way I fly is Hell; myself am hell," despairs Satan,[2] whose pride steadily leads him through introspective isolation to nihilism. The atheistic Hume, on the other hand, would coolly ascribe Satan's reaction to mere subjective attitude; whether our confinement elicits complacency or claustrophobia depends in the above passage entirely on how we feel about "ourselves." And yet "ourselves" turn out to be illusory. Like Berkeley, Hume denies the existence of an ulterior "material substratum" which Locke, following the scientists, had postulated as a cohesive underlying support for the various sensible "qualities" (color, hardness, sound, and so on) by means of which each mind subjectively interprets reality. Compelled as a result to regard perceptions as atomized "distinct existences" which are "distinct and separable, and may be consider'd as separately existent, and may exist separately, and have no need of any thing else to support their existence" (*THN*, p. 233), Hume notoriously discovers that personal identity as we habitually imagine it does not exist: "mankind . . . are nothing but a bundle or collection of different perceptions, which succeed one another with an inconceivable rapidity, and are in a perpetual flux and movement" (*THN*, p. 252).

Hume admits that practically speaking his finding is, like most epistemology, academic. Common everyday experience, in alliance with the mind's innate predisposition to associate ideas not causally connected— an alliance he variously calls "custom," "feeling," or "habit"—continues to sanction the belief that we do in fact possess an organized self. Nevertheless, Hume's finding is bound to unsettle our ethics, predicated as they are on the integrity if not the inviolability of personal identity—other people's if not our own. If there exists no definite "idea or impression of self," then what becomes of moral responsibility or even conscience as enjoined by the Delphic "know thyself"? Are we doomed to the self-withdrawal of the late Coleridge, who repudiates his lifelong glorification of "the heaven-descended 'Know thyself'" through which, he had affirmed, we shall "know God, as far as is permitted to a creature, and in God all things," and in the poem "Self-Knowledge" asks derisively: "What is there in thee, Man, that can be known?— / Dark fluxion, all unfixable by thought, / A phantom dim of past and future wrought, / . . . / Ignore thyself, and strive to know thy God!"[3]—an admonition that looks like an abandonment of metaphysics altogether? For if we cannot know ourselves, how can we possibly know anybody else, much less God? As these questions go to show, doubting the self leads, ironically, to self-preoccupation. Must we therefore suffer the fate of Rousseau in Shelley's *The Triumph of Life*, who instead of seeking acquaintance with the mysterious female "form all light" demanded only answers to himself— "Shew whence I came, and where I am, and why"[4]—and withered in the end to a solitary tree stump?

Not necessarily. In a well-known passage that Shelley's Rousseau echoes, even the relentless Hume tells when to leave off philosophizing and revert to ordinary life:

> Where am I, or what? From what causes do I derive my existence, and to what condition shall I return? . . . I am confounded with all these questions, and begin to fancy myself in the most deplorable condition imaginable, inviron'd with the deepest darkness, and utterly depriv'd of the use of every member and faculty.
>
> Most fortunately it happens, that since reason is incapable of dispelling these clouds, nature herself suffices to that purpose, and cures me of this philosophical melancholy and delirium, either by relaxing this bent of mind, or by some avocation, and lively impression of the senses, which obliterates all these chimeras. I dine, I play a game of back-gammon, and am merry with my friends. [*THN*, p. 269]

Conviviality solves Hume's philosophical perplexities, but of course only in the most unphilosophical way. As A. D. Nuttall points out, "the clouds which Nature drives away are not identical with those called up by Reason, but are rather their emotive shadows. . . . A change of mood is not an argument."[5] Hume confronts a paradox: it is true that he lacks a deducible self, but it is equally true that he cannot live with this truth about himself. These difficulties he surmounts through the even greater paradox of being quite forthright about evading them, thereby appealing for a more profoundly "philosophical" acceptance of human irrationality than academic skepticism permits. The true skeptic, he claims in Pyrrhonian fashion, is a pragmatist who escapes the self-contradictions of dogmatic skepticism by setting his doubt in perspective and discerning the limiting rationalism behind it: "I may, nay I must yield to the current of nature, in submitting to my senses and understanding; and in this blind submission I shew most perfectly my sceptical disposition and principles. . . . Nay if we are philosophers, it ought only to be upon sceptical principles, and from an inclination, which we feel to the employing ourselves after that manner" (*THN*, pp. 269–70). Here Hume's periodic need of rest from the exigencies of philosophic introspection is itself elevated into a philosophical principle. Thus the true skeptic is consistent in his inconsistency. If he appears capricious in comparison to his academic counterpart, the reason is that he acknowledges himself a man first and a philosopher only second. Among the swarm of moods and desires making up empirical experience, he sees that the impulse to philosophize is but one, and by no means the most important.

So far, we can agree with Norman Kemp Smith's interpretation of Hume as a naturalist.[6] Revising the traditional picture of Hume as a destructive skeptic, Kemp Smith claimed that it is based on a distortion. Philosophers have focused too exclusively on the pulverizing Book I of the *Treatise,* ignoring the constructive moral arguments of Books II and III which spring from the earlier epistemological crisis and may be sloganized in Hume's pronouncement, "Reason is, and ought only to be the slave of the passions" (*THN*, p. 415). Construing "passions" as "natural beliefs" in general, Kemp Smith contends that Hume's assertion is a positive one because it provides a causal theory of how belief is determined not by reason but by feeling, instinct, custom, and habit. Hume's reduction of knowledge to a psychologically conditioned "sentiment of belief" in Book I of the *Treatise* is intended to pave the way for these comforting moral surrogates in Books II and III.

Nevertheless, if reason remains forever cut off from the real, it is hard to see how certain sentiments are to be judged more valid than others. Viewed empirically, they are all sheer facts of experience, all equally part of "the way we see things." To discover that the basis of morality is not rational but sentimental—"So that when you pronounce any action or character to be vicious, you mean nothing, but that from the constitution of your nature you have a feeling or sentiment of blame from the contemplation of it" (*THN*, p. 469)—is to give up seeking a justification for ethical opinions in favor of merely explaining them in psychological terms.

And so the very empiricism Hume uses destructively to clear the ground for his system of morals finally deprives that system of any ground at all. Strictly considered, Hume never resolves the "philosophical melancholy" that overtakes him in his study toward the end of Book I; he just ignores it. Far from healing the rift that opens there between Hume the skeptical intellectual and Hume the convivial man of feeling—a rift ultimately between mind and body—the comparative laxness and conventionality of the arguments of Books II and III, whose influence in the history of philosophy has always been eclipsed by the powerful analyses of Book I, rather reemphasizes that sentiment cannot actually answer epistemological questions; it is only *felt* to do so.[7]

In modern philosophy, this rift between mind and body is generally attributed to Descartes—one of whose purposes was, however, to vindicate religion from atheistic Pyrrhonians such as Hume.[8] Now, it is true that Hume, like Locke, rejects the Cartesian *cogito* and its accompanying religious doctrine of innate ideas. But this important difference should not be permitted to obscure an even more fundamental similarity in the two men's thought. Both tend to conceive of the self in substance-oriented terms derived ultimately from Aristotle. His disdain for Descartes and the medieval Scholastics notwithstanding, Hume's notion of fully autonomous perceptions, each "a distinct and separate existent," fully suits Descartes's axiom that only "clear and distinct" ideas are true. Hume assumes no less than Descartes that the self is not a synthetic construct but must be either preexistent or else nonexistent. Descartes chooses the first alternative, Hume the second, but they both embrace the traditional paradigm of the necessary separation of our immortal soul from our perishable flesh. Simply, Hume's sensationalism forces him to recognize that such a separation precludes ever ascertaining the soul's existence.

I

In this crisis Romanticism begins—begins, however, in reversion to just those empirical elements in Hume and especially Locke which tend to resist reduction, appearing in their systems chiefly as a fertile source of inconsistencies. Indeed, Hume's sensationalism represents not so much a development of Locke's thought as a departure. As Dugald Stewart later emphasized in a number of influential works, there is much in Locke that is absolutely incompatible with sensationalism.[9] Take, for example, Locke's doctrine of "power":

> The mind being every day informed, by the senses, of the alteration of those simple ideas it observes in things without . . . and observing a constant change of its ideas, . . . and concluding, from what it has so con-

stantly observed to have been, that the like changes will for the future be made in the same things, by like agents, and by the like ways,—considers in one thing the possibility of having any of its simple ideas changed, and in another the possibility of making that change; and so comes by that idea which we call *power*. Thus we say, Fire has a power to melt gold . . . and gold has a power to be melted. . . . In which, and the like cases, the power we consider is in reference to the change of perceivable ideas. . . . Power thus considered is two-fold, viz. as able to make, or able to receive any change. The one may be called *active*, and the other *passive* power. . . . I confess power includes in it some kind of *relation*, (a relation to action or change,) as indeed which of our ideas, of what kind soever, when attentively considered, does not? For, our ideas of extension, dura- tion, and number, do they not all contain in them a secret relation of the parts? Figure and motion have something relative in them much more vis- ibly. And sensible qualities, as colours and smells, &c., what are they but the powers of different bodies in relation to our perception, &c.? . . . Our idea therefore of power, I think, may well have a place amongst other simple ideas, and be considered as one of them; being one of those that make a principal ingredient in our complex ideas of substances, as we shall hereafter have occasion to observe.[10]

"Power" is here explicitly said to be a relative idea, yet one that plays a principal role in our idea of substance. It would seem then that our idea of substance is also relative. In fact, Locke distinctly suggests that "sub- stance" is a function of our perceptual relationship with the object, of our "passive" power to objectify the object in the unified organization of our ideas about it, and of the object's "active" power to achieve such ingres- sion in us. On much the same grounds, Coleridge was to reject Descartes's "absolute and essential heterogeneity of the soul as intelligence, and the body as matter. . . . For since impenetrability is intelligible only as a mode of resistance; its admission places the essence of *matter* in an act or power, which it possesses in common with *spirit*; and body and spirit . . . *may* without any *absurdity* be supposed to be different modes, or degrees in perfection, of a common substratum" (*BL* 1:129–30). Indeed, later in the *Essay* Locke writes that "there is scarce any particular thing existing, which, in some of its simple ideas, does not communicate with a greater, and in others with a less, number of particular beings" (2:113–14). In other words, two beings, each with the same simple ideas as the other, are conceived as sharing those ideas in the form of a communication between them. The moral implications of this notion look toward the eighteenth- century doctrine of "sympathy." But in Hume and Adam Smith, sympathy remains essentially dualistic: the self mentally puts itself in the other's place by representing the other to itself through an inner image based not on their mutual involvement but on the processes of association described in the skeptical Book I of the *Treatise*. In contrast, Locke would evidently allow "communication" to operate at both the moral and epistemological levels. For him, beings do not feel *for* one another by privately representing one another's ideas or impressions—a process obviously vulnerable to the charge of solipsism. Rather, they feel *with* and *as* one another because each is already actually implicated in what the other feels, insofar as each is aware of the other at all.

In Locke's wide use of the term *idea* to include at one time or another practically all the operations of mind, one sees a characteristic looseness which makes his metaphysics less consistent than Hume's but closer to the multifarious, mixed nature of empirical experience. Hume's inconsistencies are fewer but more disturbing. For instance, Hume's chief contribution to philosophical thought was, he proudly declared, the analysis of Lockean "ideas" into two distinct kinds of perception, primary sensory "impressions" and secondary "ideas," which are "the faint images of these [impressions] in thinking and reasoning" (*THN*, p. 1). This point is established at the outset of the *Treatise* and is basic to it. And yet the distinction is less analytical than categorical; for although the relationship between impressions and ideas plainly is one of derivation, Hume observes only the sheer fact of their difference, which he says consists in an impression's greater "degree of force and vivacity."

The processive or immanent nature of experience is further eviscerated when Hume goes on to explain the development of "simple ideas" into "complex" ones:

> Were ideas entirely loose and unconnected, chance alone would join them; and 'tis impossible the same simple ideas should fall regularly into complex ones (as they commonly do) without some bond of union between them, some associating quality, by which some idea naturally introduces another . . . , nature in a manner pointing out to every one those simple ideas, which are most proper to be united into a complex one. [*THN*, pp. 10–11]

Comments Alfred North Whitehead,

> Hume can find only one standard of propriety, and that is, *repetition* . . . the frequency of ideas following upon the frequency of their correlate impressions is also attended by an expectation of the repetition of the impression. Hume also believes, without any reason he can assign, that this expectation is pragmatically justified. It is this pragmatic justification, without metaphysical reason, which constitutes the propriety attaching to "repetition."[11]

In positing as he does the individual independence of successive perceptions, Hume can find no temporal relationship between them but mere
serial order. In order for the repetition of a simple impression to produce a
complex idea, much less a self-conscious idea of the repetition itself, the
repeated impression would have to be different from the original; it would
have to be accompanied by a further impression of repetition able to
produce the *expectation* of repetition and the *habit* of expectation. Yet
Hume in rejecting knowledge of "necessary connexion" (that is, causation) explicitly asserts:

> From the mere repetition of any past impression, even to infinity, there
> never will arise any new original idea, such as that of a necessary connex-
> ion; and the number of impressions has in this case no more effect than if
> we confin'd ourselves to one only. . . . The only connexion or relation of
> objects, which can lead us beyond the immediate impressions of our
> memory and senses, is that of cause and effect; and that because 'tis the
> only one, on which we can found a just inference from one object to an-
> other. The idea of cause and effect is deriv'd from *experience*, which in-
> forms us, that such particular objects, in all past instances, have been
> constantly conjoined with each other. [*THN*, pp. 88–90]

In other words, since the manner of connection we call "cause and effect"
is not actually given in any particular impression, any more than "self" is
given in any impression, Hume traces the idea to a repetition of impressions arising from "experience." Nevertheless, in doing so he contradicts
his premise that repetition of impressions cannot ever produce "any new
idea." According to the premise, we should have no more idea of repetition, expectation, or habit than we do of necessary connection. And in that
case our ideas must in fact be, as Hume feared earlier, "entirely loose and
unconnected," joined by "chance alone."

Our analysis has demonstrated only what one would expect prima
facie. If every perception is an irreducible "distinct existence," then strictly
speaking perceptions can never repeat at all. Hume avoids this conclusion
only because, despite his repudiation of the Cartesian ego, he always
tacitly presupposes that perceptions are what the mind knows about itself
and hence can be considered as qualities attaching to a prior subject. But, it
will be objected, doesn't Hume after all reject the notion of "mind,"
declaring it to be "nothing but a bundle or collection of different perceptions"? Yes, but Hume's whole reason for positing "some bond of union
between [ideas], some associating quality" is to explain why actual *experience* usually makes sense, why as a matter of empirical fact life is not
ordinarily felt to be a phantasmagoria or perpetual delirium. Thus it seems

the notion of mind that Hume rejects is merely the superficial one he himself has been expounding.

Whitehead and his student W. J. Bate have shown how associationist psychologizing of the later eighteenth century was methodically groping toward a nondualistic view of concrete physical experience as providing a meeting ground of the self and the external world.[12] The traditional Aristotelian conception of the self as a fixed immutable "substance" was to be overturned. In the words of Abraham Tucker's *Light of Nature Pursued* (1760), whose combination of arcane theology and philosophical common sense set an example for Blake, "an act of the understanding is not so much our own proper act as the act of something else operating upon us."[13] It is his attraction toward the nondualistic position that explains how the young Coleridge could embrace the necessitarianism of William Godwin, later a mentor to the atheistic young Shelley, while at the same time preparing himself in all conscience to enter the ministry. Although Godwin's enlightened rationalism and rigid utilitarian ethic are inimical to piety such as Tucker's, like Tucker Godwin repudiates the Scholastic "distinction between the intellectual and the active powers of the mind," asking: "What indeed is preference, but a feeling of something that really inheres, or is supposed to inhere, in the objects themselves?"[14] The experiential thrust of the question becomes obvious if one considers that by "preference" Godwin means choice or free will, the very faculty Milton had identified with man's godlike autonomy from the fallen object-world (for God is reason, and "reason is but choosing").[15] Likewise, it seems the main appeal for Shelley of Sir William Drummond's *Academical Questions* was its support for construing the Humean "stream of associations" as a direct flowing of physical reality into the self in the manner of the opening stanza of "Mont Blanc," quite in spite of the skeptical sensationalism of Hume himself.[16] Tucker epitomizes the nondualistic position when he attacks Locke on empirical grounds for having

> placed our existence in a quality rather than a substance, for by the term Consciousness I cannot understand a Being, but only a power or property of some Being, nor do I apprehend a man loses his existence or personality every time he loses his consciousness, by falling fast asleep [as Hume is driven to assert in *THN*, p. 252]. . . . The only way remaining in which I can understand an identity of consciousness, is by placing it in the consciousness of the same person, in which light the idea of person must precede that of consciousness. . . . Whence we may justly conclude perceptivity and activity to be primary qualities, essential to the substances possessing them, inseparable therefrom, belonging to individuals, and not producible by any combination whatsoever of imperceptive and inactive ingredients. [1:17]

From these proto-Romantic suggestions Coleridge later draws the high Romantic inference: "intelligence is a self-developement, not a quality supervening to a substance" (*BL* 1:286).

Accordingly, our aim in Romantic narrative poetry is repossession of the rational consciousness that representational narrative takes for granted. The poems this book examines are forms of "practical activity" in Hegel's sense: "man as mind . . . is *for* himself, perceives himself, has ideas of himself, thinks himself, and thus is active self-realizedness. This consciousness of himself man obtains . . . for himself by *practical* activity, inasmuch as he has the impulse, in the medium which is directly given to him, to produce himself, and therein at the same time to recognize himself."[17] As we shall see, these poems strive not simply to represent but to lay bare before the reader the nexus of visceral feelings, intimations, and expectations (what Tucker calls "perceptivity and activity") aroused in him by the act of reading. Hume's inability to "catch *myself*" within "the perpetual flux and movement . . . of different perceptions" (*THN*, p. 252) is no cause for alarm, the authors show, because self is not, as Hume believes, a fixed entity that must either preexist perception or else not exist at all. Quite the contrary, the self constructed in Romantic narrative poetry emerges as the provisional outcome of a continuously evolving welter of perceptivity. It is merely the surface tip of the vaster underlying iceberg—or rather volcano—of immediate preconscious experience.

If the Romantic "poetry of experience" entails discovering in objects the promises and potencies we have already brought to them, as Robert Langbaum suggested,[18] it would seem the dialectical principle behind the discovery is repetition-with-a-difference. The expressive form of this principle is the spiral that M. H. Abrams sees to characterize "the Greater Romantic Lyric" whereby the poem returns to its starting point only on a new level. Whitehead's summary of his own "organic philosophy" aptly describes the axioms of Romantic narrative poetry: both posit "that experience involves a *becoming*, that *becoming* means that *something becomes*, and that *what becomes* involves *repetition* transformed into *novel immediacy*" (pp. 136–37). Or in Keats's phrase, "Nothing ever becomes real till it is experienced."[19] Hume's neglect of the immanent aspect of experience, its becoming-ness, is most conspicuous in his doctrine of memory, which he explicitly declares to be the sole "source of personal identity" (*THN*, p. 261). Hampered by his sensationalism, Hume simply sorts perceptions into three classes according to "force and vivacity": impressions, memories, ideas. The essential interdependence of all three in any act of recollection—that is, the dynamic whereby an impression repeated in memory preserves its pastness within the novel idea—is overlooked: "the memory is known, neither by the order of its *complex* ideas, nor the nature of its *simple* ones; it follows, that the difference betwixt it and the imagination lies in its superior force and vivacity" (*THN*, p. 85). Although Hume's largely unexamined notion that ideas are "derived from" impressions shows him grasping at some such interdependence between the two, as does his whole concept of habit and expectation for that matter, nevertheless in the context of his reductive sensationalism these intimations of immanence appear merely as inconsistencies.

Hume's eviscerated view of memory as just the faint repetition of a previous impression reflects his banishment of difference to an unknowable world outside the mind. As Whitehead points out, he seems to have forgotten his own earlier discussion "Of the idea of existence, and of external existence," demonstrating that "whatever we conceive, we conceive to be existent" (*THN*, p. 67). Manifestly, "necessary connexion" and "personal identity" do exist inasmuch as we can in fact conceive them. What needs answering, then, is not the epistemological question of how these ideas can be "distinguished" (discriminated) if they aren't given in any particular perception—a moot point, Hume shows, because as regards the question of existence, "reasoning concerning the *distinction* of ideas without any real *difference* will not here serve us in any stead, . . . since every object, that is presented, must necessarily be existent." Rather, we must solve the empirical question of whether these ideas are actually exemplified in the connectedness and identity of our impressions. Unlike the first, this question concerns the mind's relationship to itself and by extension the problem of its own otherness—as Shelley recognizes in his essay "On Life" and in the fragmentary "Speculations on Metaphysics."

II

The "Speculations" begin by arguing the interdependence between the mind and so-called external reality:

> We see trees, houses, fields, living beings. . . . These are perpetually changing the mode of their existence relatively to us. To express the varieties of these modes, we say, *we move, they move*; and as this motion is continual, though not uniform, we express our conception of the diversities of its course by—*it has been, it is, it shall be.* These diversities are events or objects, and are essential, considered relatively to human identity, for the existence of the human mind. For if the inequalities, produced by what has been termed the operations of the external universe were levelled by the perception of our being, uniting, and filling up their interstices, motion and mensuration, and time, and space; the elements of the human mind being thus abstracted, sensation and imagination cease. Mind cannot be considered pure. [*CW* 7:61]

The passage bears comparison with Keats's letter likening the world to a "vale of Soul-making" whose purpose is to provide the occasions by which human "intelligences," each a Leibnizian "atom of perception," can gradually "acquire identities, till each one is personally itself" (*Letters* 2:82–83).[20] Likewise, for Shelley the mind acquires identity through the antecedent "operations of the external universe"; and conversely, the components of the external universe depend for their identity upon the structuring activity of the mind. In accepting the object-world's actual presence within the mind, Shelley rejects the dualistic separation of mind and body which Locke and Hume inherited from the substance-based medieval Aristotelianism they thought they despised. Accordingly, the focus of his metaphysics is no longer the Lockean complex of ideas disclosed in consciousness but rather the complex constitution of the objectified individual as he becomes disclosed in his own consciousness. In terms of the above passage, the mind itself is the final end whereby the various "modes of existence" and their "diversities"—motion in space and change over time—become grasped into unity as concrete "events or objects"—namely, trees, houses, fields, and people seen here and now in spatiotemporal perspective by "us" or "them." Moreover, Shelley implies, to hypostatize these "inequalities" or differences of actual existence, as Newton's hypothetical atoms and infinitesimals serve to do, is to preclude all basis for a satisfactory metaphysics by abstracting the mind from the underlying activity of realization that supplies its only ground. When the Poet of *Alastor* similarly struggles toward "the perception of [his] being, uniting, and filling up" all difference, much like the poetic mind in the opening stages of *Milton*, ironically the result of such egotism is self-disintegration, for without concrete particulars there is simply nothing to think. As in Blake, abstraction leads to a void.

Extrapolating in this way from Hume's premise that "whatever we conceive, we conceive to be existent," Shelley finds the distinction between internal and external existents impossible to sustain. All we know is our own perceptions, from which we merely infer objects to be external. Thoughts may indeed differ according to their "various degrees of force" and in "the variety and irregularity of the occasions on which they arise in the mind" (much as Hume argues it is the "superior *force*, or *vivacity*, . . . or *steadiness*" of impressions that distinguishes them from ideas [*THN*, p. 629]). But contrary to Hume's axiom of the independence of successive perceptions, Shelley reasons that there can be neither "essential difference" nor "essential distinction" between thoughts, because "the principle of the agreement and similarity of all thoughts, is, that they are all thoughts" (*CW* 7:60). Building on this principle, both the "Speculations" and "On Life" proceed to apply Hume's analysis of the idea of existence to the idea of personal identity, claiming that since "nothing exists but as it is perceived," personal identity is likewise a function of perception. Within each individual mind, "On Life" asserts, the thoughts "*I, you, they*" are actually identical and indistinguishable in that they merely "denote the different modifications of the one mind" thinking them (S, pp. 474–78). Lest it "be supposed that this doctrine conducts to the monstrous presumption" of solipsism—"that I, the person who now write and think, am that one mind"—Shelley takes pains to point out the reciprocal nature of the relationship between self and other: just as each individual mind partly constitutes other people's identities, its own identity is constituted in turn by "the assemblage of thoughts . . . indicated . . . [by] the words *I*, and *you* and *they*." Solipsism is therefore ruled a contradictory position. It presupposes the existence of a distinct individual mind; yet if, as the solipsist asserts, "the solid universe of external things is 'such stuff as dreams are made of,' " then "pursuing the same thread of reasoning, the existence of distinct individual minds similar to that which is employed in now questioning its own nature, is likewise found to be a delusion."

In sum, personal identity exists for Shelley through the individual mind's attributing such identity to certain of its own "modifications," mainly for the same practical reasons Hume gives: convenience and reassurance. Conversely, "I" exist as a function of other minds' attributing such identity to certain of *their* own modifications, which they from their perspective call "you" or "they." Thus, Shelley concludes, "The words *I*, and *you* and *they* are grammatical devices invented simply for arrangement and totally devoid of the intense and exclusive sense usually attached to them."[21] Contrary to Earl Wasserman, Shelley does not deny "even the real existence of a plurality of unitary minds" by subsuming them into a theistic "One Mind"—that is to say, into Berkeley's God.[22] Rather, he denies only the existence of distinct unitary *thoughts* of other minds within the "assemblage of thoughts" that make up each individual consciousness. This distinction is crucial if the doctrine is not to result in an extreme monism or solipsism. "On Life" concludes accordingly, "It is infinitely improbable that the cause of mind, that is, of existence, is similar to mind" (S, p. 478). On one hand, each consciousness comprises however faintly the whole external world, including every person in it. On the other hand, Shelley stresses the spatiotemporal "diversities" and the "inequalities" that relativize and subjectivize the individual's relation to the world; from this perspective, the individual is constituted primarily by his personal world as disclosed in his own consciousness. The radical consequence of this doctrine is that for Shelley the individual consciousness is greater than its own identity: the self-conscious thought "I," which exists because it is perceived, doesn't include "you" and "they" in privileged fashion but is merely "a portion" of the mind's larger assembly. To put it differently, we are more than we know, but *who* we are, we are through knowing.

An important model for the phenomenological reductions that under-pin Shelley's "intellectual philosophy" is the "commonsense philosophy" of Thomas Reid propounded in his *Inquiry into the Human Mind* (1764) and *Essays on the Intellectual Powers of Man* (1785). Reid argues that our sensations constitute a language by which we interpret and know the world, but that they no more resemble the world than words resemble the objects they signify. Hume's assumption of the existence of distinct individual perceptions, the mental equivalent of Newton's irreducible atoms, thus shows him to be only "a half-skeptic": "I affirm, that the belief of the existence of impressions and ideas, is as little supported by reason, as that of the existence of minds and bodies"23 (Newton's atoms were of course equally hypothetical). Reid goes on to recognize, at least implicitly, that Hume's dismantling of personal identity is made possible by a privileging of perceptions very similar to the Cartesian privileging of the ego— ironically, in view of Hume's professed repudiation of Cartesian meta-physics.

> The form of the expression, *I feel pain*, might seem to imply that the feel-ing is something distinct from the pain felt; yet, in reality, there is no dis-tinction. As *thinking a thought* is an expression which could signify no more than *thinking*, so *feeling a pain* signifies no more than *being pained*. . . . when we attend to the sensation by itself . . . it appears to be something which can have no existence but in a sentient mind, no distinc-tion from the act of the mind by which it is felt. [*CS*, p. 183]

Most critiques of the magisterial *cogito ergo sum* are basically no different. Nietzsche, for example, points out that Descartes was entitled to assert only that thinking was going on, not that he or anybody else was doing the thinking:

> When I analyze the process that is expressed in the sentence, "I think," I find a whole series of daring assertions that would be difficult, perhaps impossible to prove; for example, that it is *I* who think, that there must necessarily be something that thinks, that thinking is an activity and oper-ation on the part of a being who is thought of as a cause, that there is an "ego," and, finally, that it is already determined what is to be designated by thinking—that I *know* what thinking is. For if I had not already de-cided within myself what it is, by what standard could I determine whether that which is just happening is not perhaps "willing" or "feel-ing"? . . . a thought comes when "it" wishes, and not when "I" wish, so

that it is a falsification of the facts of the case to say that the subject "I" is
the condition of the predicate "think." *It* thinks; but . . . even the "it"
contains an *interpretation* of the process, and does not belong to the process itself. One infers here according to grammatical habit.[24]

Reid therefore proposes, somewhat like Nietzsche, to exchange epistemology for hermeneutics. He sides with the expositors of "universal grammar," those structuralists *avant la lettre*, as against eighteenth-century
philology's numerous and fanciful attempts, based on a few hints in Locke,
to reduce all words to names of sensations. For Reid, "language is the
express image and picture of human thoughts; and, from the picture, we
may often draw very certain conclusions with regard to the original."[25]
Deductive analysis of separate mental events occurring in linear series is
replaced by a dynamic overview of immanent mental acts occurring within
a spatial system of relationships: "What we commonly call natural *causes*
might, with more propriety, be called natural *signs*, and what we call
effects, the things signified" (*CS*, p. 122). Hence the problem is no longer
one of causation but meaning. Reid explicitly recognizes this when he
declares Humean "custom" sufficient to interpret the sign only in material-object skepticism, where the sign (that is, the sensation) is constantly
accompanied by the thing signified (the object). As for skepticism toward
other minds, however, he finds "the connexion between the expression of
the countenance, &c., and the thoughts of the mind, not first derived from
experience": "When we see the sign, and see the thing signified always
conjoined with it, experience may be the instructor, and teach us how that
sign is to be interpreted. But how shall experience instruct us when we see
the sign only, when the thing signified is invisible?" (*IP*, pp. 449–50).
Accordingly, there can be no best-case test for determining what someone
"secretly" thinks. Since "the thoughts, purposes, and dispositions of the
mind, have their natural signs in the features of the face, the modulations
of the voice, and the motion and attitude of the body" (*CS*, p. 121), we are
compelled to "read" others' expressions in order to understand the language of their soul.[26] In turn, we are helped to understand our own
meanings by reading others' expressions toward us.

Since people then are books neither completely open nor closed, Reid
decides that a "first principle relating to existence, is, that there is life and
intelligence in our fellow-men with whom we converse." The reason we
believe this, he says, is simply that "their words and actions indicate like
powers of understanding as we are conscious of in ourselves" (*IP*, pp.
448–49). Thus we read another person by participating affectively in his
process of signifying his feelings, so realizing his feelings in ourselves.
Without such participation, his gestures and expressions remain alien,

mere sound and fury signifying nothing but the impersonations of Humean custom. Reid sees we must "live" our skepticism toward other minds because of our own irremediable need to have the benefit of their doubt. The question, "What is that person *really* thinking?" applies to ourselves as well.

Yet Reid does not quite manage to shake off epistemological dualism. Starting from the assertion that "the firm cohesion of the parts of a body, is no more like the sensation by which I perceive it to be hard" than gold is like the word that signifies it, he argues that sensations are "natural signs" no less arbitrary ("unaccountable and untractable") than "artificial [that is, verbal] signs" (*CS*, pp. 120–21). Reid's aim here is to show that Hume's view of the mind as a passive receptor of sense-impressions arises from a misuse of "figurative language." Hume has mistaken the metaphors he needs in order to represent the mind—metaphors based chiefly on painting, says Reid—for the mind itself:

> Conceiving, as well as projecting or resolving, are what the schoolmen called *immanent* acts of the mind, which produce nothing beyond themselves. But painting is a *transitive* act, which produces an effect distinct from the operation, and this effect is the picture. Let this, therefore, be always remembered, that what is commonly called the image of a thing in the mind, is no more than the act or operation of the mind in conceiving it. [*IP*, p. 363]

Reid's analysis finds its modern counterpart in Whitehead's exposure of "the fallacy of misplaced concreteness." Unfortunately, Reid's rebuttal of Hume only leads him into a similar error. For when he claims further that sensations are as unlike their objects "as pain is to the point of a sword" or "as the passion of anger is to those features of the countenance which attend it" (*CS*, p. 128), he is implying that one "wears" a face in as external a manner as one wears a sword. Certainly I can doubt whether my pain represents, in the sense of resembling, a sword point; but can I really doubt whether my own facial expressions resemble my anger? Not unless I am suppressing them, or playacting, or schizoid. The ultimate cause of my vexed countenance is not my anger, but something external to my mind and body together—such as the painful pricking of a sword point. In tacitly conflating sensations with perceptions in general, Reid apparently has overlooked that the body is not, like language, an arbitrary and merely conventional signifier of the mind's thoughts and feelings; unlike language, the body actually incorporates and expresses the thoughts and feelings it signifies. After all, the body *contains* the mind. Conversely, the mind does not, as Hume implies, peruse the testimony of the senses like a judge deliberating in his private chamber; rather the mind experiences firsthand the content of that testimony.

In short, Reid, no less than Hume, deprives his sensation-signs of the mediating physical "trace" that links them with the things requiring to be signified. Epistemologically, the trace corresponds to what Whitehead, in his own assault on Hume, calls the visceral "with-ness of the body in perception." Visual perceptions, for example, are not simply and automatically given; rather, "the ultimate momentary 'ego' has as its datum the 'eye as experiencing such-and-such sights.'" We see *with* the eye, and likewise "the feeling *of* the stone is *in the hand*" (*Process and Reality*, p. 118). Or as Blake categorically puts it, "Man has no Body distinct from his Soul" and "Energy . . . is from the Body" (E, p. 34). In this sense, Blake's more grotesquely anthropomorphic passages, where realms of relatively crude imaginative activity (Bowlahoola, Allamanda, and so on) are systematically located in particular bodily organs (bowels, alimentary canal, and so on), would seem intended to reenergize the disembodied perceptions drifting impotently about the Humean theater of the mind. Such mythologizing, like the medieval faculty psychology so much derided by the sensationalists, oddly enough possesses a sound empirical basis after all.

Nevertheless, Blake in more defensive moods tends to assert not so much the divinity of the human body as its contemptibleness. "I question not my Corporeal or Vegetative Eye any more than I would Question a Window concerning a Sight[.] I look thro it & not with it" (E, p. 566), concludes *A Vision of the Last Judgment*, thereby like Reid (but unlike the *Songs of Innocence*) slighting the body's artistic role in representing and expressing the testimony of the senses. Shelley reveals the same ambivalence. His abortive "Catalogue of the Phenomena of Dreams, As Connecting Sleeping and Waking" in "Speculations on Metaphysics," attentive as it is to the visceral element in perception, illustrates bizarrely the consequences of neglecting the visceral quality of such attentiveness itself. "I have beheld scenes, with the intimate and unaccountable connexion of which with the obscure parts of my own nature, I have been irresistibly impressed," the poet stridently announces (CW 7:67). As we shall see, his dizzying double "with" expresses not only "with-ness of the body in perception," but a further uncanny, because unacknowledged, with-ness of the material world within the perceiving body, which manifestly has been impressed by that world in some way. Does Shelley here gaze outward upon external scenes; or as their seemingly preestablished consonance with his inner nature suggests, are the scenes inscapes constitutive of himself qua beholder? Both evidently, for it appears the striking feature of these occasions is the sense of interconnectedness or with-ness as such. The difficulty of expressing so elusive a perception accounts for the catalog's unstable tone. By their very inappropriateness, the elaborate syntax and oratorical suspension of the sentence we've been considering only underline the essentially private nature of the author's perplexity, exposing his self-absorption and making it seem less than surprising that he should be so "impressed" with himself.

In his influential essay "On Method," Coleridge similarly extrapolates the dual aspect of the self from "an obscure sensation." He relates how the ordinary practical-minded "man of trade," who "is called into action from without, in order to appropriate the outward world, . . . at once discovers and recoils from the discovery, that the *reality*, the *objective* truth, of the objects he has been adoring, derives its whole and sole evidence from an obscure sensation . . . which compels him to contemplate as without and independent of himself what yet he could not contemplate at all, were it not a modification of his own being."[27] Thus Coleridge attempts to defeat skeptical sensationalism by a Platonic embrace, demonstrating that it was all along contained within the idealist position which "realistically" recognizes that "in every act of conscious perception, we at once identify our being with that of the world without us, and yet place ourselves in contradistinction to that world" (*Friend* 1:497). He spares no effort in establishing the basic compatibility between his method and the inductive method of Bacon, "the British Plato" falsely appropriated by the sensationalists in support of their system: "With him, . . . as with us, an idea is an experiment proposed, an experiment is an idea realized" (*Friend* 1:488–89). Since for Coleridge the laws by which an intelligible order is found in nature are not physical but "spiritual"—for they reflect the nature of the human mind, itself a reflection of the Creator's mind—Baconian induction turns out to be virtually a form of Protestant meditation.

The affirmations of "On Method" reverberate throughout the similarly transcendentalist *Defence of Poetry* (in which Shelley, for the first time, also extols Bacon). In the essay "On Life" and the "Speculations on Metaphysics," however, Shelley's more deductive approach seems indebted rather to the thoroughly un-Platonic Reid, whose commonsense philosophy can be seen to provide an empirical basis for Coleridge's argument:

> If a man run his head with violence against a pillar, . . . to speak in the common language of mankind, he feels nothing in the stone, but feels a violent pain in his head. It is quite otherwise when he leans his head gently against the pillar; for then he will tell you that he feels nothing in his head, but feels hardness in the stone . . . and accordingly, he instantly

fixes his attention upon the thing signified; and cannot, without great difficulty, attend so much to the sensation as to be persuaded that there is any such thing. [*CS*, p. 120]

One hopes he was able to establish this distinction without repeated experiment. Reid's point is that sensation does not automatically disclose the existence of external objects; rather, since externality or "outness" (to use Coleridge's term) is itself a type of sensation, it is not fixed but varies in degree. In a Rousseauvian passage that finds echoes in "On Life,"[28] Reid goes on to assert that children notice this sensation owing to its novelty for them, but eventually they succumb to the adult's "habit of inattention which has been gathering strength ever since we began to think." Hence, "what a philosopher by pains and practice must attain" is "to attend to this fugitive sensation, to stop its rapid progress." This difficult arresting of the "rapid and perpetual stream" of thought and the ensuing "passage from sensation to reflection" are precisely what Shelley enjoins in the section of the "Speculations" entitled "Difficulty of Analyzing the Human Mind" (*CW* 7:64). Like Reid, who refuses "to use the sensation as a sign, and to pass immediately to the . . . signified," but instead "makes [the sensation] a *distinct object of reflection*" that has no "name in any language" (*CS*, p. 120), Shelley's philosophizing repeatedly carries him to "that verge where words abandon us" (*S*, p. 478), because it compels him to recognize that "We are ourselves . . . depositories of the evidence of the subject which we consider" (*CW* 7:63).

So, Shelley claims, "it imports little to inquire whether thought be distinct from the objects of thought. . . . *external* and *internal*, as applied to the establishment of this distinction, . . . is only an affair of words" (*CW* 7:65). Far from leaning toward solipsism, Shelley emphasizes that interconnectedness with the world is the primary, albeit elusive, report of experience. "Life, and the world, or whatever we call that which we are and feel, is an astonishing thing" (*S*, p. 474) only because we are so accustomed to dichotomize between the first pair of terms and the second. The above-cited passage from Coleridge's essay "On Method" suggests, for example, that not only am I in my study but my study, as a portion of my experience, is in me. Blake's pervasive anthropomorphism whereby a mythological figure (say, Urizen) is simultaneously identified with a state of mind (detached introspection), a particular bodily part which engenders that state (the reifying eye), the environment which that part appropriates (the wasteland of Ulro) and specific historical figures inhabiting that environment (William Pitt, Scofield) similarly depicts reality as an interlocking between "life, and the world" on one hand and "that which we are and feel" on the other. Yet there remains a further turn of the screw. I am in my study and my study, as part of my experience, is in me; but since my experience is necessarily particular and limited, it exists in turn as part of the larger world outside my study. Hence, Coleridge hints, the "obscure" and "fugitive" sensation of interconnectedness can produce an uncanny "recoil" rather than the easy oceanic feeling one might expect. We realize that we can become what we behold.

Shelley's "Catalogue of the Phenomena of Dreams, as connecting Sleeping and Waking" offers an extraordinary instance of such recoil. As in *Alastor*, the object of attention is a dream that has encroached upon reality:

> I was walking with a friend, in the neighborhood of [Oxford], engaged in earnest and interesting conversation. We suddenly turned the corner of a lane, and the view, which its high banks and hedges had concealed, presented itself. The view consisted of a windmill, standing in one among many plashy meadows, inclosed with stone walls; the irregular and broken ground, between the wall and the road on which we stood; a long low hill behind the windmill, and a grey covering of uniform cloud spread over the evening sky. It was that season when the last leaf had just fallen from the scant and stunted ash. The scene surely was a common scene; the season and the hour little calculated to kindle lawless thought; it was a tame uninteresting assemblage of objects, such as would drive the imagination for refuge in serious and sober talk, to the evening fireside, and the dessert of winter fruits and wine. The effect which it produced on me was not such as could have been expected. I suddenly remembered to have seen that exact scene in some dream of long[1]——
>
> [1]Here I was obliged to leave off, overcome with thrilling horror. [Shelley's note] [CW 7:67]

Not least remarkable about the passage is its curious stylistic development. In seeking to analyze his experience, apparently a species of déjà vu, it seems Shelley gradually falls into a constrained self-consciousness that reenacts the former split between Shelley the Oxford walker and Shelley the dreamer of that scene. The account opens with a starkly graphic depiction almost visionary in its dreariness. In fact, it directly recalls the two "spots of time" passages of Wordsworth's *Prelude* (Book XII, 208–335). In the first, the "bare common" and beacon that Wordsworth says "formed, in truth, an ordinary sight" reappear in Shelley's "plashy meadows" and windmill forming "surely . . . a common scene"; the second spot's "old stone wall" and "one blasted tree" above "the meeting-point of two highways" are discernible in the stone wall nearest Shelley's lane and the "scant and stunted ash." But Shelley's scene illustrates how feeling comes in aid of feeling only in a negative, ironic way. Unlike

Wordsworth, Shelley does not objectify himself in his present role as memoirist by acknowledging that the episode elicits "inward agitations" when recollected now, years later.[29] Instead, he represses his sense of disturbance in a series of affectedly gothic insinuations. The formalized "last leaf" (compare *Christabel*'s patently symbolic "one red leaf, the last of its clan" [49]) and the cozy abstractions of "the evening fireside, and the dessert of winter fruits and wine" have no basis in the actual Oxford setting but are evidently embellishments added by the "lawless thought" of the overwrought writer. Indeed, his somewhat stilted proposal of taking "refuge in serious and sober talk" is redundant, given his claim of being already quite comfortably "engaged in earnest and interesting conversation."

It is the writer's histrionic distortions of his original Oxford walk, distortions generated by his retrospective knowledge that the walk would culminate in a sense of déjà vu, that produce the uncanny feeling in him. In thus conflating the Oxford setting with his (ostensibly) remembered dream about that setting, Shelley drops his usual awareness of writing as a mediating act that transforms what it transcribes. He seems to be naively seeking an immediacy beyond language, beyond mimesis—a charge frequently leveled against his poetry. And yet the context here remains coolly practical. As an empirical experiment on the "difficulty of analyzing the human mind" (*CW* 7:64), the purpose of the dream catalog is, like *Alastor*, to demonstrate by skeptical reduction that introspection cannot offer privileged access to experience because it, too, is a form of experience.

The result is an epistemological collapse similar to Hume's. Shelley's meticulous description, instead of clarifying the dream scene's original "connexion . . . with the obscure parts of [his] own nature," becomes itself obscurely assimilated to the scene. And so we cannot tell the dreamer from the dream. The poet commits the Humean error of confusing an "impression of a repetition of impressions" with an actual "repetition of impressions." In other words, he runs together an impression of déjà vu with the uncanny reality which that impression seems to betoken; in terms of the essay "On Life," he mistakes a "thought upon which [another] thought is employed, with an apprehension of distinction" for an external "object of thought"—that is, a "*thing*" (S, p. 478). In consequence, the Oxford walker's momentary sense of depersonalization springing from the belief that his dream had become a public reality is rehearsed anew, but with extra horror this time because, like the increasingly "intimate and unaccountable connexion" between Christabel and *her* waking nightmare, or between Los and his creation Urizen, the dream's recurrence now occurs "with open eyes" as though by evil fate. In sum, there is repetition without insight. Moreover, this vicious circle extends beyond the historical Shelley's immediate situation alone someplace transcribing his dream. When Mary had the "Speculations" published years after Shelley's death, she subjoined to his closing footnote an editorial comment of her own: "This remark closes this fragment, which was written in 1815. I remember well his coming to me from writing it, pale and agitated, to seek refuge in conversation from the fearful emotions it excited. No man, as these fragments prove, had such keen sensations as Shelley" (CW 7:67). Of course, such behavior only repeats, outside the text, the poet's preceding description of the Oxford scene as "driving the imagination for refuge in serious and sober talk." Even if Shelley actually did nothing of the sort, the self-defeating way Mary attempts to impose closure on the fragment by appending a second note to his is clearly the beginning of an infinite regress.

If the refugee from the dream catalog suffers a touch of associative delirium, the reason is his failure to "apprehend the distinction" that separates his original experience from his recollection of it, framing the first within the second.[30] Such an apprehension of difference corresponds to what, following Whitehead, I have been calling the visceral "with-ness of the body in perception," and it is ultimately the only evidence we have against solipsism. Boswell's celebrated anecdote of Dr. Johnson's mighty rebound from the stone whose materiality Berkeley had denied likewise affirms it is the felt resistance and intractableness of things that finally satisfies us of their existence outside the mind.[31] Coleridge recognizes as much when he links the similarly physical "obscure sensation" that he says underwrites the subject-object relationship with the apprehension of "outness." And so, implicitly, does Hume when he appeals to "force and liveliness" as the final criterion for distinguishing true impressions from the delusions of imagination. In an early letter of March 1734 to the famous Dr. Arbuthnot seeking advice for an apparent nervous collapse, Hume literally proves on his own pulse the crucial importance of bodily with-ness in perception:

> having read many Books of Morality . . . & being smit with their beautiful Representations of Virtue and Philosophy, . . . when I was about 18 years of Age, there seem'd to be open'd up to me a new Scene of Thought, which transported me beyond Measure, & made me, with an Ardor natural to young men, throw up every Pleasure or Business to apply entirely to it. . . . I was infinitely happy in this Course of Life for some Months; till at last, . . . all my Ardor seem'd in a moment to be extinguish'd, & I cou'd no longer raise my Mind to that pitch, which formerly gave me such excessive Pleasure.[32]

Subsequently, the young scholar found his stoic "Reflections against Death . . . & all the other Calamities of Life" useful only "when join'd with an active Life; because [then] the Occasion being presented along with the Reflection, works it into the Soul, & makes it take a deep Impression, but in solitude they serve to little other Purpose, than to waste the Spirits, the Force of the Mind meeting with no Resistance, but wasting itself in the Air." In the same way, the Poet of *Alastor*, smitten by a beautiful image conjured from his extensive researches, ends by "wasting [his] surpassing powers In the deaf air" (288–89).[33]

Such self-disintegration resembles the fate of the solitary Humean skeptic whose ratiocinations on association of ideas serve simply to dissolve those associations, which are "*to us* the cement of the universe . . . the only links that bind the parts of the universe together, or connect us with any person or object exterior to ourselves."[34] Indeed, the cement of common sense provides a touchstone throughout the *Treatise* by offering the isolated, introspective author a sense of solidarity with his reader.[35] At times, his need to elicit the audience's sympathetic willingness to follow the argument even takes precedence over strict reasoning. Consider, for example, the distinction Hume himself considered one of his most original, that between "memory," which we "believe" because it is based on primary "impressions," and "imagination," which gives rise to secondary "ideas"; the latter we merely "entertain" as fictions or delusions because, being merely "derived from" impressions, they are "fainter" and less "lively." At the beginning of the *Treatise*, Hume glibly asserts that the distinction between impressions and ideas is too obvious for discussion, being the same as "the difference betwixt feeling and thinking," which "every one of himself will readily perceive" (*THN*, pp. 1–2). Struggling to uphold this highly problematic dichotomy against a welter of exceptions such as sleep, fever, madness or "violent emotions," in all of which he admits "our ideas may approach to our impressions: As on the other hand it sometimes happens, that our impressions are so faint and low, that we cannot distinguish them from our ideas," a cornered Hume finally takes his stand upon the plainest bedrock of empirical apologies: "An idea assented to *feels* different from a fictitious idea. . . . And this different feeling I endeavour to explain by calling it a superior *force*, or *vivacity*, or *solidity*, or *firmness*, or *steadiness*."[36] Thus the distinction between impressions and ideas, memory and imagination, feeling and thinking, is proved, Hume argues, by feeling alone, not by thinking. This line of— thinking? No: feeling—is circular, yet there is no real alternative to it. He who thinks otherwise doubts his own feelings, "the only links that . . . connect us with any person or object exterior to ourselves" (*THN*, p. 662). As one sees from Hume's later portrait of the misanthrope as "altogether insufficient to support himself; [so] that when you loosen all the holds, which he has of external objects, he immediately drops down into the deepest melancholy and despair" (*THN*, p. 352), epistemological skepticism leads to a collapse of the psyche.

It appears, then, that with-ness of the body in perception has its moral counterpart in what Hume, having dismissed the epistemological problems of the *Treatise* Book I as mere intellectual riddling without ethical consequence, calls "sympathy." Just as association of ideas "is a kind of ATTRACTION, which in the mental world will be found to have as extraordinary effects as in the natural" (*THN*, pp. 12–13), so through the mechanism of sympathy operating in social relationships it is "as if our ideas acquir'd a kind of gravity from their objects" (*THN*, p. 435). Thus in isolation, Wordsworth's "Nutting" tells in a passage whose Shakespearean pun reverberates throughout *Alastor*, "The heart luxuriates with indifferent things, / Wasting its kindliness on stocks and stones, / And on the vacant air" (41–43). As the author of the dream catalog also attests by his apparent desperate need of his wife's company, the heart loses its essential human "kindness" if it cannot find a respondent of similarly human "kind."

III

Such affectless narcissism represents, at the emotional level, the equivalent of Hume's failure to acknowledge otherness or novelty or difference at the epistemological level. Blake's abhorrence of abstract memory is essentially a rejection of the Humean principle of the undifferentiated repetition of distinct sensa, which he views as part of the Newtonian program to reduce experience to mathematic uniformity. Hume's simplistic concept of repetition reappears in Hartley, where it is criticized by Coleridge as allowing only "delirium," pure sensation without any differentiating awareness of externality:

> our whole life would be divided between the despotism of outward impressions, and that of senseless and passive memory. . . . one or other of two consequences must result. Either the ideas, (or relicts of such impression,) will exactly imitate the order of the impression itself, which would be absolute *delirium*: or any one part of that impression might recall any other part, and . . . *any* part of *any* impression might recall *any* part of any *other*, without a cause present to determine *what* it should be. [*BL* I:111–12]

This is the phantasmagoric world of the Ancient Mariner, a world devoid of the hypotactic connections required for coherent storytelling. In contrast to Coleridge's "man of education" whose speech reveals a unifying method "grounded on the habit of foreseeing, in each integral part, or (more plainly) in every sentence, the whole that he then intends to communicate," the simple Mariner can relate his voyage only through a process of total recall tantamount to actually reliving the events in their original unpatterned sequence. "Listen . . . to an ignorant man, . . . whether he be describing or relating," the essay "On Method" invites:

> We immediately perceive, that his memory alone is called into action; and that the objects and events recur in the narration in the same order, and with the same accompaniments, however accidental or impertinent, as they had first occurred to the narrator. The necessity of taking breath, the efforts of recollection, and the abrupt rectification of its failures, produce all his pauses; and with the exception of the *"and then,"* the *"and there,"* and the still less significant, *"and so,"* they constitute likewise all his connections. [*Friend* 1:448–49]

On the other hand, repetition recognized as such entails awareness of the difference between oneself and the repeated event. The act of recollection objectifies the self, securing it the minimum degree of self-identity needed in order to confront the recurrence as a further event, however familiar, in the individual's continuing life history. Shelley's *Alastor* can be seen as a demonstration *a contrario* of the necessity of this process. Instead of possessing his dream maiden as a means of self-development by making her his muse, the Poet is possessed by her, so succumbing to self-absorption in the most literal sense: his regressive musings on the maiden eventually assimilate him to his own deliquescent dream world. Blake's *Milton*, on the other hand, painfully affirms the redemptive role of historical difference. Milton's bright pilgrimage of sixty years can be rectified and fulfilled only through his successor Blake, who is thereby brought to acknowledge the merciful gap between the mortal visionary and the object of his vision.

Keats's letter to Bailey of November 22, 1817, helps clarify how repetition can serve to objectify a self, provided it introduce a saving difference. The reason Keats here rejects the "consequitive reasoning" of the philosopher and yearns "for a Life of Sensations rather than of Thoughts" is that the philosopher's "hunger after Truth" as something fixed and immutable precludes the more immediately human goal of "having what we called happiness on Earth repeated in a finer tone and so repeated—And yet such a fate can only befall those who delight in sensation." Unlike the simple repetitions of mathematics which supply the model for Humean association, such "spiritual repetition" includes difference. It produces not uniformity but intensification, as the memory of some former h͏͏ becomes superimposed with "fine suddenness" upon the experience oɪ a like pleasure in the present:

> have you never by being surprised with an old Melody—in a delicious place—by a delicious voice, felt over again your very speculations and surmises at the time it first operated on your soul—do you not remember forming to yourself the singer's face more beautiful than it was possible and yet with the elevation of the Moment you did not think so—even then you were mounted on the Wings of Imagination so high—that the Prototype must be here after—that delicious face you will see. [*Letters* 1:184–85]

It isn't clear whether the second sentence, "do you not remember . . .," exhorts the friend to remember his very first encounter with the melody, or rather his subsequent one, in which case he is being asked to remember his previous recollections of the first encounter. The confusion recalls Shelley's dream catalog, much as the passage in its entirety—especially Keats's enigmatic summation, " 'It is a Vision in the form of Youth' "—recalls the youthful *Alastor* Poet's vision of a beautiful singing poetess whose "prototype" (Shelley's Preface also uses this term) he, too, seeks in the hereafter. Yet the Shelleyan *mise en abîme* springs from the Poet's pursuit of his maiden "Beyond the realms of dream": "He overleaps the bounds" (206–07) of accustomed reality, so undermining the necessary "apprehension of distinction" between the two realms. Since Humean custom remains in place for Shelley—"Mind . . . cannot create, it can only perceive" (S, p. 478)—the result is déjà vu, a regressive false consciousness where novel experiences are merely assimilated to the past. In the Keatsian waking dream, on the other hand, such intimate connections between dreams and reality are not uncanny anomalies, inexplicable departures from normal reality; more positivistically, these novel experiences supply the material for constructing a new reality compounded of the so-called dreams and reality both. Keats does not simply recall by association all the "surmises and speculations" the old melody elicited from him before; because his mind recognizes self-consciously this "repetition of its own silent Working," it gains the "reward" of being able to manipulate the surmises "in a finer tone" nearer its desire. Analogously, the letter's Shelleyan echoes can be seen as part of a "grand march of intellect" (*Letters* 1:282) whereby Imagination is gradually remaking the world in its own image. Insofar as the letter reflects Keats's recent reading of *Alastor*, published the year before and based in large measure on *Endymion*, published the year before that, it shows that his poetic vision has assumed a Lamia-like life of its own, eliciting the self-conscious admiration of its creator (Keats's implied criticism of Lycius is that Lycius's admiration of Lamia lacks precisely this sort of self-consciousness). Like the listener of the delicious melody, Keats experiences with fine suddenness the repetition of his mind's own working in the form of Shelley's *Alastor*.

The letter recalls Schlegel's famous *Athenaeum* fragment number 116. Here Schlegel hails a poetry simultaneously self-creating and self-destroying, skeptical and idealistic, which he terms "the romantic kind of poetry, . . . the only one that is more than a kind, that is, as it were, poetry itself: for in a certain sense all poetry is or should be romantic": "It alone can become, like the epic, a mirror of the whole circumambient world, an image of the age. And it can also—more than any other form—hover at the midpoint between the portrayed and the portrayer, free of all real and ideal self-interest, on the wings of poetic reflection, and can raise that reflection again and again to a higher power, can multiply it in an endless succession of mirrors."[37] The twin aspects of Schlegelian repetition-with-a-difference are refinement and realization. They are reflected respectively in Keats's claim that all intense passions are, like Adam's dream, both "a Shadow of reality to come" and "creative of essential Beauty": such passions not only foreshadow but actually create whatever afterlife each of us shall have. His much greater religiosity notwithstanding, Blake also elevates poetry to the status of supreme fiction when he urges the constructive role of Imagination: "Let every Christian as much as in him lies engage himself openly & publicly before all the World in some Mental pursuit for the Building up of Jerusalem" (E, p. 232).[38] Accordingly, Keats solves the problem of Milton's influence much as Blake does: in the only way possible, by seeing the grand precursor as less an Oedipal rival for limited poetic territory than a brother creator of the infinite realm of Imagination. So, for example, when Keats writes that "Adam's dream . . . seems to be a conviction that Imagination and its empyreal reflection is the same as human Life and its spiritual repetition" (*Letters* 1:184–85), the conviction to which he refers is, if not Adam's, then probably Milton's (see *Paradise Lost* V, 574–790)[39] and certainly his own. The dream is, as Newell B. Ford said, "not merely an analogy but a *proof* of the prefigurative agency of imagination,"[40] if only because it has itself undergone a process of "spiritual repetition" in the course of literary history. From the Bible to *Paradise Lost* to *Endymion*, *Alastor*, and the emphatically un-Miltonic *Lamia*, the persuasive beauty of the image has been progressively refined until it has become "conviction," an enduring and essential part of poesy not only for Keats but also (if he succeeds) for *his* successors. Keats's argument is the more compelling for being unabashedly ex post facto:

"What the imagination seizes as Beauty must be truth—whether it existed before or not."

The Romantics strive to prove this claim upon our pulses. By deploying a series of subnarratives that repeat the same basic plot across a range of narrative styles, the poems we shall examine continually double back on themselves, compelling the reader to recognize his own activity in constituting the narrative as a unified whole. The poems establish a cycle of "spiritual repetition," similar to the process of Freudian transference, whereby the reader is empowered to repossess the unacknowledged "surmises and speculations" he first projected onto the narrative, so gaining the freedom to realize them "in a finer tone." Since each poem ends by dramatizing our own experience of the several preceding subnarratives, we are brought to see that its action was all along taking place inside ourselves. In turn, the poem as text appears most limitedly self-referential during this final stage. With its mimetic powers now fully undermined, it can no longer usurp the ordinary daily immediacies it was designed to reveal. In Coleridge's words, the reader realizes that he was contemplating "as without and independent of himself what yet he could not contemplate at all, were it not a modification of his own being." Thus placed "withoutside," as Blake puns in *Jerusalem*—placed, that is, simultaneously without and inside the poetic heterocosm, hence lifted into the space of a visionary Moment without any limiting sides at all—we can see that "There is an Outside spread Without, & an Outside spread Within . . . / . . . / An orbed Void of doubt" (18:2–4). The epistemological anxieties of the narrative's early stages resulted, we now see, from the self-division inherent in the Humean search for a fully distinct and independently existing perception of personal identity that might be somehow external to the self actually engaged in the search.

Since repetition is always complicated by an intervening temporal difference, the form of these poems is not circular but spiral. In order to show the reader how far he has come, the narrative constantly turns and looks back at itself even as it travels forward. In this way, the hermeneutic circle—the search for some final or foundational meaning, "what the text knows about itself"—is correlated with the continuing activity of the searcher.[41] The sequence of subnarratives can be considered as an inductive series of tests at locating a ground of knowledge; and yet this ground continually eludes the reader because, contrary to expectation, it is never identified with any specific place, character, or event in the poem. The omphalos-like well and its attendant Spirit in *Alastor*, the Eternal Bard's Song in *Milton*, Don Juan's confrontation of cannibalism, and Christabel's equally horrified discovery of naked Geraldine's "mark of shame" and "seal of sorrow"—each of these seemingly climactic events turns out to be merely a provisional stage in our reading. After all, how could an originary ground of knowledge possibly occur *within* the narrative? In the end, therefore, the reader sees that the narrative action, and indeed the objectified poem itself, exists nowhere but within himself. And with this acceptance of an inward difference or otherness he is forced to relinquish the whole solipsistic fantasy of coinciding perfectly with himself, of possessing self-knowledge in separation from the finite, temporal conditions of human life.

Irony and
False Consciousness

Artificial signs signify, but they do not express; they speak to the
understanding as algebraical characters may do, but the passions,
the affections, and the will, hear them not: these continue
dormant and inactive, till we speak to them in the language of
nature, to which they are all attention and obedience.

> *Thomas Reid*, An Inquiry into the Human Mind
> on the Principles of Common Sense, *chap. IV, sect. ii*

The Romantic attempt to marry the warring contraries temporality and
repetition, immediate experience and its literary representation, can be
clarified by glancing at the concept of Romantic irony, whose history
reveals a curious, and of course ironic, dialectic of revaluations. For
Friedrich Schlegel, inventor of the term, Romantic irony unites opposites
in a "beautiful confusion" that actually surmounts the law of noncontra-
diction, based as that law is on self-identity $(p = p)$ rather than becoming
(if p is to realize itself, it must become something different from what it
now is, and there must theoretically be a point in the process where p is
both p and not-p). As Anne Mellor argues, ironic indeterminacy can be
regarded as an exuberant affirmation of human freedom, whose restless
strivings are seen to embody the contradictions of life itself. Unlike recent
dark interpreters anxious to identify Romantic irony with the skeptical
practices of Derridean deconstruction, Mellor emphasizes its celebratory
enthusiasm for creation:

> Having ironically acknowledged the fictiveness of his own patternings of
> human experience, [the ironist] romantically engages the creative process
> of life by eagerly constructing new forms, new myths. And these new fic-
> tions and self-concepts bear within them the seeds of their own destruc-
> tion. They too die to give way to new patterns, in a never-ending process
> that becomes an analogue for life itself. The resultant artistic mode that
> alone can properly be called romantic irony must therefore be a form or
> structure that simultaneously creates and de-creates itself.[1]

This accurately captures the tone of much Romantic theorizing about
irony, but it tends to minimize irony's transcendental tendency to conflate
art and life, poetry and politics, forgetting that its relationship to the latter

terms is indeed only "analogical." When such conflation occurs, the ironist's ability to "deconstruct his mystifications of the self and the world" (p. 5) turns out to be just one more mystification.

For example, in *The Marriage of Heaven and Hell*—the work I will take as exemplary of this problem—Blake's rampant perspectivism annihilates any distinct autobiographical presence in order to express a purely impersonal and possibly amoral "Energy . . . the only life." Yet this energy serves to undermine not only established authority but also any position from which authority might be criticized or reformed. And so the perplexities of self and world, denied the empirical basis that gave them a more than merely intellectual urgency, are not demystified but merely subsumed into irony's endless regress, now become virtually synonymous with textuality. Thus, if on one side I reject Mellor's espousal of the Romantic ironist's own self-representations, on the other side I disagree even more sharply with David Simpson's attempt to identify Romantic irony with the indeterminacy of the hermeneutic circle. In the ironist's "studied avoidance . . . of determinate meanings" and "refusal of closure," Simpson finds "the provision of a linguistic sign which moves towards or verges upon a 'free' status, and the consequent raising to self-consciousness of the authoritarian element of discourse. . . . Unable to achieve a metacomment, we are trapped in a perpetual present, where causality and temporality are completely suspended."[2] The Derridean drift of this argument is that irony's surplus of different meanings is disclosed as a single simultaneity that can be identified with language itself, language finally liberated from its bondage to the particular mediating discourses of society, history, knowledge, and power; *il n'y a pas d'hors texte*. Schlegel's point, however, is that the ironist occupies his infinite variety of positions only successively; what matters is the journey, the "process" or the "becoming," not the arrival, which can be only provisional anyway. Indeed, it is the diachronic, ongoing nature of the Romantic ironist's quest for self-realization that leads the later Blake to regard irony's unlimited freedom as a false consciousness, a rhetorical disguising of the temporal conditions in which the real quest must be played for mortal stakes.

Schlegel's acutest critic, the young Kierkegaard, similarly accuses the Romantic ironist of disregarding the claims of history by confounding

> the temporal ego with the eternal ego, and as the eternal ego has no past, so neither does the temporal [as far as the ironist is concerned]. Insofar as irony should be so conventional as to accept a past, this past must then be of such a nature that irony can retain its freedom over it, continue to play its pranks on it. . . . Authentic history, on the other hand, wherein the true individual has his positive freedom because in this he has his premises, must be dispensed with.[3]

Kierkegaard views ironic indeterminacy in Hegelian terms as absolute negativity." For him, the ironist indeed believes in the exi: an absolute ethical truth, but because he knows only what that trut... .s not, his awareness has no ethical import and constitutes, practically speaking, a mere denial of actuality. Kierkegaard's critique of the Romantic ironist is developed along the lines of Hegel's critique of "the beautiful soul": "because he lives completely hypothetically and subjunctively, his life finally loses all continuity. With this he wholly lapses under the sway of his moods and feelings. His life is sheer emotion . . . as the ironist has no continuity, so the most contrary feelings are allowed to displace each other. Now he is a god, now a grain of sand" (pp. 300–01). The Devil of *The Marriage* would retort that Kierkegaard's charge of "negativity" only reduces a genuine contrariety to the polarized negations of his own Christian orthodoxy. Blake, of course, vigorously endorses such "displacements" of feeling as being essential to the redemptive dynamics of imaginative perception—seeing infinity in a grain of sand is precisely what enables us to become God. So, somewhat differently, does Schlegel, who terms this aspect of irony "caprice" or "hovering." For Schlegel, the ironist's metamorphoses are a form of self-overcoming; by actually confronting each new facet of the self that his irony raises to consciousness, the ironist detaches himself from it, thus gaining a precarious freedom from the fixed and definite self-as-object.

Kierkegaard, however, goes on to give the argument a typically Hegelian twist: "[The ironist's] feelings are as accidental as the incarnations of the Brahma. . . . Feeling has therefore no reality for the ironist." Thus the life of pure emotion swallows itself up, ending in aestheticism and "boredom." Since the ironist denies the reality of whatever cannot be subsumed by the self, he lacks anything to feel toward or about. Why then should the ability of Schlegel's ironic "romantic kind of poetry" to "hover at the midpoint between the portrayed and the portrayer . . . on the wings of poetic reflection" necessarily "raise that reflection again and again to a higher power,"[4] intensifying the original image rather than debasing and enfeebling it? What saves such poetry from being mere wishful thinking and distinguishes, say, the Keatsian Adam's "true" dream of Eve from the *Alastor* Poet's destructive dream of *his* maiden?

More recently Paul de Man's influential essay "The Rhetoric of Temporality" has added to Kierkegaard's revision of Schlegel a new twist of his own. Accepting Kierkegaard's description of irony as essentially devoid of affirmation, de Man nevertheless claims that its refusal to embrace the "bad faith" of "symbolism," the belief "in a world where it would be possible for the image to coincide with the substance," permits a brave existential confrontation of man's "authentically temporal predicament."[5] I have suggested that the Romantic poet's striving for such a confrontation leads him to double the narrative back on itself, to image within the poem its own means of production, namely writing and reading. By thus representing the poem *as* representation, he exposes and neutralizes its inevitable tendency to usurp the natural immediacies he seeks to reveal. Indeed, Schlegel explicitly recognizes the necessity of "artistic reflection and beautiful self-mirroring": "In all its descriptions, this [romantic] poetry should describe itself, and always be simultaneously poetry and the poetry of poetry" (Firchow, p. 195). The result is not formal stasis or infinite regress, but a process of decreation which leads back, as Mellor suggests, to the ever-renewing particulars of concrete human life and thence to what Schlegel calls "the clear consciousness of eternal agility, of an infinitely teeming chaos" (Firchow, p. 247).

In an important sense, though, de Man values irony for just the opposite reason Schlegel does (however inconsistently). In his view, it is not immersed in the life process but, like all literary structures, irrevocably cut off from reality; the distinctiveness of irony is its poignant, comic recognition of its estrangement. So whereas for the transcendental idealist Schlegel irony supplies our supreme source of freedom, for the skeptical rationalist de Man this freedom takes place merely within the prison-house of language. And yet de Man apparently sees no contradiction in supporting his argument with a citation from Schlegel's farewell address to readers of his journal the *Athenaeum*, entitled "On Incomprehensibility." After surveying several types of irony, Schlegel finally reaches "the irony of irony":

> Generally speaking, the most fundamental irony of irony probably is that even it becomes tiresome if we are always being confronted with it. . . .
> For example, if one speaks of irony without using it, as I have just done; if one speaks of irony ironically without in the process being aware of having fallen into a far more noticeable irony; if one can't disentangle oneself from irony anymore, as seems to be happening in this essay on incomprehensibility; if irony turns into a mannerism and becomes, as it were, ironical about the author; if one promises to be ironical for some useless book without first having checked one's supply and then having to produce it against one's will, like an actor full of aches and pains; and if irony runs wild and can't be controlled any longer.
>
> What gods will rescue us from all these ironies? The only solution is to find an irony that might be able to swallow up all these big and little ironies and leave no trace of them at all. I must confess that at precisely this moment I feel that mine has a real urge to do just that. But even this would only be a short-term solution. [Firchow, p. 267]

Schlegel's transcendental buffoonery asserts no less than Kierkegaard the ultimate tediousness of irony. Evidently the irony of irony is that, for all its proliferating indeterminacy, irony must *end*—this is, after all, a farewell address—arbitrarily and, as the bathetically ironized speaker shows, without dignity. Where irony ends is in its beginning, for as the spirit of self-criticism, its purpose for Schlegel is not the aesthetic one of generating enclosed heterocosms, but the practical one of furthering the growth of the world-soul by transforming repetition and narcissism into difference and self-consciousness. Since Romantic poetry is "a progressive, universal poetry," its dialectics already encompass everything he can possibly say about it, so that his enthusiastic speculations at some point cease to be mere commentary and become instead an actual contribution to the poetry's growth. In this way, the poet-philosopher's words become performatives, speech-acts akin to the Logos whose secular partners they are (not rivals, as Coleridge is at pains to explain in the final pages of *Biographia Literaria*). A similar positive tautology enables Hegel to present the *Phenomenology of Mind* as a long, winding (if not long-winded) account of the spirit's travails toward self-unity, whose final purpose is to induce self-unity in anyone able to discern the work's underlying cogency. It follows that the poet-philosopher of the world-soul exerts more than his reason in trying to "have" ideas; he engages his entire being in realizing them through the appropriate, world-historically necessary expression (hence Schlegel's seemingly contradictory emphasis on the need of "self-restriction"; *Lyceum*, number 37). Although for Schlegel irony's endless regress resists any ultimate Hegelian synthesis, irony's infinite eternal becoming is dependent, in the last count, on the distinctly finite temporal beginnings and endings of writing and reading.

De Man, on the other hand, sees the ironist as a spectator whose sole activity is the paradoxical one of resisting the allure of all worldly activity by observing his own temptations, and so ironizing them, too. Through this endlessly repeated "*dedoublement*," which "carried to the extreme . . . is a consciousness of madness" arising from destruction of his actual "empirical self," the ironist asserts "the necessity of not becoming the dupe of his own irony and discovers that there is no way back from his fictional self to his actual self" (pp. 216–19). But Schlegel's passage demands this assertion be qualified: there is no way back for the ironist except the temporary one of ceasing to write and rejoining the world of becoming, thence to begin writing again with fresh inspiration.

For de Man's distinction between the ironist's "mad self" and that part of himself which "proceeds to reflect on his madness thus objectified" ultimately breaks down. If the ironist must be continually ironizing his own insights lest they become falsely subsumed into his original empirical self, then is his ensuing self-isolation and vertigo really any different from the madness he seeks to evade? However much irony involves the awareness that "there is no escape from the prison-house of language," that awareness entails by the same token the realization that literary irony cannot actually be "lived" any more than dogmatic skepticism about the existence of the material world can be practiced without schizophrenia. The prison-house of language resembles Hume's philosophical study in this respect, and its paralysis seems no less artificial than Hume's melancholy. Precisely because it is so self-conscious, then, the irony of irony is Janus-faced; it looks not only toward textuality but toward the exigencies of practical ordinary existence outside the text. From this viewpoint, Schlegel's farewell address goes to show what, ironically enough, de Man himself demonstrates in his book's central essay, "The Rhetoric of Blindness": namely, the critic's difficulty in opening the doors of perception is that the doors are revolving, so that if he systematically pushes his insight far enough, the darkness closes behind him once again.[6] Schlegel shares de Man's Humean vision of reason undermining itself, yet unlike de Man he finds the result to be not entrapment within a "rigorous" (de Man's favorite adjective) rationalism but on the contrary a comic return to the concrete human world in which rationalism plays a merely limited role—in Hume's terms, the world of dinner, backgammon, and good company.

On another level, though, de Man has anticipated these objections. For the terms of his analysis do not remain fixed but undergo a development strikingly similar to that of the narrative poems we'll be examining. As his essay proceeds from the section "Symbol and Allegory" to "Irony," de Man forgoes the historical analysis by which the symbolist "myth of organic totality" was demystified in favor of allegory.[7] The first section concludes having established that whereas "in the world of the symbol it would be possible for the image to coincide with the substance," allegory involves a more authentic representation of temporality and the necessary distance of signs from their origin: "The meaning constituted by the allegorical sign can consist then only in the *repetition* . . . of a previous sign with which it can never coincide, since it is of the essence of this previous sign to be pure anteriority" (p. 207). In discussing irony, however, de Man will be using texts that are already "demystified . . . and ironical," and so do not attempt to conceal their "temporal predicament"; thus he can begin the essay's second section, he says, with a direct examination of "the structure of the trope itself" (p. 211). Indeed, a historical analysis would be positively misleading because irony "becomes conscious of itself as it shows the impossibility of being historical," figuring most often as an attack on the "claim to speak about human matters as if they were facts of history."

On one hand, therefore, de Man rejects history with the ironist; on the other hand, he embraces it by asserting the historical fact of the ironist's rejection. How can he escape contradicting himself? By writing a text that is itself ironical. His observation on irony in general perfectly applies to his own essay: "it seems to be only in describing a mode of language which does not mean what it says that one can actually say what one means" (p. 211). Only by disclosing his position obliquely through a progressive repudiation of what might be called the "symbolist" conception of irony can de Man avoid totalizing irony in the usual symbolist fashion; hence the pains he takes to dispel the view of irony as a kind of unraveling able to move so rapidly from local to universal effects, or from the empirical self to the "representing" or "linguistic self," that it can create a Coleridgean translucence of the latter in the former and thereby offer genuine self-knowledge. In short, it is only by organizing his essay into two seemingly opposed sections that de Man escapes the paradox of attempting to "rescue a coherent historical picture at the expense of stated human incoherence" (p. 222). Just as Schlegel defines irony as the "refusal to treat any stage . . . as definitive," de Man cannot rest his argument at the end of section one with a simple rejection of symbolism in favor of allegory, its traditional opposite. Rather, he must push on toward the recognition of irony as itself a mode of symbolism which, because it acknowledges the temporality of discourse and does not confuse its own fictional constructs with "actual reality," can supply a more authentic contrary to allegory than the symbol. In this way, "The Rhetoric of Temporality" avoids reifying its insights into a "simultaneity" or "totality" whose critical representations would neglect their own reliance upon figurative language. The essay is indeed ironical; but its progressive organization, based on the author's awareness of its necessary temporality, makes it ultimately an allegory of irony whose meaning, according to the definition of allegory given earlier, "can consist then only in the *repetition* . . . of a previous sign with which it can never coincide, since it is of the essence of this previous sign to be pure anteriority." Hence de Man warns that any attempt to return the essay's meaning to history or actuality is subject to "renewed blindness." By the same token, however, the essay's allegorical status means that de Man's last position cannot be final, any more than can Schlegel's in "On Unintelligibility." And in this sense, the essay does indeed return critic and reader to Schlegel's "infinitely teeming chaos" of becoming, the source of the essay's own rhetoric of temporality.

I

The liminal, not to say contradictory, nature of Schlegelian irony whereby it constitutes at one and the same time textuality and the end of textuality is on display in Blake's *The Marriage of Heaven and Hell*. If the work's exploded form can be seen to represent the infinite, self-escalating consciousness of the Romantic ironist, nevertheless that form also represents a continual denial of the actual empirical context within which the finite consciousness of the historical author evidently wishes to operate (as the opening references to Swedenborg make clear). Not until *Milton* does Blake achieve a narrative of "temporality" able to demystify the ironic consciousness of *The Marriage*, ordering its ironies into the progressive narrative arrangement that de Man terms "allegory."

Let me begin by pointing out that Blake nowhere rejects the sensationalist premise that all knowledge comes from experience. Quite the opposite—his quarrel, as he sees it, is with Locke's unempirical reduction of experience to mathematical uniformity through denial of the principle of difference or novelty. In "There Is No Natural Religion" and "All Religions Are One," Blake locates difference within the mind as a faculty of perception he terms "Poetic Genius" without which man would "stand still, unable to do other than repeat the same dull round over again."[8] Similarly, his abhorrence of memory, specifically "the Reasoning Memory," is limited to the word's somewhat technical sense in Hume, where it denotes the undifferentiated repetition of identical perceptions. Blake himself extolled diligent copying of the old masters in engraving and painting; and his myth, which culminates when the characters all re-identify themselves as fallen parts of the One Man, obviously makes a form of recollection (similar to Platonic anamnesis) the key to redemption.

By recognizing difference or otherness to be an irreducibly mysterious fact of immediate sense experience, Blake in effect beats the sensationalists at their own game. The letter to Trusler of August 23, 1799, sounds surprisingly Keatsian in speaking of "Imagination, which is Spiritual Sensation" (E, p. 703). Like Coleridge, what Blake despises is not sensationalism broadly construed, but its Hobbesian strain of reductive materialism which he sees as precluding a creative moral will. The fall whereby Los, resting from the labor of creating Urizen, succumbs to pity and becomes the horror he beholds illustrates the reductionist view of mimesis as a passive molding of the mind by sense-impressions mysteriously derived from without. At this stage, Los accepts only the sacrificial first half of Blake's proposition that "God becomes as we are, that we may be as he is" (E, p. 3), ignoring the redemptive second half which is the whole purpose of the first. Coleridge and Shelley similarly detect hypocrisy in the eighteenth-century conception of sympathy as a particularly intense domination of the mind by a painful external object, a process of suffering whose virtuousness is seen to lie precisely in its impotence, its poignant inefficacy in a universe of mechanism. The "forced unconscious sympathy" that transforms Christabel into Geraldine reappears in the self-deluded Prometheus' capitulation to the Furies: "Whilst I behold such execrable shapes, / Methinks I grow like what I contemplate / And laugh and stare in loathsome sympathy."[9] The source of such degenerative mirrorings, the metamorphosis in *Paradise Lost* of the devils into snakes— "horror on them fell, / And horrid sympathy; for what they saw, / They felt themselves now changing"[10]—makes clear how they are all at bottom travesties of God's creation of man in his own image.

One suspects the special sarcasm Blake reserves for Locke reflects his frustrated awareness of how close they are in terms of approach while diverging hugely in their fundamental assumptions. Compare, for example, their accounts of knowledge acquisition. Repudiating the doctrine of innate ideas, Locke describes "The Steps by which the Mind attains several Truths":

> The senses at first let in particular ideas, and furnish the yet empty cabinet, and, the mind by degrees growing familiar with some of them, they are lodged in the memory, and names got to them. Afterwards, the mind proceeding further, abstracts them, and by degrees learns the use of general names. In this manner the mind comes to be furnished with ideas and language, the materials about which to exercise its discursive faculty.[11]

The Marriage of Heaven and Hell depicts the same process of development, the big difference being that Blake's Mind doesn't start out empty but contains all of so-called external reality. What we term knowledge is therefore really a forgetting, as in Plato's doctrine of remembrance:

> The ancient Poets animated all sensible objects with Gods or Geniuses, calling them by the names and adorning them with the properties of woods, rivers, mountains, lakes, cities, nations, and whatever their enlarged & numerous senses could perceive. . . .
> Till a system was formed, which some took advantage of & enslav'd the vulgar by attempting to realize or abstract the mental deities from their objects. . . .
> Thus men forgot that All deities reside in the human breast. [E, p. 38]

No less than Blake, Locke's Baconian attacks on Scholastic jargon acknowledge the tendency of language to calcify and prevent accurate perception of the world it purports to represent: "Because men would not be thought to talk barely of their own imagination, but of things as they really are; therefore they often suppose their words to stand also for the reality of things" (2:11). His observation "how great a Dependence our Words have on common sensible Ideas; and how those, which are made use of to stand for Actions and Notions quite removed from sense, have their rise from thence, and from obvious sensible Ideas are transferred to more abstruse

Significations" (2:5)—his examples being that "spirit, in its primary signification, is breath; angel, a messenger"—suits well with Blake's conviction
that the origin of the world we know and experience, including even its
transcendent aspects, is "the Body." The susceptibility of Locke's examples to a materialist interpretation did not escape Leibniz, who criticized
their impious tendency, but Locke's own assumption, that man in his
present state is confined to a world of sense, is of course orthodox. Another
product of that assumption is Locke's nominalism, which leads him to
make the potentially expressivist point that linguistic meaning depends
upon shared social processes of rectification and adjustment. This seems a
paradox only because, as A. N. Whitehead and more recently Hans
Aarsleff have argued, the traditional reading of the *Essay* underestimates
the importance it allows to "reflection," concluding—as Locke specifically did not—that since reflection is chronologically secondary to sensation, the capacity for reflection must be reducible to the effects of sensation.[12] As we have already seen, it is not Locke but his successor, Hume,
who draws this conclusion.

The Marriage's description of the five-chambered printing-house in
Hell, an allegory of artistic creation, likewise embraces a sensationalist
psychology inasmuch as it locates creativity within the five sensory regions
of the author's body. Blake's version of "the method in which knowledge
is transmitted from generation to generation" (E, p. 40) is a parody of
Bacon's account of "the transmission of knowledge":

> Let us now proceed to the art of Transmitting, or of producing and ex-
> pressing to others those things which have been invented, judged, and laid
> up in the memory; which I will call by a general name the Art of Trans-
> mission. This art includes all the arts which relate to words and discourse.
> For although reason be as it were the soul of discourse, yet in the hand-
> ling of them reason and discourse should be kept separate, no less than
> soul and body.[13]

Similarly, when Blake writes that "in the first chamber was a Dragon-
Man, clearing away the rubbish from a caves mouth," he recalls Locke's
Epistle to the Reader, which modestly asserts that "in an age that produces
such masters as . . . the incomparable Mr Newton, . . . it is ambition
enough to be employed as an under-labourer in clearing the ground a little,
and removing some of the rubbish that lies in the way to knowledge"
(1:14). Might the Dragon-Man be Locke, whose reductive system assists
more imaginative beings in making "the inside of the cave to be infinite" by
demonstrating despite itself the mysterious integrity of mind, the fact that
thought is irreducible to sensation? Shelley, at least, views his role as
metaphysician in this way; echoing Locke's passage, he calls philosophy a

ground-clearing "pioneer for the growth of ages" that "destroys error, and the roots of error," leaving "a vacancy" (S, p. 477) which can then be apprehended as a space of inspiring potentialities. Locke's picture of the mind yields endless fragmentation: the "testimony of the senses" must be examined by other senses, which must be examined in their turn, and so on. In contrast, Blake affirms throughout his writing that what exists at the center of every man is not an infinite regress of senses but an infinitely expanding imagination. His allusions to Locke and Bacon are therefore ironical, of course, but the reason Blake even bothers to parody them is that his own emphasis on bodily energy resembles their sensationalism enough to be mistaken for it. Locke's rubbish clearing having engendered a system of its own, Lockeanism has itself become part of the rubbish the poet needs to clear off, thereby like Shelley "melting apparent surfaces away, and displaying the infinite which was hid" (E, p. 39).[14]

II

The Marriage's moral critique parallels its epistemological one. Just as the reified perceptual categories of subject and object are to be abolished, so are the reified moral categories of good and evil. As the relevant discussion in Milton's *Areopagitica* proclaims, "that which purifies us is trial, and trial is by what is contrary. . . . Good and evil we know in the field of this world grow up together almost inseparably . . . as two twins cleaving together. . . . And perhaps this is that doom which Adam fell into, of knowing good and evil, that is to say, of knowing good by evil (Hughes, p. 728). In Blake's construal, our knowledge of good and evil as qualities separate and unrelated—that is, as Negations, "what the religious call Good & Evil" (E, p. 34)—is mere rationalization after the fact; in actual experience, we encounter both simultaneously. (As we'll see, Coleridge's *Christabel* similarly deconstructs the pious polarization of good and evil, showing like *The Marriage* that each term contains the other in a covert way: not only do the two women begin to seem doubles, but as Christabel increasingly internalizes Geraldine's evil, Geraldine conversely appears less demonic and more motivated by ordinary human emotions.) What has happened is that one term in the opposition—the Good—has been falsely privileged over the other, the cause of this being our own fallenness. To put it differently, the reason the mind simplistically conceives good and evil to be polarized absolutes is that it is itself a corrupt, warring mixture of the two without realizing it.

The solution to this problem is religious conversion. As a work of Schlegelian irony, however, *The Marriage* also portrays such mental warfare as a sign of "Energy . . . the only life" and hence as vitally "necessary to human existence," and the more intense the better. In this sense, the only conversion required or even possible is the self-transcendence that comes, as de Man says, from simply observing the conflict so as to reenact it on a higher, more self-conscious level. The problem is that, as Kierkegaard argued vis-à-vis Schlegel, this is a purely negative goal devoid of actual ethical implications. Likewise, Blake's balanced critique of the British tradition of reductive sensationalism is subverted by his irony's antinomian striving to transcend "the Body" and identify the indeterminacy of rhetorical self-consciousness with the unshackled energies of a genuinely world-consuming apocalypse. One thus agrees with Leopold Damrosch, Jr., that Blake is "a dualist who wishes he were a monist"—if not throughout his work, at least in *The Marriage*. For Damrosch, "the concept of Negation is a desperate measure intended to rescue the contraries by banishing from them whatever is irredeemably corrupt. But the act of banishment vitiates the whole meaning of contraries."[15] True, and yet without Negations, Blake's axiom "As the eye, such the object" is liable to the imputation there's nothing bad but thinking makes it so. In that case, innocence must dwindle to a fugitive and cloistered virtue based on ignorance of evil, and eventually to practiced ignorance—that is to say, hypocrisy, the very crime of which Blake is accusing his audience.

III

This tension between a commitment to the ethical imperatives of religious prophecy and a desire to glorify the imagination's freedom from worldly compromise is apparent in the form of the work. *The Marriage* not only parodies the polite reader's beliefs, it strives to shatter the value system that stands behind them. Like most eighteenth-century satires, *The Marriage* is a moral satire with a serious purpose; unlike them, *The Marriage* satirizes morality itself. In simple terms (such as appear only occasionally beneath the bold intellectualizings of *Paradise Lost*), the traditional Christian argument for improved moral behavior claims it was the passions that prevented reason from ruling man and so prevented man from serving God. For Blake, on the other hand, the blame lies with conventional morality, which by repressing the passions has perverted them into cold, hypocritical shadows of reason. Yet *The Marriage* doesn't simply stand accepted Christian values on their head. The Devil's neatly inverted perspective is ingenious—"It indeed appear'd to Reason as if Desire was cast out. but the Devils account is, that the Messiah fell. & formed a heaven of what he stole from the Abyss" (E, pp. 34–35)—but as a number of commentators have recognized, the Devil often seems no less partisan and domineering than, by his own lights, God is. "For this history has been adopted by both parties": that God and the Devil share the same Bible, the one reading white where the other reads black, wickedly undercuts God's privileged status, but Blake's larger irony is that any history that thus polarizes reason and energy is itself a product of reason. As he says elsewhere, in equivocal worlds, up and down are equivocal; therefore, to invert the established order as the Devil does isn't to overcome that order but merely reify it.

Consider then the problem of determining the work's unity. Although one can pretty confidently identify the genre of *The Marriage* (and also its precursor, *An Island in the Moon*) as seriocomic Menippean satire dating back to Petronius, Lucan, and other classical Dialogues of the Dead, such satire is, as Mikhail Bakhtin says, inherently "multi-styled and multi-toned," a basically antiformalist hybrid of "inserted genres: novellas, letters, oratorical speeches, symposia, and so on; also characteristic is a mixing of prose and poetic speech."[16] Thus the question of *The Marriage*'s unity reappears, writ large now as the question of the unity of so diverse a genre. Moreover, the work opens with an "Argument" which, instead of being the usual prose summary of an ensuing poem, is a *poem* that obliquely explains the reluctant conversion of the "meek . . . just man" to the howling outcast prophet who evidently has composed the ensuing *prose* writings. And yet those writings, a bewildering collection of gnomic proverbs, shocking polemic, visionary anecdotes, and terse myths of creation and fall, are so disparate, even incompatible in form and style that they eventually subsume the Argument as just one more fragment in the general melee. By undermining the Argument's logical priority as an authorial introduction, Blake forestalls dismissal of *The Marriage* as merely the product of an eccentric solitary's disaffection ("Blake rejects conventional Christianity? So what—as a conventional Christian, I reject him"). Thus denied the intentionalist fallacy and its attendant complacencies, we are forced to shift focus from what the author has become to what Christianity has become—a much larger problem that includes ourselves.

Blake achieves his desired transvaluation of values (a goal less Nietzschean than it is antinomian puritan) not by saying one thing and meaning the opposite but by deconstructing apparent contraries, revealing their primordial unity within the mind. Should we regard the Devil of *The Marriage* as deluded when in plates 4–6 he lays down the law in a parody of God's commandments, thereby appearing equally authoritarian? Are we meant to see the orderly manner in which his argument develops as a contradiction of his thesis, which exalts energy, not reason? Notwithstanding his brilliant critique of *Paradise Lost*, is the Devil then a character just as damaged and self-aggrandizing as Milton's Satan? The illustration to plate 4, showing the Devil chained by the ankle to flames emerging from

a turbulent blue ground which is evidently the burning lake of Milton's
Hell, certainly suggests so. Or are these diabolical contradictions perfectly
in character: imbued as he is with energy, why shouldn't the Devil reason
inconsistently and unfairly?[17] For example, his tour-de-force indictment
of Jesus for breaking God's commandments indeed seems rationalistic in
its effort to demonstrate systematically that Jesus broke all ten of them,
even "murder[ing] those who were murderd because of him" (E, p. 43).
But despite a few tongue-in-cheek sophistries, the Devil's basic point here
is sound enough: the Bible tells that Jesus knowingly broke a number of the
commandments, believing as he did in the superiority of love over law.
Perhaps then the Devil is Blake's vehicle for carrying reason to excess,
making it undermine itself and become energy.

Elsewhere the Devil's inability to go beyond conventional good and evil
is more plainly exposed. Whereas his notorious "Note" on *Paradise Lost*
sees Milton as fettered by a value system which as a "true poet" he
unconsciously rejected, *The Marriage* on the whole takes Milton's repudiation of that system to be open-eyed and exemplary. Contrary to the
usual view reiterated by Harold Bloom in his commentary to the standard
edition, the Note reveals not Blake's, but Blake's Devil's sense of "the
declining movement of creative energy in *Paradise Lost* from the active of
the early books to the passive of the poem's conclusion, where all initia-
tives not a withdrawn God's own are implicitly condemned" (E, p. 897). In
fact, *The Marriage* repeatedly affirms its author's abhorrence of the same
historical corruptions that Milton, in the tradition of the Old Testament
prophets, boldly condemns in the closing books of his poem. In Book XI,
Michael's account of the period preceding the Deluge lets Milton launch
an attack on time-servers who have used the Revolution for selfish ends:

> Those . . . in acts of prowess eminent
> And great exploits . . .
> Shall change thir course to pleasure, ease, and sloth
> . . .
> So all shall turn degenerate, all deprav'd,
> Justice and Temperance, Truth and Faith forgot;
> One Man except . . .
>   . . . hee of thir wicked ways
> Shall them admonish, and before them set
> The paths of righteousness . . .
>   . . . denouncing wrath to come.
>   [XI, 789–818]

"The one just Man" is Noah, here presented as a type both of Christ and
the poet himself. *The Marriage* opens with another, more distinctly apoc-

alyptic Deluge about to cut loose: in "burdend air" thick with thunder and lightning, "Hungry clouds swag on the deep" (E, p. 33). Building on the passage from *Paradise Lost*, Blake's Argument goes on to portray religious hypocrisy as a final collapse of values which completes the process of moral degeneration begun in Milton's day. Now, says Blake, "the villain" has "left the paths of ease" Milton described and has usurped "the perilous path" of righteousness, driving "the just man" into "the wilds" beyond the social pale. Indeed, only one hundred lines from his poem's end, Milton himself vehemently asserts that such a reversal of values is already taking place. Michael warns Adam how the self-proclaimed representatives of God will take it upon themselves to enforce by secular means the spiritual laws of conscience, thereby degrading those laws and unwittingly doing the work of Satan. The church shall become prey to

> Wolves,
> Who all the sacred mysteries of Heav'n
> To thir own vile advantages shall turn
> . . .
> Then shall they seek to avail themselves of names,
> Places and titles, and with these to join
> Secular power, though feigning still to act
> By spiritual, to themselves appropriating
> The Spirit of God. . .
>   . . . and from that pretense,
> Spiritual Laws by carnal power shall force
> On every conscience . . .
>   . . . So shall the World go on,
> To good malignant, to bad men benign.   [XII, 508–38]

The mythological passages in *The Marriage* (plates 5, 11, and 16) describe just such a legalistic counterreformation leading to the hegemony of Reason. And yet the Devil claims "Energy is the only life." How then could Reason get the strength to control Energy? Blake sketches an answer by dividing humanity into two classes, Prolific and Devouring. The Prolific would naturally dominate the Devouring, parasites who live off their energy, except that the current value system considers restraint of desire the highest good. Since the Devouring are inherently better at restraining themselves than are the Prolific, they have been able to turn their weakness into an insidious strength.

Insofar as *The Marriage* takes up where *Paradise Lost* left off, Blake appears fully aware that the principle of desire and self-integrity he terms Imagination closely resembles the principle of "choice" and conscience that Milton terms Reason, the chief difference being for Blake that his principle is identified with Christ, Milton's with God the Father. Milton is everywhere careful to distinguish Reason, our means of ascertaining God's truth, from the prideful perversities of rationalization, one of Satan's main weapons of temptation. It is Blake's Devil who fails to recognize this distinction. Blake himself perfectly accords with it: "Self Evident Truth is one Thing and Truth the result of Reasoning is another Thing[.] Rational Truth is not the Truth of Christ but of Pilate[.] It is the Tree of the Knowledge of Good & Evil" (E, p. 621). As J. A. Wittreich, Jr., discerns, "Blake's Devil may be more enlightened than his Angel; but he never exhibits the enlightenment characteristic of the true visionary."[18] If Blake's Devil is therefore imperfect, it is evidently because he has suffered the same fall as he says happened only to the Messiah. For if "Reason and Energy . . . are necessary to Human existence" (E, p. 34), so that the collapse of either of these contraries vitiates the human whole, then it must vitiate the other contrary as well.

In thus refashioning the myth of the Fall into an allegory of mental fragmentation, Blake radically develops the heterodox implications of Milton's theodicy. Whereas in *Paradise Lost* God utilizes Satan as a way of turning evil into still more good, in Blake's work this symbiotic relationship deepens, temporarily for the worse, into a genuine interdependence between coequals. Hence if the Devil of *The Marriage* is corrupted by his exultance in a still traditionally fiery Christian Hell, conversely the traditional Christian Heaven which the Eternals inhabit in *Milton* seems, Beulah-like, to impair their vision of human wholeness: they fail to comprehend the Bard's Song, much as their counterparts within the Song, the Great Solemn Assembly in Eden, mistakenly convict Rintrah instead of Satan. Further, the poem's opening description of Milton in terms of his own rendering of the Devils in Hell ("pondring the intricate mazes of Providence / Unhappy tho in Heav'n" [E, p. 96; compare *Paradise Lost* II, 555–69]) ironically insinuates that each Eternal gets the same afterlife he imagined, imperfectly, of course, while on earth—in Milton's case, a labyrinthine realm of predestinarian speculation. But if Reason *and* Energy have fallen, how can we trust whoever it is that has brought to light the limitations of these characters? It is at this point that Blake's irony returns to ironize him; history dissolves, and with it the tradition of prophetic denunciations that was meant to mediate and contextualize the violence of Blake's attack on the Evangelicalism of his day. Wittreich discovers in *The Marriage* "a larger consciousness . . . aware of subtleties that his devil does not perceive" (p. 215), but it is difficult to identify that consciousness with any specific authorial persona. "Blake the true visionary" remains hidden in the interplay of contrary perspectives; his language generates an infinite, increasingly self-conscious series of meanings above and beyond the empirical William Blake. Indeed, for the author thus to express by self-annihilation more than he actually intends seems tantamount in *The Marriage* to prophecy itself. At the same time, if "Every honest man is a Prophet[;] he utters his opinion both of private & public matters / Thus / If you go on So / the result is So" (E, p. 617), so that it is only by speaking out in no uncertain terms against particular evils that one's moral vision can in fact become prophetic of the future, then such indeterminacy is bound to look disturbingly quiescent.

In *A Rhetoric of Irony* Wayne Booth sets out to combat radical indeterminacy of meaning: "pursued to the end, an ironic temper can dissolve everything, in an infinite chain of solvents. It is not irony but the desire to understand irony that brings such a chain to a stop."[19] Booth's enemy solvents resemble the corroding fires of Blakean Energy; what he calls "learning where to stop" Blake calls "the bound or outward circumference of Energy," beyond which lies a merely adventitious territory formed by the inertness of objects not yet ironized by the creative mind. For "Reason or the ratio of all we have already known. is not the same that it shall be when we know more" (E, p. 2).[20] In other words, Reason is not a fixed possession of the knower but simply the outcome of the act of knowing, an act that by altering the knower also alters his reason. Blake's irony thus denies not only the independent existence of the object-world but also the ability of language to represent it, finally suggesting that physical reality is itself just representation. The myth of the ancient poets on plate 11 shows explicitly that Nature, a calcified mental projection that now resists internalization, is nothing but a dead metaphor. The same holds for *The Marriage*'s own status as an art object. Blake's elusiveness places him both inside and outside his writing—inside it, because he always seems to be insinuating some further meaning just beyond our ken; outside it, because for this reason we can never pin him down to any final meaning—so that responsibility for closure is shifted to the reader, who ends the work by summarily projecting onto it an image of his own (perhaps transformed, perhaps retrenched) empirical self and deciding, for now at least, that *that* is who the author is.

Since Blake's aim, like Schlegel's, is not to present ideas about the world of becoming but to stimulate participation in it, obviously any attempt to explain or describe such participation would be self-defeating. Hence the reader is treated as a contrary; he confronts not a chaos that negates all perception but a darkness visible that is designed to baffle his *habits* of perception, thereby rousing the faculties to act. On the other hand, *The Marriage*'s disjointed organization and the Devil's bewildering peremptoriness suggest the author has no real interest in reaching an audience. Blake's letters and marginalia seethe with Swiftian contempt for opponents, whom he regards less as marriageable contraries than as enemy negations: "What is Grand is necessarily obscure to Weak men. That which can be made Explicit to the Idiot is not worth my care" (E, p. 702; note the "necessarily"). Or as the author tells the Angel in *The Marriage*: "we impose on one another, & it is but lost time to converse with you whose works are only Analytics" (E, p. 42). But if Prolific and Devouring are therefore not only portions of the universal mind but actual classes of people opposed as "separate" and irreconcilable "enemies" (E, p. 40), then how is humanity to be redeemed? If the Devouring are to be considered weak innately and immutably, then isn't the author succumbing to the same predestinarianism he condemns in Swedenborg and Milton, and consequently accepting severe constraints on his prophetic role? One wonders if Blake's refusal to speak in propria persona attests not energy and inspiration but a Wizard of Oz-like attempt to hide his human vulnerability behind the impressive supernatural machinery of his myths. And yet Blake *is* fallen: in this sense, his inconsistencies ultimately confirm rather than undermine his main argument that the fall of reason necessarily affects energy as well.

Although the Reason-Energy dialectic never reaches a final synthesis, its permutations can be seen to reveal a pattern of unresolved ambivalence toward physical existence. On one hand, the very intensity of Blake's desire to affirm Imagination embitters him toward the object-world, that infuriatingly persistent delusion. Especially in his late writings, the withdrawing, defensive stance that results sounds distinctly Platonic:

> I assert for My self that I do not behold the Outward Creation & that to me it is hindrance & not Action[.] it is as the Dirt upon my feet[,] No part of me. [E, p. 565]

> Natural Objects always did & now do Weaken deaden & obliterate Imagination in Me. [E, p. 665]

On the other hand, the only way of returning to Eternity is by exploiting the object-world as a means toward expanded sense perception, seeing infinity in a grain of sand:

> I feel that a Man may be happy in This World. And I know that This World Is a World of Imagination & Vision. . . . Some Scarce see Nature at all But to the Eyes of the Man of Imagination Nature is Imagination itself. [E, p. 702]

Only the latter attitude, with its emphasis on sensible experience, permits that selfless, actively contrary relationship to earthly life which Blake implicitly sees to be a reenactment of God's human incarnation. What generates the irony in Blake's work is the way each of these attitudes inevitably elicits the other, yielding Romantic irony when the author's empirical self remains concealed, as in *The Marriage*, and dramatic irony when he is externalized and narrativized in the Prophetic Books as a specific character like Los.

Blake's Escape
from Mythology:
Self-Mastery in *Milton*

*Everywhere nature first confronts us in more or less hard
form. . . . How can we, so to speak, spiritually melt this
apparently hard form, so that the unadulterated energy of things
fuses with the energy of our spirits, forming a single cast? We
must go beyond form, in order to regain it as comprehensible,
living and truly felt . . . for without bounds the boundless could
not be manifested; if there were no harshness, mildness could not
exist, and if unity is to be made palpable this can only be done
through singularity, isolation and conflict.*
Schelling, "Concerning the Relation of the Plastic Arts to Nature"

The central problem of this chapter is epitomized by the printing-house in
The Marriage of Heaven and Hell depicting "the method in which knowledge is transmitted from generation to generation."[1] We have seen how
the passage parodies the Baconian concept of "the advancement of learning." Blake here does not exalt the creation of art forms, as has often been
claimed, but shows how unimaginative people use them, and hence their
deficiency and liability to perversion.[2] The passage portrays a journey
through the author's mind, a five-chambered zoo inhabited by the Senses.[3]
These creatures, although mystifying to the reader (the brain and its
operations can be surgically exposed to view without rendering any less
elusive the phenomena of mind), are nonetheless clearly engaged in a
common pursuit; despite their wildness, it appears they all labor sub-
missively at some larger enterprise (namely, mind). At this point, then, the
creative process remains unified and continuous. Once the "living fluids"
of this forgelike brain are "cast into the expanse" and there "receiv'd by
Men," however, they harden into metal books and become punctiliously
"arranged in libraries." The forms for transmitting knowledge—books—
prove to be most tame compared to the fantastic bestial energies that begot
them. This irony dominates the text's material "trace." *The Marriage*
proffers numerous resemblances, even mergings, between the illuminated
script, its various arabesques and flourishes, and assorted human figures

and tableaux, often the same size as individual letters or words of text. Does this reveal the Logos-like presence of the human body energizing the writing, or does it show the human form vegetating into the dead letter? So long as text, flourishes, and tableaux are regarded sequentially, the sequence can run in either direction.[4]

I

Blake's rather Gnostic view of the written word as entailing fragmentation of the mind's creative unity is hardly unique. It is shared in some measure by anybody who has ever felt a thought to be greater than its expression. Still, there is a vast difference between writers who enjoy an invigorating disquietude toward their finished oeuvres ("the next will be better") and those who must struggle with a genuinely anxious ambivalence about the value of writing at all. The exuberance of *The Marriage of Heaven and Hell* notwithstanding, it appears the works of the mid-1790s, especially their attempted résumé and consolidation in *The Four Zoas*, carry Blake further and further in the direction of the second attitude. The supernatural mythology that is merely implicit in *The Marriage* because it is volatilized for the most part by the author's intense personal Energy (it emerges chiefly through the Blake-Devil's "Memorable Fancies," flippant public renditions of his still largely unrevealed, more seriously private imaginings)[5] now begins to calcify into a cluster of self-isolated individuals. Spinning outward and down from their life source in the creative mind, Blake's miserable titans assume concrete form only at the very limit of entropy, earth. Thus the same fall that reduces the poet's boundless inner energy to a set of discrete figures also furnishes, via this externalization, a comprehensive means of locating and identifying those figures: a grand mythology of the uncreating word. One sees from this that much of Blake's mythology is a compensation—but an insidious one, for the control it supplies him is largely illusory. Manipulate it as he may, especially in *The Four Zoas*, Blake's elaborate "grammar of the Imagination" never quite offsets the debilitating realities of fallen self-expression so much as it gestures back at them with reemphasis.

The Four Zoas represents a deliberate attempt at confronting this dilemma. It fails mainly through its shapelessness reflecting too honestly the author's divided motives. The poem's huge bulk and scope, its consolidation of the Prophetic Books, above all the basic patterning of its narrative on the Christian model of fall and redemption suggest an enormous effort at affirmation. Yet what the narrative affirms is the parodic view of form as springing from fall and fragmentation; Creation only gratifies the Zoas' megalomania and shields them from the now-unendurable intensities of Eternity. Thus Blake's attempt to surmount the problem of fragmentation by writing a poem about it becomes itself part of the problem. One reads his perplexity in the story of Los. Like the mythologist, Los fabricates life forms. Although he knows his creations are merely provisional—come the apocalypse, all things will be one—circumstances compel him to ignore this truth. Since earth lies in imminent peril of Eternal Death, he cannot take time to assess his work but must forge on blindly without rest. And yet this well-intentioned urgency is potentially disastrous, for if Los loses sight of the main end, Eternity, his misguided industry will serve to usher in eternal death just as well as torpor would have done. Indeed, Los's endowing the specters with bodies makes them more, not less, capable of evil, so that he must refashion them all over again. Apparently he is defeating himself—hence his racking self-doubt.

It is no coincidence that the composition of *The Four Zoas* evinces much the same floundering on the part of Blake. Written piecemeal, perhaps as largely unpremeditated reportage of contemporary military and political events,[6] the poem was evidently intended to capture history in the making, even to become itself a direct part of the upheavals it records. The question here is how to end such a poem. Possibly, considering his occasionally millennialist rhetoric, Blake expected that the end of history as we know it would shortly end it for him.[7] But it didn't, and so the poet toiled on, increasingly disturbed by lack of direction, as his extensive revisions suggest.[8] Like Los, Blake becomes lost in immediate labors of organization and alienated from their ultimate goal. A collapse of perspective ensues: the poet's personal strivings toward unity, namely a completed poem, gradually displace those of the Universal Man, not dissimilar yet vastly more important. Blake avails himself little of the dramatic irony which, as the successful presentation of Urizen goes to show, could make us identify with his titans while recognizing that their pathetic efforts at self-integration only underscore their loss of humanity. In consequence, he seems throughout *The Four Zoas* to be exhibiting the giant warriors as evidence of his own Ossianic imaginative strength, when, after all, their size mainly indicates the monumental proportions of man's misery and self-conflict. Similarly, the constant multiplication of mythological personae attests not the author's prolificness, as Blake enthusiasts used to suppose, but the anxiety of the Universal Man compulsively struggling to conceal the inner void made by his fragmentation—a labor of evasion that fragments him all the more.

Blake's evident abandonment of *The Four Zoas*—whether or not he ultimately intended to engrave it, the existing manuscript is plainly something less (or more) than a finished copy—no doubt rescued the poem from the process of calcification depicted in *The Marriage of Heaven and*

Hell. But of course a rescue so desperate is failure by any other name. Ultimately Blake does make Los succeed, but only through a paradox. In the Eighth Night abruptly enters Satan, Lord of Spectres, who rapidly hypostatizes so much darkness that he bursts the Limits of Contraction and Opacity within which the narrative has been taking place and falls out of the poem. The reifying Selfhood actually reifies itself out of the personality; his epiphany is suicide. Ostensibly, Satan's defeat leaves Los victorious. But if Satan defeats himself, Los could hardly find his post facto victory personally very satisfying; his sudden transformation into Luvah renders such satisfaction moot, anyway. So instead of a climactic encounter between the antagonists Satan and Los, the poem offers only their separate epiphanies. Yet Blake had good reason for avoiding this encounter. Face-to-face with Satan, Los might not have withstood his archenemy; after all, what is Satan but a mass of spectrous forms that Los himself created? Blake's evasion is even more telling in view of his identification with Los. For may we not suppose that Los's specious consummation of his long-suffering labors accurately reflects the factitiousness of Blake's apocalyptic Night the Ninth, a finale imposed without real mastery of his poem's difficulties?[9]

II

Nevertheless, it is only by countenancing such ambiguities that one can overcome them. Self-doubt thrives on the effort to pretend it does not exist. In actuality, says Blake, self-doubt cannot exist, being a contradiction or Negation,[10] but evidently one must look hard at it in order to make it disappear. This we do at the end of *Milton*, where Satan forfeits his illusory existence acquired through *The Four Zoas* and stands fully exposed as the formless "Trembling & fear, terror, constriction; abject selfishness" (38:39) lurking about Milton's and Blake's and every man's "outline of identity" (37:10). Thus *Milton* strives toward an unqualified affirmation of concrete human life. In the closing scene Blake repossesses his mythology as direct personal vision, thereby returning to a new form of the vigorous self-expression of *The Marriage of Heaven and Hell*. And as we shall see, the entire preceding course of the poem works to make possible this final scene in all its passionate apprehension of particularity.

The circumstances of *Milton*'s composition are well-known.[11] Suffice it to say that Blake's dilemma vis-à-vis his patron Hayley, critical as it was to his material welfare, seems to have assumed even greater proportions for him privately. The letter to Butts of January 10, 1803, discloses grave anxieties intensified by the poet's fear of having compromised his artistic, and therefore spiritual, integrity. Breaking away from the dangerous security of Hayley's patronage thus could represent for Blake a triumph over internal doubts having little to do with Hayley or Felpham in direct fact. "I have indeed fought thro a Hell of terrors & horrors (which none could know but myself.) in a Divided Existence," he told Hayley himself on December 4, 1804; "now no longer Divided. nor at war with myself I shall travel on in the Strength of the Lord God as Poor Pilgrim says" (E, p. 758). In overcoming Felpham's temptation of corporeal ease, Blake had asserted as in earlier days the autonomy of Imagination and the precedence of his poet's calling: "I have proved that I am Right & shall now Go on with the Vigor I was in my Childhood famous for. . . . My Enthusiasm is still what it was only Enlarged and confirmd" (E, pp. 719–20).

Yet the characteristic exuberance of these letters is expressed in quite new tones of brotherliness and humility. As his last remark suggests, Blake's recovered enthusiasm necessarily differed from the enthusiasm that had been lost, for the struggle of recovery had altered the man himself. Perhaps not by coincidence, Blake now begins to develop a doctrine of provisional States through which the individual passes on pilgrimage to renewed unity:

> Distinguish therefore States from Individuals in those States.
> States Change: but Individual Identities never change nor cease:
> You cannot go to Eternal Death in that which can never Die.
> . . .
> Judge then of thy Own Self: thy Eternal Lineaments explore
> What is Eternal & what Changeable? & what Annihilable!
> The Imagination is not a State: it is the Human Existence itself.
>
> [32:22–32][12]

Although his youthful Devil's repudiation of external form cannot be sustained, it remains for Blake to master the corollary development of a flexible human relation to form. In *Milton* he turns upon himself the dramatic irony merely latent in *The Four Zoas*. Through a series of mergings, the various mythological figures belie their apparent autonomy and ultimately reveal themselves to be extruded personae of the man William Blake. Thus reintegrated into a human being, the poet, for all his mortal weakness, is literally seen to surpass his wildest imaginings. *Milton* is Blake's exploration of his own mythological "lineaments," culminating in his arrival at the "Individual Identity" that underlay them all and indeed made the whole exploration possible. The poem comprises a series of states of mythological nonbeing leading finally to disclosure of "the Human Existence itself": the inspired Blake living in Felpham who has just completed *Milton*.

Studies of *Milton*'s structure tend to distinguish several narratives within the poem, each of which is considered to repeat a fundamental pattern of prophetic awakening and descent. As James Reiger observes: "Rhetorically, *Milton* exists on four levels of discourse, corresponding to the four worlds of Blake's myth. . . . The utterances of any higher realm are only partially intelligible to the inhabitants of the worlds below it. That is the central stylistic problem of the poem."[13] This needs a caveat, for what the poem's visionary finale suggests is that none of the worlds of Blake's myth is fully real, precisely *because* they all entail style. How to expose the Logos underlying actual everyday human life and indeed all human expression, poetry included, without simply reducing it to these mundane appearances—that is the question. Hence Susan Fox's emphasis on the poem's basic "structural principles" is perhaps slightly but crucially misplaced. Fox quotes Michael Riffaterre summarizing Roman Jakobson: "the recurrence of equivalent forms, parallelism, is the basic relationship underlying poetry." Then she one-ups him: "Parallelism is more than that in *Milton*; it is the theme of the poem realized concretely as its narrative structure."[14] But if the arrangement of *Milton* shows anything, it is that the poem's recurrent "forms" ("the four worlds of Blake's myth") are not genuine logical equivalents; Blake stresses that they are not interchangeable. Strictly speaking, then, parallelism is not the theme of the poem but only a technique. It is Blake's provoking *use* of parallelism that enables him to dramatize his real theme, self-annihilation, a theme paradoxical to earthly sense and thus expressible only indirectly.

I am suggesting that *Milton* progressively uses up its various narrative styles so as to unveil its theme without ever actually embodying it. Each style merely provides a means to the next, until finally style itself is called into question and, as W. J. T. Mitchell sees, *Milton* the poem self-annihilates just like Milton the character.[15] *Milton*'s parallelism is purely functional. It is the rehearsal of a single prophetic pattern on several levels that serve, first, to expose the animating truth behind the pattern (the Logos of the conclusion), but that also signal the falseness of reducing this truth to any of the vehicles that shadow it forth (the mythopoeic Bard, the mythological Los, the various spiritual figures of Milton, or the historical character William Blake in Felpham garden circa 1800). Such parallelism we might term "sublime allegory" according to Blake's definition: "Allegory addressd to the Intellectual powers while it is altogether hidden from the Corporeal Understanding" (E, p. 730). I previously suggested that the synchronic hybrid form of *The Marriage* embodies the contradictory nature of Schlegelian irony—its denial of temporality in favor of "an infinite eternal becoming." Claims Schlegel, "It is equally fatal for the mind to have a system and to have none. It will simply have to decide to combine the two."[16] As a poem that systematically destroys its mythological system, *Milton* combines these two requirements, but unlike *The Marriage* it does so in order to reconfront, rather than attempt to transcend, the temporal conditions of human existence.

Hence *Milton*'s narrative is as paradoxically incorporeal as its theme. The different journeys of the Bard, Milton, Los, and Blake all link up through the gradual merging together of these protagonists, yet the single extended journey that results doesn't go anywhere at all: *Milton* ends within the same Felpham garden that S. Foster Damon showed to be allegorically concealed within the Bard's Song.[17] Meanwhile, though, the stylistic context becomes changed utterly, from obscure mythology to a comparatively detailed naturalistic presentation of human life. What kind of journey returns to its starting point, only on a new level? A spiral. Unlike "the Greater Romantic Lyric," however, *Milton* spans not years but a single moment. This flattens the spiral, precluding spacious open-ended meditation back and forth through time such as M. H. Abrams finds in "Tintern Abbey" and Coleridge's conversation poems.[18] Yet as we've seen, the result for Blake is not circular repetition of the journey. Since the cosmic mythology of the Bard's Song, the poem's point of departure, is of much vaster scope than the concluding particularized depiction of the author's house and grounds in Felpham, it appears the path of *Milton* forms an eddy. Moreover, since Felpham was in reality the place where Blake composed the poem, as eventually he tells us at 36:21–24, *Milton* eddies toward a center which is also its source. In sum, the poem describes a Vortex:

> The nature of infinity is this: That every thing has its
> Own Vortex; and when once a traveller thro Eternity.
> Has passd that Vortex, he perceives it roll backward behind
> His path, into a globe itself infolding; like a sun:
> Or like a moon, or like a universe of starry majesty,
> While he keeps onwards in his wondrous journey on the earth
> Or like a human form, a friend with whom he livd benevolent.

[15:21–27]

The vortex is essentially a process that delineates the coming to grips with and mastering of ordinary fragmented experience. Even as the mental traveler circles involvedly about some local "thing," such as a poem, he is also progressing steadily toward an apex that will free him to continue his life journey. He thus avoids entrapment within the products of his "concentration"; these come to be regarded merely as means of continuing the journey. Although a vortex seems engulfing at the open end ("infinity"), it appears in retrospect a solid object, that portion of ourselves we have lived through and can never reenter ("a human form"). As the afterthought of the last line insists, the sense of loss is great. Yet there is a corresponding gain in self-perception; "for man cannot know / What passes in his members till periods of Space & Time / Reveal the secrets of Eternity: for more extensive / Than any other earthly things, are Mans earthly lineaments" (21:8–11). The configuration of the poem works to dramatize this basic law of providence. Whether or not we agree with J. A. Wittreich, Jr., that *Milton* progresses from shadowy types to truth specifically by virtue of belonging to the genre of "epic prophecy,"[19] passage through the *Milton* vortex clearly does generate a crystallization of awareness, as the cosmic Bard's Song is discovered in retrospect to the projection of a particular bard, William Blake. If the human poet cuts a modest figure alongside the sublime Bard, nevertheless he is not belittled; the contrast arises only because man is sometimes unequal to his own desires. So eternity, which at first seemed a vast self-enclosed universe, is found in the end to concentrate within the author's mind.

The course of *Milton*, then, is a progressive compression of form leading to the internalization of form as vision, thus liberating the poet from his work.[20] What we could call *Milton*'s "Living Form" (E, p. 270)— its symbiosis of style and narrative—appears literally as a form of subjectivity. The poem's growth in self-expressiveness ineluctably suggests that the figure who comes into focus as William Blake was present imperceptibly throughout the rest of the poem as well. That is, when Blake suddenly appears in Felpham garden repossessing his mythology as personal vision, we can only conclude that for the whole preceding course of the poem he must have been lost *within* the mythology. Lacking "outline of identity," he couldn't possibly have entered the narrative as a distinct individual possessing mental acts of his own, and yet he was all the while struggling to do and be just this. The author, we realize, had succumbed to the entropy of becoming what you behold. *Milton* was his way of getting back inside his visionary self.

If *Milton* shows the poet progressively becoming himself, logically the beginning of the poem should show him furthest from his goal. "He," however, must be taken figuratively in this case: if the poet has scarcely begun to become himself, who or what is he? The question defines our experience of plates 3–7. Far from viewing the author Blake incorporated into his poem as a definite human figure ("a human form" such as the conclusion presents), here one apprehends merely unmediated intention, an inchoate "authority" gesticulating *through* the broken verse paragraphs, not expressing itself by means of them. These plates represent the engulfing end of the *Milton* vortex. Yet the effect is not simple confusion but rather darkness visible, inarticulateness made explicit. The narrative disjunctions thwart the narrative and all critical attempts to make sense of it as well,[21] but they do communicate an unmistakable force of will. What we seem to confront is a kind of stammering, the speech act reduced to physical impulse. In light of the author's palpable absence from his text, it is perhaps appropriate we call in a surrogate to help establish a basis of understanding. Consider Nietzsche's discussion of the experience of "willing":

> Willing seems to me above all something complicated. . . . In all willing there is, first, a plurality of sensations, namely, the sensation of the state "away from which," the sensation of the state "towards which," the sensations of this "from" and "towards" themselves, and then also an accompanying muscular sensation. . . . [Second,] in every act of the will there is a ruling thought—let us not imagine it possible to sever this thought from the "willing," as if any will would then remain over! Third, the will is . . . above all an affect, and specifically the affect of the command. That which is termed "freedom of the will" is essentially the affect of superiority in relation to him who must obey: "I" am free, "he" must obey. . . . But we are accustomed to disregard this duality, and to deceive ourselves about it by means of the synthetic concept "I" . . . to such an extent that he who wills sincerely believes that willing suffices for action.[22]

Broadly speaking, *Milton* reveals a development similar to the one outlined here. The poem progresses from a confusing plurality of sensations entailing the gradual disclosure of a ruling thought—namely, "William Blake"—to a triumphant sense of self-mastery and renewed power. The opening plates primarily exhibit obscure first-stage "sensations." But they do so in as highly specific a manner as Nietzsche's analysis would suggest.

The passages composing plates 3–7 form two sets: (1) pieces of an epic narrative that subsequently becomes the Bard's Song (4:1–20, 5:1–4), and (2) everything else. The second set is not random, however, but has two defining features: first, the general familiarity of the material, which presents either scenes from London (4:21–28, 5:38–6:35) or interpolations of Blake's previous mythologizing (all of plate 3, 5:5–37); and second, the material's apparent total irrelevance to the proposed theme of the narrative, the Three Classes of Men. In set 2, then, is represented Nietzsche's "sensation of the state 'away from which'": the selfhood of accumulated past experience (the historical Blake's life in London, his previous writings) which is to be overcome through self-annihilation (hence the irrelevance of these passages to the work at hand). Set 1, the narrative bits, gives on the other hand "the sensation of the state 'towards which'": the new poem, whose successful performance will revitalize the poet's identity. The narrative disjunctions embody "the sensation of this 'from' and 'towards' themselves" and its "accompanying muscular sensation." They manifest the disruptiveness of the speech act *as* an act, the effort needed to wrest oneself out of oneself and so create new possibilities for growth—possibilities that are not actualized until plate 7, when the Bard begins to sing in earnest.

The success of this effort is measured by the seven-times repeated "Mark well my words! they are of your eternal salvation."[23] Is this the Bard addressing his epic audience or the author warning baffled readers not to throw the book down? Initially (2:25) there is no way of telling; the line lacks a determining context. Yet by plate 7 it has occurred no fewer than three times. Such insistence is necessary presumably because the Bard's words indeed do *not* appear of our eternal salvation. The abrupt injunction only makes us more forcibly aware how far *Milton* is from containing a persona who might plausibly be speaking with such self-assurance. Once the Bard's Song becomes continuous on plate 7, however, the phrase is henceforth heard as his. If we continue to detect in it the author's personal voice, it is only indirectly, via the Bard's, in the same way as we learn of Blake's residence at Felpham via the Bard's epic allegory. So it appears the author has finally submerged himself in the Bard persona. The first few "Mark well my words!" sound self-important, like a strident parody of the somewhat firmer admonitions of Milton's epic voice. By contrast, the final two repetitions seem to reveal a distinctly new tone of seriousness and authority. They evince the growth in self-mastery that Nietzsche sees as springing from a successful act of the will: " 'I' am free, 'he' must obey." It is by some such development as this that the inchoate would-be author of plates 3–7 evolves into the Bard, a collective entity more resembling the legendary Homer than the supremely individualistic Milton, but one who can at least speak and be recognized.

But why should *Milton*'s speech act be so much more conspicuously effortful than any other poem's? Most simply, because the whole of *Milton* takes place within a single moment of inspiration; the poem scrutinizes at length mental acts occurring in a flash. A more detailed reply is suggested by the ambiguities of the invocation. As Harold Bloom noticed, the Daughters of Beulah "delight" but they also offer "delusions" (2:1–5; E, p. 910). Like patrons, the Daughters are a necessary evil; by refreshing the pilgrim's hunger and thirst they enable him to continue his spiritual journey, yet these refreshments are also temptations to abandon the journey altogether. The poet's capsule history of Beulah can therefore be seen to summarize the mythology leading up to and necessitating *Milton*:

> . . . Come into my hand
> By your mild power; descending down the Nerves of my right arm
> From out the Portals of my Brain, where by your ministry

The Eternal Great Humanity Divine. planted his Paradise,
And in it caus'd the Spectres of the Dead to take sweet forms
In likeness of himself. Tell also of the False Tongue! vegetated
Beneath your land of shadows: of its sacrifices. and
Its offerings; even till Jesus, the image of the Invisible God
Became its prey; a curse, an offering, and an atonement. [2:5–13]

The agents of "Eternal Great Humanity Divine" are modestly unnamed, but the "sweet forms" that represent him clearly refer to Los's labors in *The Four Zoas* "to fabricate embodied semblances in which the dead / May live" (E, p. 370), and by extension to Blake's own attempt at constructing a mythological pantheon. The poet appears fully aware of the greenhouse effect to which his mental garden is dangerously prone. "The False Tongue" is evidently an uncontrollable mythological language which has usurped the human realities originally providing its inspiration ("even Jesus") and destroyed itself as a result, thus becoming a curse *and* an atonement.

The invocation tells not simply that *Milton* is to be the product of misleading muses; it indicates further that the poet acknowledges their necessity to himself. Either he must accept his unreliable mythological tongue, at least provisionally, or forever hold his peace, for it seems the tongue cannot be made true but by process of use. The inarticulateness of plates 3–7 reflects the poet's search for a new mythology with which to begin the new poem, a search inhibited by his inexorable awareness of the potential falsity of mythology. We see him attempting a variety of styles recalling the *Book of Los* and *Urizen* (plate 3), *Visions of the Daughters of Albion* (5:19–37), also *Jerusalem*, Chapter One (plate 6). The fact that they all prove false starts indicates he isn't comfortable with any. This helps explain why Blake cut his splendid preface when he added plates 3, 4, and 5 to the two previously completed versions of the poem: its aggressive confidence clashes with the effect of stammering anxiety that was evidently the reason for these plates.[24]

Finally, on plate 7 the narrative disjunctions cease and the Bard takes control of *Milton*. Apparently the Muses of Beulah approve of his Song. So they should, for the style of the Bard's Song is the style of *The Four Zoas*, their most recent inspiration: hermetic mythology concealing autobiographical material within a cosmic outer narrative. The loose forked tongue of *The Four Zoas* is where Blake left off before beginning *Milton*; by now accepting this tongue as the only one he's got, Blake will perhaps be able to make it speak true, thus recovering poetic control. The story of Leutha, a digression little regarded by most commentators, implies as much.[25] Calling herself "the Author" (11:35) of Satan's sin, Leutha claims she alone is responsible for his losing control of the harrow and Phaeton-like razing of earth. Damon has shown that the Blakean harrow can be seen as a vehicle of poetry which plows "lines" into the poet's mental garden, enabling the specters to vegetate into mythological forms. Leutha would therefore seem to be allegorizing a failure of authorship we have already noticed. It is moving to regard as the Blake of *The Four Zoas* her brave but cupidinous Satan struggling to master a self-imposed task that only gets harder the more he resists it, until finally he defeats himself, blackening the earth he desired to glorify and quicken.

Yet this comparison, set up after all by the Blake of *Milton*, is also ironic. The allegory of Satan and Leutha, his muse—for she, too, is a seductive Daughter of Beulah—parodies the inspiration of *Paradise Lost*. Having followed his muse "Into the Heav'n of Heav'ns," the Miltonic poet in Book VII requests a safe journey home:

> Return me to my Native Element:
> Lest from this flying Steed unrein'd, (as once
> Bellerophon, though from a lower Clime)
> Dismounted, on th' Aleian Field I fall,
> Erroneous there to wander and forlorn.
>
> . . .
>
> Standing on Earth, not rapt above the Pole,
> More safe I sing with mortal voice.[26]

Satan-Blake suffers just such a dismount, and with consequences fully as damaging as Milton indicates: for the author of *Milton*, the runaway tongue of *The Four Zoas* is a form of wandering erroneous and forlorn. But this fall is not irreversible. In the end, *Milton* displays its author standing on earth, not lost within the impersonal vastnesses of the Bard's Song, and singing more securely with his own mortal voice. Thus the falling Blake reaches the same destination Milton reached without falling; he only takes a more roundabout route. This twisting fortunate fall is Blake's passage through the vortex of the poem *Milton* itself.

Meanwhile, the Leutha-muse's nocturnal temptation of Satan-Blake is a mere travesty of Milton's "Celestial Patroness, who deigns / Her nightly visitation unimplor'd, / And dictates to me slumb'ring, or inspires / Easy my unpremeditated Verse" (IX, 21–24). In a different context, Erdman, as we have seen, finds excessive unpremeditation to be precisely the cause of *The Four Zoas'* foundering. Although any chronological grouping of the various Nights remains hypothetical, it appears each new narrative sequence necessitated painstaking revision of all the rest of the narrative before the two could be brought into alignment.[27] One step forward, two steps back: inspiration in this case is perhaps more facile than "easy."

There is further irony in the fact that Milton's lines accompany a demand for "answerable style" with which to complete the last, most recognizably human part of his argument—the eating of the apple and its consequences—whereas the mythology of *The Four Zoas*, we have seen, is a style unanswerably oblique. In thus adopting the style of *The Four Zoas* but then making it discredit itself, Blake stresses the temporariness of the Bard's Song. Evidently the poet of *Milton* is using the Song as means to an identity beyond the Bard persona, who of course is unaware of the parodies, and its indirectness enables him to avoid exposing his intentions prematurely.

The cosmos of the Bard's Song is an inner space. Los, Rintrah, Palamabron and Satan, whatever else they may be (pace Damon and Erdman), personify aspects of the universal poetic mind. In terms of the concomitant psychological allegory, Satan's fall is a purging of preoccupying self-doubts; by causing limits of contraction and opacity to be established (10:1–11), it provides the minimum of imaginative unity needed in order for the poet to look beyond himself to the announced story of Milton. Out of sight, out of mind: the obstreperous Satan actually disappears through his own breach in the psychic decorum (9:19–52). However, so as not to preclude the possibility of his future redemption and the ultimate reunification of humanity, Satan is not destroyed but repressed, thus becoming cathected as a remote but ubiquitous anxiety. His fall is an apparent rise to power over the earth created to sustain him in his eternal death. These events recapitulate the penultimate Eighth Night of *The Four Zoas*, but in *Milton* they are merely preliminary. The function of the Bard's Song is to externalize Satan from the poet's mind in order that he may then be discovered by Milton. Thus the Satan of corrupted Puritanism which the dead poet goes to redeem we see to be the living poet Blake's Satan of personal self-doubt. If the poetic mind behind the Bard's Song is too uncertain of himself to embrace Satan directly, he may yet do so indirectly by embracing Milton.

But not without struggle, as plates 14–22 show. The story of Milton's descent to earth demands relinquishing the egocentric mythology of the Bard's Song. No longer able to hide behind his titans, the poet is simply thrust naked into the narrative, generating a crisis of confidence that threatens to end not just the Bard's Song but the poem itself. Milton's objective, we are told, is "Albions land: / Which is this earth of vegetation on which now I write" (14:40–41). Instantly the mythological curtain falls back—too late, though, to prevent a comparison of the two poets hardly reassuring for Blake. When the above-cited passage on the vortex next appears (15:21–27), it only reemphasizes the author's need of humility. The "human form, a friend with whom [the traveller thro Eternity] livd benevolent" recalls Hayley and Blake's rueful realization that "Corporeal Friends are Spiritual Enemies" (4:26)[28] who obstruct one's spiritual journey unless abandoned. In context, however, the traveler is Milton; Blake merely watches him from earth below. It would seem that as Hayley was to Blake, now Blake is to Milton; like Hayley, Blake has become an expedient in a greater poet's mission. Hence when he again breaks into the narrative to declare how Milton entered his left foot (15:47–49), the ensuing account of the consequences focuses exclusively on Milton: his heightened self-awareness, his confrontations of the Shadowy Female, Urizen, and Rahab-Tirzah. Blake, evidently none the wiser for this merging, is ignored. So, although one might expect Blake as a poet to identify with Milton, there follows a startling outburst of despair in which he explicitly associates himself with the freezing clay of unredeemed Urizen:

> O how can I with my gross tongue that cleaveth to the dust,
> Tell of the Four-fold Man, in starry numbers fitly orderd
> Or how can I with my cold hand of clay! . . .

Here, in the dead waste and middle of the poem, with the poet apparently too feeble to pen another word, comes an about-face:

> . . . But thou O Lord
> Do with me as thou wilt! for I am nothing, and vanity.
> If thou chuse to elect a worm, it shall remove the mountains.   [20:15–19]

The difference between the two passages is the difference between looking back toward a lost world—the Bard's mythological cosmos—and looking ahead to whatever might eventually replace it, namely earth. Like Phoebus' reply to the despairing poet of *Lycidas* (". . . But not the praise"), Blake's tone shift is all the more abrupt for arriving at a line ending; and yet it also serves to complete the line and continue the poem, thus seeming necessary and providential. In both cases the poet appears to discover, in his moment of doubt, an answering voice in some deeper stratum of himself. For Blake, the virtue of this voice is precisely its un-Homeric, un-Bard-like humility. By thus reconciling himself to an outwardly restricted role in the poem—a role heroic only in the obedient Miltonic sense of "standing firm" against temptation[29]—Blake begins to accept his Urizenic need to be remade in Milton's image. In an unprecedented style of direct address, he intimately enjoins us to share his awareness of the redeeming vulnerability of the life principle:

> Seest thou the little winged fly, smaller than a grain of sand?
> It has a heart like thee; a brain open to heaven & hell,
> Withinside wondrous & expansive; its gates are not clos'd,

I hope thine are not: hence it clothes itself in rich array;
Hence thou art cloth'd with human beauty O thou mortal man.
Seek not thy heavenly father then beyond the skies:
There Chaos dwells & ancient Night & Og & Anak old.   [20:27–33]

What dwells beyond the skies is mythology, "the Seat Of Satan" (20:37–
38), an unregenerate disguising of the human which Blake now casts off.
By contrast, the microcosmic fly stands at the other end of the *Milton*
vortex, the infinitely small point at the tip where the mind repossesses its
projections as lively acts of vision. Restricted Blake's role may be, but at
least it is now overt and unambivalent. In a crucial affirmation, he tells
how "all this Vegetable World appear on my left foot / As a bright
sandal . . . / I stooped down & bound it on to walk forward thro' Eternity" (21:12–14). Blake's difficulties in reaching this resolution recall
Satan on the last leg of his journey from Hell in *Paradise Lost*:

> Satan now in prospect of Eden, and nigh the place where he must now at-
> tempt the bold enterprise which he undertook alone against God and
> Man, falls into many doubts with himself, and many passions, fear, envy,
> and despair; but at length confirms himself in evil, [and] journeys on to
> Paradise. [The Argument, IV]

Having survived his crisis of confidence, Blake—who together with
Milton appears as Satan to the now obviously impeded perception of
Palamabron and Rintrah—can commence his final descent to Earth for the
unmasking of the "real" Satan, the anxious usurper of whom the Bard
sang.

The ensuing description of Los's world in plates 22–30 consolidates
Milton's new style of immediate address. It is a return to mythologizing
after the disjunctions of plates 14–21, but mythologizing now in the
service of personal prophecy by Blake as author telling how poems get
written. The redemptive Moment in which "the Poets Work is Done"
(29:1) extends systematically the vision of sportive "Minute Particulars"
that became available in the fly passage of plate 20. Blake is no longer the
Sons of Los but Los himself; thus from 25:66 to the close of Book One, the
Father's exhortations to his Sons are simultaneously seen to be mythological explications controlled by the author. Unlike the Bard's Song, however, the mode of these plates is not autobiographical concealment; the
Los persona does serve as a vehicle of positive self-expression. As the
prophetic statement of their merging shows—it begins as Blake's but ends
by being attributed to Los (22:12–26)—Blake speaks not delphically
through Los but rather *as* Los. And yet, although this is evidently an

improvement over the Bard's Song, the ultimate goal is for Blake to speak directly as himself.

For despite its splendors, Los's world can be only provisional. Although his Sons' ingenuity makes them masters of mundane space and time (28:44–29:36), the Sons are emotionally limited and their realm of artistry therefore insufficient. Los's apocalyptic winepress operates with a distinct indifference to human life, as occasionally in their frenzy the pressers trample and drown one another. Conversely, the merciful artisans who fashion forms for the feeble doubting Spectres appear ignorant of their charges' fates: Rahab simply weaves them back into "The veil of human miseries" (29:62). If Los's world supplies the means of redeeming human life, as almost all readers agree, nevertheless Blake's point would seem to be that except in certain supreme moments of vision one cannot actually dwell there and be human. The space for ordinary human dwelling is apparently earth.

Hence Blake-Milton's discovery that he must modify his journey of self-annihilation to include the more positive act of bringing Ololon to life. Ultimately, Ololon is the intimacy denied expression by John Milton and implicitly William Blake in their relationships on earth, particularly those with women.[30] Union with Blake teaches Milton that "the Three Heavens of Beulah were beheld / By him on earth in his bright pilgrimage of sixty years / In those three females whom his Wives, & those three whom his Daughters / Had represented and containd ... / ... also Milton knew: they and / Himself was Human" (15:51–17:6). Milton's new knowledge is the prerequisite for his eventual transformation. One can look back on one's public life as a Rintrah prophet-reformer, see its errors and resolve, still in character, to reform them too; this is to be just before the law. But the yearning to realize a portion of one's humanity that one never knew to exist even potentially, much less erroneously, implies a change of the character itself; this is self-annihilation in the radical sense of conversion, the transformation of oneself though love into Christ, as the conclusion reveals.[31] Milton therefore cannot already know at the outset of his descent that there is something missing from his pilgrimage of sixty years which needs redemption. Gradually, his approach to earth opens his eyes.

Thus the arousal of Ololon, the poet's human potential, is also gradual. *Milton* is arranged to present her in phenomenological fashion as an obscure object of desire occasioned by the poet's awakening and meaningful solely in terms of it. Accordingly, our first sight of Ololon, on plate 21, is just a glimpse. "A sweet River, of mild & liquid pearl, / Namd Ololon" (21:15–16) groggily decides to descend into Beulah; the significance of this is unclear, but plainly it somehow follows from and reflects the union of Blake and Milton immediately preceding. Then comes Blake-Milton's further union with Los and journey through his realms of imagination (22–29). Our perceptions thus heightened, when plates 30–36 shift back to Ololon she appears proportionately more distinct. Now, Ololon is the collective personality of all her Sons and Daughters. When finally she steps out the other side of Beulah into Felpham garden, "as One Female, Ololon and all its mighty Hosts / Appear'd: A Virgin of twelve years" (36:16–17). Like the poet himself, Ololon is becoming a progressively more human being. She has passed through a series of mythological lineaments or States, which are not themselves her individual identity but rather the path to it.

The editing of *Milton* resembles a D. W. Griffith movie climax. Across a great Space—earth—a pair of estranged lovers are seen straining with one instinct toward an embrace; meanwhile, the poem cuts back and forth between them, looking through the eyes of each at the other figure coming into view, ever more urgently desired. Milton and Ololon, it seems, are converging on a single point. As the curiously mundane illustration to plate 36 (prosaically subtitled "Blake's Cottage at Felpham") shows, their inspired reunion takes place, finally, as nothing more or less than a moment of vision in the mind of the historical William Blake, who walked in the garden one spring dawn while his wife, "sick with fatigue" (36:32), remained indoors. So it appears that every day is a means of gathering in human potential (35:42–47) and thus a foreshadowing of the apocalypse to which it actually brings us one step closer (42:16–43:1).

What makes possible such exuberant mundaneness is the final dispersal of *Milton*'s mythology, revealing with enhanced beauty the concrete particulars that evidently have been standing behind it all along. The "Vision of the lamentation of Beulah over Ololon" (31:45, 63) derives from nothing more exotic than the common birds and flowers of an English spring morning. Like the pagan gods of Milton's Nativity Ode or the pastoral tribute of flowers in *Lycidas*—poetry whose poignant futility the description of Ololon specifically recalls[32]—Blake's similarly unredeemed tongue of Beulah burgeons most plaintively while in process of falling silent. Yet despite this ironic awareness of suffering and loss, *Milton*'s lyricism here is primarily an exultant survey by the author, in person, of the brave new world he is about to inhabit. We are *told* that Ololon's music is really a lament at her impending womanhood and sounds like a glad song of spring only because men's ears are clogged; nevertheless, what the poem actually describes is not the lament but the song. The tongue of *Milton*, then, is evidently no longer Beulah's but the mortal author's own.[33]

Pointedly, Blake reports that when the virgin Ololon entered his garden he "address'd her as a Daughter of Beulah" (36:27). In other words, she is his muse, the invocation's generalized Daughters of Beulah now compressed into human form. They have finally obeyed his opening summons to come into his physical person from out the portals of his mythologizing brain (2:1–15); simply, Blake had no idea at the time how arduous that journey would be and how tremendously important for himself. Thus it appears the whole of *Milton* has taken place within the poet's single dawning moment of insight into the human truth behind the myth of his muses. The poem itself was merely the route to this realization. So when Blake writes his friend Thomas Butts from Felpham on April 25, 1803, disclosing "the Grand Reason of my being brought down here," he barely mentions the "long Poem" he has probably just about completed but instead stresses the "Spiritual Acts" embodied in its composition: "I have written this Poem from immediate Dictation twelve or sometimes twenty or thirty lines at a time without Premeditation & even against my Will. the Time it has taken in writing was thus renderd Non Existent. & an immense Poem Exists which seems to be the Labour of a long Life all producd without Labour or Study" (E, p. 728–29). Such a poem is a vortex: it is merely provisional, a means to life. Or more precisely, considering the unmistakable time and labor required to produce it, we might say that such a poem is, like the vortex, a potential barrier to life which succeeds, paradoxically, through the poet's attaining enough inspiration to surmount it. After all, necessary as *Milton* seems to have been for Blake in retrospect, the task was voluntarily, even defiantly chosen; materially speaking, Blake's efforts could have been much better employed in service to corporeal friend Hayley, as both well knew. Like any freely willed challenge, therefore, what the poem provided was an opportunity for self-mastery—and also its converse, self-annihilation.

With his muse so close at hand, Blake is able to experience the action of *Milton* directly as personal vision, thus taking control of the narrative in propria persona. Since there is no doubting his inspiration now, his concealment of anxieties by mythology is no longer necessary, and so mythology, indeed *Milton* itself, is sloughed off as just one more Satanic covering of the human which the poet must annihilate in order to become fully himself. "This is a false Body: an Incrustation over my Immortal / Spirit," Milton tells Ololon and points to Satan (40:35). Accordingly, Milton, "collecting all his fibres into impregnable strength" (38:5), compresses himself into his actual seventeenth-century "outline of identity," steps out from Satan's bosom and exposes him as the usurper, contradiction itself, a mere parody of the human (39:25–27). Somewhat less grandly, the smaller figure of Blake achieves a similar victory with respect to his own mythology. He annihilates it—the machinery at 38:50–39:9 and 42:7–12 combines the thunder and lightning of biblical epiphanies with that of opera and fireworks[34]—and the energy released by this combustion instead of being dispersed is then recovered as Ololon, unmediated inspiration. To put it another way: what Blake experiences walking in his garden is the concussive impact of the poem's imploding mythology, the charged significance of its annihilation for himself as author (it literally knocks him to his senses). He sees not a hallucination but, as he puts it elsewhere, an "Intellectual Vision." That is, the implosion is a "realization" in both main senses of the word. It is Blake's *recognition* of his personal Satan, self-doubt cloaked in mythology; and what follows from this, it is also the repossession of the poet's emanation, Ololon, Blake's *actualization* of the mythologically projected portion of himself.

Yet the Miltonic repossession produces an apotheosis; Blake's, merely a reawakening. Being already dead, Milton is a step ahead of Blake, who can recover Ololon in a temporary way until tomorrow but cannot altogether redeem her. So it would seem the struggle toward full self-integration is one that can never be final while we are still in life. Milton ascends to eternity the same instant fainting Blake hits solid earth, there to continue the life pilgrimage his predecessor has just completed. But henceforth Blake must be his own guide. For, once the two poets appear in the garden as distinct human figures, it is plain that their union is over. Milton's merging with Ololon is mildly reflected in Blake's life when he collapses and awakens reconciled with his own "sweet Shadow of Delight" (42:28), his hitherto sick and refractory wife who previously remained indoors unaware of his visions; but for the most part, says Blake, the "wondrous acts" of the great pair remained "by me unknown / Except remotely" (40:2–3).

Yet if Milton now abandons Blake in order to become Jesus, we also see that Blake no longer needs Milton because he has finally become, by great effort, himself. Evidently Blake has been in Felpham throughout the poem; the long journey he undertook was only to get there more fully. So where Milton leaves off, Blake begins, and the effect is mixed. Denied a Miltonic apotheosis, wistfully Blake recognizes that the alternate route to eternity, apocalypse, is also at present unavailable. In a very major respect, then, unfulfillment is the order of the day. Prophecy can become actual in the sense of becoming explicit, these last plates show, but it cannot replace actuality. Albion's awakening will doubtless prove most inspiring when it happens, but a proleptic narrative of the event at this point would only falsify the poem, which concludes by humbly entering history as a document in the life of its author. For if Blake let Albion walk forth now, he would equally have to admit all the rest of the mythology that Albion comprises, so throwing the poem back to the Bard's Song. Staunchly, *Milton* lets him slumber. But although Albion's time is not yet come, the final paragraph and accompanying illustration demonstrate that Blake's time, and the *beginning* of the time for apocalypse, are now.[35] In the end, therefore, Blake's difficult submission to earthly life confers a subdued fulfillment of its own: namely, a *vision* of Milton's much greater fulfillment in which he cannot share.

The one goal everybody has been striving toward is briefly attained when Milton embraces Ololon and becomes

> One Man Jesus the Saviour. wonderful! round his limbs
> The Clouds of Ololon folded as a Garment dipped in blood
> Written within & without in woven letters: and the Writing
> Is the Divine Revelation in the Litteral Expression.   [42:11–14][36]

Ololon's consummation redeems Milton from entrapment in her demonic parody, Rahab's rigid cloak of Puritan errors. "My Garments shall be woven of sighs & heart broken lamentations," crows Rahab; "I will have Writings written all over it in Human Words / That every Infant that is born upon the Earth shall read / And get by rote as a hard task of a life of sixty years" (18:6–14). Like the interwoven narratives of *The Four Zoas*, Rahab's writings, which include even the living word of God once it is made matter for memory only, do not serve human life but entangle and bind it. By contrast, Ololon's cloudy garment, which interpenetrates the wearer and spells with his blood, is virtually impalpable. Like *Milton* itself, then, Ololon's paradoxical covering of words only reveals the more explicitly the naked human truth in which, for Blake, all imagination subsists: Christ as Logos, here seen to be the vital principle of human being which every individual identity innately strives to express through its particular life and works, and yet also strives to become in spite of itself (poets only more deliberately so than others).

Finally, Blake collapses. For an anticlimactic "moment" (small "m" now) he appears in his "mortal state" (42:26) outstretched upon the garden path, the path Milton has just trod. Then *Milton* ends and the author, it seems, actually passes beyond his poem into the daily realities awaiting him just outside the last line, "To go forth to the Great Harvest & Vintage of the Nations" (43:1). Having emerged from his mythological vortex through an apex of vision, Blake thus resumes his earthly pilgrimage. Ultimately even the visionary remains divided from Jesus, the object of vision, by his own body. In inspired Moments he may surmount this last of all Satanic coverings, but short of suicide he can hardly annihilate it for good. Hence the reintegration of Blake's human self at the end of *Milton* is really an escape from the poem and readiness to write another. Of all its peculiarities, perhaps the strangest thing about *Milton* is that it self-destructively gets itself out of the way as it proceeds, so clearing the way for the thoroughly logocentric *Jerusalem*.

III

A mythological poem that proceeds by annihilating mythology neatly supplies its own conclusion—but where does one go from there? The next poem, if there is to be one, must somehow be made to annihilate continually from the start. Having realized through *Milton* that the creative process entails a perpetual sending forth of new "emanations" even though its ultimate aim is to repossess them all, Blake in *Jerusalem* struggles to write in full face of this perplexity. His characteristically strenuous solution is continually to re-create his continually self-annihilating mythology. *Jerusalem* is therefore a return to mythology, but mythology tempered and qualified by Los's need to subjugate his Spectre and remain personally self-unified before he can attempt to awaken Albion, the unified humanity that is the end of every artist's labors.

The reason this struggle particularly dominates Chapter One is that the poet of *Jerusalem* must confront doubt fully at the outset of writing. Imbued, now, with the ineluctable awareness that he also stands in Satan's bosom, Blake cannot repeat the gradual lifting of mythological veils that made *Milton* essentially just a preparing for this confrontation. Hence Los's struggle, unlike the earlier combat between Palamabron and Satan which it resembles, is not preliminary to his main endeavor but an integral and constant part of it. The smithy hammering away at the dread furnaces of vision, patiently "measuring out" "minute particulars" with "beats" upon his anvil, is a picture never far from view (among several such passages, see 56:18–24)—a patent allegory of Blake himself composing *Jerusalem* and contending, as Chapter One tells, with the nightmare of solipsistic isolation in a London grown paranoid from years of war and repression. He is "Striving with Systems to deliver Individuals from those Systems" (11:5), the paradox being that since he strives both *against* systems and *by means of* them—for the "with" is ambiguous—what endures is not the systems but only the striving itself. This is not, however, the infinite eternal becoming of *The Marriage of Heaven and Hell* all over again. Since the poet of *Jerusalem* acknowledges the immediate felt reality of historical and psychological states of suffering, however delusive such phenomena may ultimately prove, he is not seeking to surmount or escape the limitations of empirical existence but to work through them: "I must Create a System, or be enslav'd by another Mans" (10:20).

Such running in order to stand still is reflected in the form of the poem, heterogeneous yet broadly unified. *Jerusalem* takes the different styles through which *Milton* evolved and presents them all simultaneously: Albion and Los jostle alongside biblical figures, personified British cities, and great men of European intellectual history, as well as obscure contemporary individuals such as Scofield whose significance in the poem is purely autobiographical. The result is ceaseless ferment, mythology expanded to bursting. So, for example, those tedious catalogs matching British counties with Hebrew tribes, their typological counterparts (15:30–16:60, 71:10–72:52), can be seen as systematic demonstrations of the versatility of *Jerusalem*; they represent mythology in the act of self-annihilation, that extreme limit of formlessness where personification verges apocalyptically on Adamic naming. Such passages are evidently poetry's closest approach to the redeemed Zoas' conversation "in Visionary forms dramatic which bright / Redounded from their Tongues . . . / In new Expanses, creating exemplars of Memory and of Intellect / Creating Space, Creating Time . . . / . . . / . . . & every Word & Every Character / Was Human" (98:28–36): the language of the indwelling Logos, a plastic mythology of spontaneous self-expression in which creative word and act are one.

Nonetheless, despite the protean formlessness of its mythology, *Jerusalem* is not a chaos. On the contrary, the poem discloses a distinctly human shape, only "human" in a sense so thoroughgoing as to overwhelm mere individualism. With the poet's mythology now undermined through its implied contrast with the language of the Universal Man (the reunified Zoas), we look *through* the mythology to its organizing central source, the historical William Blake. But what, after all, is this presence—"William Blake"? Only an idea, we see, for in reality no one, no matter how isolated or visionary, is ever quite cut off from the shared earthly circumstances of experience. *Jerusalem*'s directly autobiographical material (Los at the anvil, the fight with Scofield and ensuing trial for sedition, the quarrel with Hayley) is therefore only the limiting "outline of identity" of a life experience ultimately inseparable from the gigantic surrounding contours of Albion himself—that is, the overall life experience, social, political and intellectual, of early nineteenth-century Britain. If *Milton* expresses Blake's struggle to overcome preoccupying self-doubts and recover his rightful place in the world, then *Jerusalem*, in Morris Eaves's words, "follows the work of art outward toward the audience by extending the metaphor of expression itself: if the artist expresses the work of art, then the work of art also expresses its audience."[37]

Thus Blake, having in *Milton* repossessed his mythology as direct personal vision, is able to go on projecting it despite its internalization. *Jerusalem* takes up and inverts Milton's vision in *Areopagitica* of a London filled with warfaring Christian humanists whose industrious mental activity must sooner or later rouse the whole nation. "Behold now this vast City," urges Milton: "The shop of war hath not there more anvils and hammers waking, . . . than there be pens and heads there, sitting by their studious lamps, musing, searching, revolving new notions and ideas wherewith to present, as with their homage and their fealty, the approaching reformation" (p. 743). Milton's city swarms with thoughtful men; Blake's is a man swarming with citified thoughts. "I behold London," he answers Milton, "a Human awful wonder of God! / He says . . . / . . . / Awake Albion, awake! and let us awake up together. / My Houses are Thoughts: my Inhabitants; Affections, / The children of my thoughts" (34:29–34). *Jerusalem*'s humanized universe springs from its free-form mythology, no longer calcified but returned to its original molten state in *The Marriage of Heaven and Hell* as "living fluids" of the poet's mind. Nevertheless, as I have tried to show, the return is not a simple one. The poet has recovered the expressive vigor he originally lost through the entropy of creation only because his mind has, in effect, turned inside out. Whereas the young Blake-Devil's living fluids circulated within a private cavern surrounded by an "expanse" full of Devourers, those of the *Jerusalem* poet wash easily back and forth across the expanse itself—all six thousand years of it, from London to Jerusalem—swallowing the Devourers in vision. If the *Milton* vortex supplied Blake with a provisional means to concrete human life, *Jerusalem*, expanding inward from *Milton*'s apex, serves to embrace the new world of visionary experience in all its diverse plenitude. "I rest not from my great task!" the poet exclaims upon commencing his new poem,

> To open the Eternal Worlds, to open the immortal Eyes
> Of Man inwards into the Worlds of Thought: into Eternity
> Ever expanding in the Bosom of God. the Human Imagination. [5:17–20]

Self-Doubt and
Doubt of Others

For as the eye sees not itself, unless by reflection in a glass, so
neither can we know our own internal features, unless by
beholding the counterparts of them in other persons.
  Abraham Tucker, The Light of Nature Pursued, *pt. I, chap. xxiv.*

Hume's ethics of sentiment, summarized with deliberate shock in the precept "Reason is, and ought only to be the slave of the passions,"[1] indeed provides a proto-Romantic escape from the problem of reason's inefficacy, but it fails to resolve the problem. The Humean philosopher either must abandon his speculations altogether or eventually tumble once more into the paralyzing melancholy from which sentiment has offered relief. This schizoid split between reason and feeling, mind and body, the Romantics aim to surmount by showing that although the two are distinct, they cannot be separate, for the mind is nowhere if not in the body. Similarly, the symbiosis of style and narrative in *Milton* and the other Romantic narrative poems we shall examine, and the strangely formless form that results, can be seen to demonstrate the cognitive status of feeling and its interdependence with reason. The authors' core premise, stemming from the associationist exploration during the half-century after Hume of various less than fully conscious shades and habits of thought, is that consciousness depends on and presupposes experience—not the other way round, as presumed by Descartes's cogito and Hume's distinct, independently existing perceptions. Inasmuch as their narratives disclose an initially dim, visceral groping *toward* consciousness, all the authors would concur with William Godwin (whatever they might think of his necessitarianism) that "thought may be the source of animal motion, and at the same time be unattended with consciousness. . . . Consciousness is a sort of supplementary reflection, by which the mind not only has the thought, but adverts to its own situation, and observes that it has it."[2] As Blake emphasizes in telling how Milton entered into his foot,

> But I knew not that it was Milton, for man cannot know
> What passes in his members till periods of Space & Time
> Reveal the secrets of Eternity: for more extensive
> Than any other earthly things, are Mans earthly lineaments.[3]

Since experience occurs in time, these narratives refute Descartes's postulate that "I am, I exist, is necessarily true each time that I pronounce it, or that I mentally conceive it."[4] One needn't endorse the self-objectifying ego of German transcendentalism to see that in temporal terms Descartes is *not* the same whenever he mentally conceives himself because he becomes modified each time, however slightly, by his own previous act of reflection. Coleridge points out the roots of this position in traditional British empiricism, significantly in one of the few original passages in a section of the *Biographia Literaria* lifted almost entirely from Schelling. "The assertion of Hobbes and Hartley . . . that all real knowledge supposes a prior sensation" is perfectly true in a nonreductionist sense, he claims; "for sensation itself is but vision nascent, not the cause of intelligence, but intelligence itself revealed as an earlier power in the process of self-construction."[5] Similarly, as I tried to show in chapter 2, the early Blake's emphasis on the body as the source of imaginative perception reflects a nondualistic view of Lockean sensationalism as providing the very basis for "Imagination which is Spiritual Sensation" (E, p. 703).[6]

The dualistic metaphysics finds its counterpart in the neoclassical attempt to define the relation of wit and its virtual twin, expression, to nature. In Pope's formulation:

> True Wit is Nature to advantage dress'd,
> What oft was thought, but ne'er so well express'd;
> . . .
> But true Expression, like th' unchanging Sun,
> Clears, and improves, whate'er it shines upon,
> It gilds all objects, but it alters none.[7]

Expression here is the added embellishment that makes nature decent and presentable; it is, says Pope, "the dress of thought." If wit is a form of perception, then nature's priority as the object of perception is taken for granted, even if we understand the word in its broadest sense to mean not just physical nature but whatever is given, the nature of things, human nature included. Indeed, the assumption of a cosmic union between human and physical nature is crucial to a main paradigm of Augustan nature poetry, the *discordia concors*; remove it, and the poet's comparisons of the two realms, lacking a meaningful basis, lose all decorum, cease to be a set of necessary and predetermined correspondences and become merely a discrete series of illustrations. It is equally crucial, however, that because the poet simply accepts this underlying conformity between man and nature, its existence cannot ever complicate the way he actually views nature, so that for practical purposes he can consider the two realms distinct and separate. After all, if he did see the human and the natural as identical, how could he possibly draw the analogies requisite for his poetry?

This contradiction in the Augustan *discordia concors* becomes glaring in an explicitly ideological work like Pope's *Essay on Man*. The poem begins by establishing a "vast Chain of Being" extending from God to man to beasts. But since man is just a link in the chain, and "What can we reason, but from what we know? / . . . or can a part contain the whole?" it follows that " 'Tis but a part we see, and not the whole." In short, man's knowledge is limited to what he can observe within his own sphere of creation: "Through worlds unnumbered though the God be known, / 'Tis ours to trace him only in our own" (I, 18–60). Nonetheless, the poet goes on to *project* all of creation by considering man as an absolute defined by his relation to the other two spheres. Epistle II commences:

> Know then thyself, presume not God to scan;
> The proper study of Mankind is Man.
> Placed on this isthmus of a middle state,
> A Being darkly wise, and rudely great:
>
> . . .
>
> He hangs between; in doubt to act, or rest;
> In doubt to deem himself a God, or Beast;
> In doubt his Mind or Body to prefer.   [II, 1–9]

From this viewpoint, God and beast, mind and body, reason and self-love are contraries fighting a tug-of-war for the human soul, itself essentially an oxymoronic combination of contraries. Rather paradoxically, it turns out the reason man's knowledge is so limited is that he already contains in himself all the things he wishes to know and yet fails to realize it.

This accords well with the strain of nonsensationalist epistemology in Locke's *Essay* whereby, as chapter 1's discussion of "power" showed, our ideas of objects are considered to be aspects of our perceptual relationships with them. In the context of Pope's *Essay*, however, that epistemology secretly suggests that the being who closes the Great Chain, binding it into a perfect circle, is not God but man. By abstracting God from any direct role in human affairs, Pope's deism allows him to avoid drawing so drastic an inference. For a radical anthropomorph like Blake, on the other hand, such a self-confrontation provides the very basis for prophecy: "He who sees the Infinite in all things sees God. He who sees the Ratio only sees himself only. Therefore God becomes as we are that we may be as he is" (E, p. 3). Pope's unacknowledged assumption of an interdependence, within his concept of a divinely sanctioned "Nature," of human "spiritual" nature and physical nature is again seen in the *Essay on Criticism*, which propounds the familiar hierarchy of poetic styles—high, middle, and low—based on the principle that "diff'rent styles with diff'rent subjects sort" (II, 322). Pope here implies the primacy of subject matter over style; the one is simply there, the other should conform to it. And yet the codification of a hierarchy of such correspondences would be absurd were it not believed to reflect a prior, basically idealist harmony between man's mind and the nature of things.

Whereas the Augustan discordia concors maintains the separation of the human and physical realms even while tacitly asserting their cosmic union in a higher nature, the Romantic poet actively explores this contradiction. If the poet already belongs to the human realm he is concerned to distinguish from the physical, and if his analogies between the two therefore occur within that realm, then what saves them from being mere self-projections? Such is the epistemological question we associate with Hume. The Romantics answer it by showing that since the observations on which the poet founds his analogies are events occurring in a specific time and place, his human realm contains an internalization of the physical. For the Romantics, then, one cannot proclaim truth, depict a landscape or bewail lost innocence without in the process revealing something significant about oneself. What makes such self-description meaningful, and not solipsistic, is the way it publicly objectifies the process by which the poet's experience is raised into consciousness and articulated. The poet is always present at least implicitly as the perceiver of the narrative, the events of which are presented relatively to his own developing awareness. Through this contrary method, *Milton* offers a redemptive countermovement to the preoccupation of the earlier Prophetic Books with fall and fragmentation. If those narratives remain, in Coleridge's terms, unmethodized discourse that reflects "passive impressions" of external circumstances based on the "habitual submission of the understanding to mere events and images as such, independent of any power in the mind to classify or appropriate them,"[8] then the great achievement of *Milton* is that there Blake squarely confronts the mutual dependence of the poet and his myth.

Here I must hazard some generalizations whose grossness is justified only by their heuristic purpose. Broadly speaking, narratives composed according to the neoclassical concepts of wit and nature tend to present the dramatic action as a series of events already known, selected, and arranged by an ulterior consciousness, typically the omniscient narrator. Cognition of the narrative is presupposed; the reader stands outside the dramatic action, which it is his role to analyze and judge by bringing to bear upon it a similarly preestablished hierarchy of moral-social values.[9] Like the mind as postulated by the dualistic metaphysics of Descartes and Hume, author and reader are isolated, ideal, timeless subjects whose thought is directed outward to an external universe of fixed objects. Each event or character is, as Hume says of the mind's perceptions, "a distinct existence, and is different, and distinguishable, and separable from every perception, either contemporary or successive" (*THN*, p. 259). In the same way, the neo-classical reader remains focused on the given contents of his reading, which does not actually dramatize the process of representation by which those contents have been brought before him.

Consider, for example, the celebrated opening couplet of Dr. Johnson's *Vanity of Human Wishes*: "Let Observation with extensive View, / Survey Mankind, from China to Peru."[10] Rightly admired by F. R. Leavis for its "unevadable concreteness" and "irresistible weight of representative human experience,"[11] Johnson's poetry nevertheless hardly owes these qualities to its imagery, Leavis's usual touchstone. Indeed, the couplet is remarkably, although typically, impersonal. "Observation" is no actual human subject but a hypostatization, placeless and bodiless, conjured by tautology from its ostensible attributes, "Survey" and "View." Thus raised beyond physical space, the poet achieves the God's-eye perspective of a Mercator map projection or of a Laplacean ideal observer able to discern both hemispheres at once (China and Peru are near antipodes). A similar development occurs with respect to time, as the poem's various historical particulars are lifted from their contexts and made exemplars of a universal moral truth: "all is vanity." Johnson's many personifications, circumlocutions, and pleonasms still hold fast, barely, to their empirical origins, as the scattering of proper and place-names vividly goes to show; *The Vanity of Human Wishes* doesn't simply reveal the effects of abstraction, it dramatizes the process itself. Yet without specific location in time and place there can be nothing for an abstract personification to do except passively exemplify itself. As Johnson himself observed of poetic allegory: "Fame tells a tale and Victory hovers over a general or perches on a standard. . . . To give them any real employment, or ascribe to them a material agency, is to . . . shock the mind by ascribing effects to non-entity."[12] "Observation" is accordingly a pleonasm, a rhetorical figure produced by the tacit suppression of an actual human figure—the poet—able to feel, think about, and handle things as well as observe them. Stemming as it does from language's usurping tendency, such a personification is in a sense specious, an impersonation. Since Observation can *only* observe, with impressive range but without power to change anything, one suspects that for all its air of aloofness it remains just another part of the general vanity below.

Such impotency is the subject of the grand fourth book of Pope's *Dunciad*, a reversed progress-poem where the personifications that supply the language of poetry steadily calcify, through the "uncreating word" of the goddess Dulness, into inert word-objects that impede all dramatic action. But if nothing takes place, there is nothing to tell; and so the narrator's capacity for poetic vision grows increasingly clouded until the poem finally self-destructs in primordial chaos. As in Blake, Pope's image for the tendency of perception to coalesce into an unparticularized object separate from the percipient is the vortex; and as in Blake, the image implies a critique of Newtonianism, the application of mechanistic determinism to personal human life. Dulness, the core of the vortex, represents not the material limitations of earthly existence but the unimaginative acceptance of materiality as the defining condition of man's *moral* world. No less than Blake's Satan or Shelley's Jupiter, Dulness embodies a failure of perception and is therefore fundamentally unreal, a paradox. As Blake and Shelley would agree, it is our own resigned embracing of Dulness that gives her life, our life. And as Pope would agree with Blake and Shelley, a universe redeemed from Dulness is no transcendent pie-in-the-sky free from gravitation and death—a world impossible to imagine, hence liable to become only another excuse for remaining inert—but one that arises from an awakened appreciation of the familiar, now seen with eyes unbedimmed by anxious fatalism.

Pope added Book the Fourth to *The Dunciad* in 1742, fourteen years after publication of the first three, at a time when the leap tide of Augustan confidence had already begun to recede, revealing mid-century shoals of poetic doubt. Its inclusion transformed the poem from self-assured corrective satire aimed at the author's assorted enemies and rivals—many in number but of trivial importance, mere gnatlike irritants—into prophetic denunciation of the genuinely appalling force of anarchy seen to underlie their behavior. Whereas the earlier books assume the existence of a public hierarchy of moral-social values able to validate the poet's criticisms of the trespassing dunces, Book the Fourth envisions a collapse of all values, and thus the end of meaningful communication. In discerning how Dulness replaces the complex unity between the Augustan poet and his audience with mere inchoate uniformity—"We hang one jingling padlock on the mind" (IV, 162), the dunces titter insidiously—Pope can be seen to anticipate Blake's attack from a far deeper wilderness on the similarly mind-forged manacles of his day.

Gregory Bateson famously remarked that schizophrenia is the outcome of Hume's frankly impracticable skepticism toward the existence of the material world. Hume's skepticism toward personal identity heightens the anxiety if that is possible; for when introspection calls personal identity into doubt, it is also calling itself into doubt, thereby shattering any lingering illusions of cozy withdrawal from an admittedly unknowable external world into a separate, interior realm of self. We've seen how Hume uses a stage metaphor to explain his inability to discover his own personal identity. Notice, however, the dunceish paralysis that pervades the passage:

> For my part, when I enter most intimately into what I call *myself*, I always stumble on some particular perception or other, of heat or cold, light or shade, love or hatred, pain or pleasure. I never can catch *myself* at any time without a perception, and never can observe any thing but the perception. . . . The mind is a kind of theatre, where several perceptions successively make their appearance; pass, re-pass, glide away and mingle in an infinite variety of postures and situations. . . . The comparison of the theatre must not mislead us. They are the successive perceptions only, that constitute the mind; nor have we the most distant notion of the place, where these scenes are represented, or of the materials, of which it is compos'd. [*THN*, p. 253]

Lost amid the phantasmagoria of this magic-lantern show, Hume becomes a detached spectator to his own perceptions. But plays have authors. Even if one stops short of Berkeley's incautious religious solution to the problem, Hume's metaphor is bound to raise the specter of mind control (here lies the paranoid aspect of Humean schizophrenia).[13] Thus, although we cannot tell where Hume's mental theater is, the absence of anyone demonstrably responsible for the show at least enables us to specify its type: theater of the absurd. The facts that we can control our perceptions by *taking* thought; that such an act underlies Hume's whole analysis, based as it is on introspection, a special state of attentive withdrawal which as it is not particularly spontaneous or habitual (that is precisely why he privileges its report) requires deliberate effort in order to be sustained; that the feeling of such exertion is bodily, Hume's body being of course the ultimate location of his mental theater—all this is ignored.

Hume's passage well expresses the curious theatricality of much eighteenth-century personification, its double movement of urbane distance and affective identification.[14] The consequences of Hume's scenario can be observed in Collins's "Epistle to Sir Thomas Hanmer," in which well-known scenes from Shakespeare's history plays are re-presented so as to isolate for intensive sympathy their principal dramatic emotions. Thus Antony of *Julius Caesar*

> . . . in Tears approv'd,
> Guards the pale Relicks of the Chief he lov'd:
> O'er the cold Corse the Warrior seems to bend,
> Deep sunk in Grief, and mourns his murther'd Friend!
> Still as they press, he calls on all around,
> Lifts the torn Robe, and points the bleeding Wound.   [127–32][15]

One notes the character's increasing frozenness, culminating in a pose of statuesque rigidity (Collins's characteristic elision of the preposition in the last line heightens the impression of arrest). Similarly, the portrayal of Coriolanus begins with a complex, turbulent figure torn between "impatient wrath," injured honor, filial affection, and "the Roman's pride," but ends by reducing him to a balanced pair of gestures, a virtual personification of that favorite eighteenth-century device, antithesis: "O'er all the man conflicting passions rise, / Rage grasps the sword, while Pity melts the eyes" (133–34). What the "Epistle" represents is not Shakespeare's characters themselves (Collins never presumes to rival his master), but the audience's remembered perceptions of those characters, perceptions dissevered from the actual event that elicited them (reading the play or seeing it performed), pushed front-stage and highlighted with a preternatural degree of distinctness. Reading the poem, we are not seeing Shakespeare; we are seeing ourselves seeing Shakespeare—in short, we are *savoring* Shakespeare with the discrimination of a connoisseur.

Thus does Collins illustrate the central paradox of Humean sensationalism, which asserts that the "testimony" of the senses is perused within the private chamber of the mind, but neglects the fact that this process requires the existence of a second, mental set of senses able to perceive the report of the first set. Much has been made of Collins's Platonism, notably by A. S. P. Woodhouse, who argued that the aim of the Odes is to seize the underlying universal "idea" of an emotion and purge it of the limiting particulars through which it is variously experienced by each person.[16] The opposite view seems nearer the truth: Collins's personifications express his uncanny sense that in the universe of Humean sensationalism, where "every distinct perception, which enters into the composition of the mind, is a distinct existence, and is different, and distinguishable, and separable, from every other perception" (*THN*, p. 259), being the mental equivalent of Newton's irreducible atom, one's innermost thoughts and feelings can function mechanistically without needing an actual human person to "have" them.[17] From a Blakean viewpoint, one could say the person's total involvement, mind and body, in the act of perception, his actual participation through perception in the inner constitution of the object, is in Collins identified exclusively with the reasoning "Ratio" able only to compare objects *already* perceived. In a process analogous to that which Alfred North Whitehead terms "the fallacy of misplaced concreteness," the Ratio then appropriates the total human form to itself, and the result is abstract personification. The creation of a coherent myth of human identity was left to Blake. Yet as we've seen, Blake, too, is led to realize that inasmuch as his mythological system exists by reason of the mind's fall into disunity, the only action he could represent would always be psychological in a merely pejorative sense, a prelude to the more impressive but indescribable deeds of the reintegrated Albion. At the same time, the poet's repressed awareness of the separation between mind and body, self and other, returns *within* the mythology as a constant splitting apart of characters into new personae (chiefly specters and emanations), making reintegration all the more difficult.

Meantime, Collins travels further down the path of Pope's prophecy. Says Wallace Jackson of Collins, Gray, and the Wartons: "Paradoxically, while they searched for the wonders within the mind, they created no myth of human identity to which such wonders could be referred. To speak metaphorically, they created a stage on which to present their actors [that is, the abstract personifications of emotion], but no action in which they could participate."[18] The result is paralysis and fragmentation; the poet becomes the horror he beholds. When in the "Ode to Fear" Collins confronts Fear's "unreal scene" of "shadowy shapes" and exclaims, "Like Thee I start, like Thee disorder'd fly. / . . . / Who, Fear, this ghastly Train can see, / And not look madly wild like Thee?" (2–25), he is asserting his outward resemblance to Fear, not their empathic union. The poet's goal is the kind of inspired identification with another that he associates with the creative sympathy of Shakespeare; but inasmuch as he grows to fear Fear, his mirror image, it seems he only exacerbates his initial sense of self-division. It could hardly be otherwise: since the poem takes place entirely within Fear's "world unknown" (1), there is literally nothing for the poet to fear but fear itself.[19]

But although the dramatic content of Collins's Odes attests a chilling loss of affect, their plot structure shows an urgent striving to recover immediacy. Studies of British Romanticism are notorious for treating the poets of Sensibility as "pre-Romantics" struggling against the uniformizing strictures of Newtonian rationalism, but too compromised by Augustan anxieties about social decorum to win through to the high-Romantic belief in the autonomy of the individual imagination. To this view the present chapter is manifestly no exception. My aim, however, is not to condemn these poets by Romantic criteria they themselves helped to create. Especially in Collins and Gray, the judgment of failure is often part of a determinism built into the very structure of the poem, whose successful completion paradoxically hinges on such failure. As belated progress-poems whose purpose is to depict the "westering of culture" from ancient Greece and Rome to the England of Shakespeare and Milton and onward to the New World, their odes achieve success by demonstrating Pyrrhically the historical necessity of their own defeat. Of course, so neatly internalized a failure has its compensations: at the same time as it elicits pathos for the doomed poet, it offers him a unified, even organic arrangement of his poem. By tracing their announced subject through history, the poems transport the poet from the distant past to the present moment of composition. In this way they ultimately reveal themselves to be invocations, the titular personification being the muse through whom the poet hopes to surmount his paralysis. And yet the wish is never taken for the deed; Collins never presents his Odes as anything but timorous preludes to their "real," as yet unwritten successors. Ironically, the very need to summon inspiration implies unacceptable weakness: if you have to ask, you can't afford it. The Odes thus conclude in melancholy acquiescence to a determinism holding that the possibilities for poetry have been exhausted by the giant bards of the past; it only remains for the modern poet to acknowledge this fact by terminating his poem.[20]

Where does this leave Collins? The "Ode to Pity" gives an answer. Having for several stanzas withheld her favors, Pity finally takes pity on the poet (how can she else?). Thus inspired, his "thoughts" proceed to "design" her temple. The poem then concludes with his encapsulation:

> There let me oft, retir'd by Day,
> In Dreams of Passion melt away,
>   Allow'd with Thee to dwell:
> There waste the mournful Lamp of Night,
> Till, Virgin, Thou again delight
>   To hear a British Shell!   [37–42]

"Shell" is a poeticism for the grand tortoiseshell lyres of Britain's bardic past; by contrast, it seems the only shell Collins has got is the private one into which he is withdrawing, snail-like. "There" is no place in the actual world but the Humean theater of the mind, a secluded chamber which the preceding stanza explicitly says will be interior decorated with scenes from tragic drama à la "Epistle to Sir Thomas Hanmer." Thus removed, the poet will "melt away" much as the Humean spectator, having by introspection detached himself from his own body, finds his sense of personal identity to be dissolved. Offsetting this loss are the poet's intensified daydreams of poetic glory, narcissistic compensation for his anxieties of influence. Nevertheless, the gain is clearly secondary, for the daydreams are doomed never to be realized. Locked inside his literary temple, the poet has deprived himself of anything to become inspired *about* except poetry, the very source of his anxieties.

If Blake's "Song," "Memory, hither come . . ." in *Poetical Sketches* represents the luxurious narcissism typical of such Penseroso sampler-poems, then the "Mad Song" immediately following illustrates how easily indulged melancholy can pass into genuine mental disturbance. In willfully confining himself to the nocturnal half of the daily cycle, the "Mad Song" speaker reaches toward the same darkly sorrowful pleasures as Collins and so many other meditative-Miltonizing poets of Sensibility. And yet those pleasures are found to be merely an attenuated version of the morning's spontaneous delights; instead of attaining a suitably "poetic" refinement of his emotion, the speaker merely experiences the "howling woe" and "frantic pain" of solipsistic despondency. Like Milton's Satan "self-condemn'd to eternal woe," he has denied himself all possibility of a creative, and hence redemptive, relationship with his pain. Blake parodies the despondency inherent in the progress-poem as early as "To the Muses" (1783); in *Milton*, as we've seen, he undermines it from within. For the ending of *Milton* is not necessitated by the precursor poet as by some inexorable external force, the literary equivalent of gravitation; rather it develops as the author's long-sought personal affirmation of the eternal present moment as the source of inspiration.

The establishment of an objectified public role for the poet is central to the work of Gray. By compelling the reader to recognize his own sympathetic collaboration with the poem's abstract personifications of emotion, Gray opens the Romantic possibility of viewing them as sundered personae of a larger human identity embracing poet and reader alike. Consider, for example, the development of the "Ode on a Distant Prospect of Eton College." The nightmarish horde of personifications seen hovering about the schoolboys at play in the valley below are "vulturs of the mind" not only of the Eton-educated poet but of fallen mankind generally. The scene recalls our first glimpse of Paradise through the cormorant eyes of Milton's Satan, who is shut out from Eden much as the poet is shut out from his paradisiacal childhood Eton. Accordingly, the poet's black predictions of the children's future convey a distinctly misanthropic relish that makes one wary:

> Alas, regardless of their doom,
> The little victims play!
> No sense have they of ills to come,
> Nor care beyond to-day:
> Yet see how all around 'em wait
> The Ministers of human fate,
> And black Misfortune's baleful train!
> Ah, shew them where in ambush stand
> To seize their prey the murth'rous band!
> Ah, tell them, they are men!

> These shall the fury Passions tear,
> The vulturs of the mind,
> Disdainful Anger, pallid Fear,
> And Shame that sculks behind;
> Or pineing Love shall waste their Youth,
> Or Jealousy with rankling tooth,
> That inly gnaws the secret heart,
> And Envy wan, and faded Care,
> Grim-visag'd comfortless Despair,
> And Sorrow's piercing dart.[21]

And so on for another twenty-five lines. Although obviously intended as timeless universals, the personifications multiply with so little connection to the immediate physical scene that they come to seem projections of the poet's purely personal sufferings. The gist of this catalog of miseries is that the children are sadly deluded; but inasmuch as the children are not "men" at all but boys, it is the poet's morose preoccupation with life's misfortunes that seems deluded and childish.

The recognition of this irony supplies the reversal that completes the poem:

> Yet ah! why should they know their fate?
> Since sorrow never comes too late,
> And happiness too swiftly flies.
> Thought would destroy their paradise.
> No more; where ignorance is bliss,
> 'Tis folly to be wise.   [95–100]

The poet realizes his anxieties are premature and foolish: it is impossible for the boys to anticipate their fate without falling into precisely the adult self-consciousness he wants to warn them against. Regarded abstractly as "men," "the little victims" are damned if they do watch out, damned if they don't. As living children, however, they aren't damned at all but more confidently innocent than we can even imagine. The "thought" that most directly threatens their paradise would therefore appear to be that of the jealous excluded poet—specifically, it is his projected personifications composing the "murth'rous band" of Sin and the "griesly troop" of Death (81–84), the two earthly allies of Milton's Satan. Yet although cut off from childhood's paradise, the poet is no longer isolated. His exclusion is no different from every other adult's, as we ourselves tacitly admit when we consent with relief to his stoical reassertion of decorum ("No more").[22] Hence the dramatic irony that earlier separated our view of the children from the poet's now reaches out to encompass us, too. If Gray cannot find redemption in a typically Romantic consecration of fallen experience, it is nevertheless a similarly dialectical return to society that leads him to affirm at least the solidarity of shared alienation.

The *Elegy Written in a Country Churchyard* strikingly extends this affirmation, somber as it is. As the poet-speaker gradually disappears amid the gathering twilight, his corresponding meditative withdrawal serves to universalize his voice until, through an extraordinary series of pronoun shifts, we finally hear it as uttered within the calm of our own thought. He begins by telling how the homeward-returning plowman "leaves the world to darkness and to me" (4). As the landscape "fades . . . on the sight," the poet's darkening mind turns appropriately toward the graveyard, passing from observation of what is (the Poussin-like opening scene) to contemplation of what was but is no more (the lives of the buried peasants; 17–28) to speculation on what might have been (the wasted potential of "Some village-Hampden . . . Some mute inglorious Milton . . . Some Cromwell"; 45–76). At this point of greatest removal, when the poem throngs with abstract personifications (Ambition, Grandeur, Honour, Flatt'ry, Knowledge, Penury), a countermovement commences. As Dr. Johnson saw, with the four stanzas beginning "Yet ev'n these bones . . ." (77) the poet's sentiments sweep outward to embrace not only the peasants but mankind generally:

> For who to dumb Forgetfulness a prey,
> This pleasing anxious being e'er resign'd,
> Left the warm precincts of the chearful day,
> Nor cast one longing ling'ring look behind?
>
> On some fond breast the parting soul relies,
> Some pious drops the closing eye requires;
> Ev'n from the Tomb the voice of Nature cries,
> Ev'n in our Ashes live their wonted Fires.   [85–92]

The "voice" is plainly of universal scope, as the first-person plural shows. The *Elegy* thus prepares to turn upon itself:

> For *thee*, who mindful of th' unhonour'd Dead
> Dost in these lines their artless tale relate;
> If chance, by lonely contemplation led,
> Some kindred Spirit shall inquire *thy* fate,
>
> Haply some hoary-headed Swain may say, . . .   [93–97; my italics]

To paraphrase the Swain: We used to see him looking more and more melancholy every day; then one day we missed him, and next day saw him dead on a bier. "Thee" refers to the poet. Who then is addressing him?

Evidently the "voice of Nature" itself, speaking coextensively with the poet, author, and reader.[23] If in traditional elegy the poet cannot consider his friend's death without in some measure imagining his own, here Gray secures an additional intensity by compelling the reader to project himself into the *poet's* imagined death.

Having thus sloughed off his solitary persona, Gray proceeds to bury him through false surmise. With the introduction of the hypothetical Swain telling some kindred persona how the poet was adopted into the churchyard, the poem's reversal becomes complete: instead of a poet contemplating the graves of peasants, now a peasant contemplates the poet's grave. And so the dead poet, "a Youth to Fortune and to Fame unknown" (118), actually joins the mute inglorious Miltons with whom he had earlier identified. Even more ironically, it appears to be his "forlorn," even "craz'd" (107–08) musings on them that cause his death in the first place.[24] A third stage is reached when the Swain enjoins, "Approach and read (for thou can'st read) the lay" (115) engraved on the poet's tombstone, and the poem then proceeds to its closing section, the Epitaph. Again, to whom does "thou" refer? It cannot be the poet, as was the case twenty lines earlier, for he is now supposed to be dead. A logical answer would be that the Swain is addressing the poet's "kindred Spirit." And yet we have seen that both of them are only conjectures of the common "voice of Nature" belonging to dead poet, author, and reader alike. The line must therefore be addressed directly to ourselves *as* readers. Such heightened immediacy dramatizes the poet's need to "cast one longing ling'ring look behind," an appeal to posterity aimed nowhere if not at the reader, his survivor, his semblable.

Thus the *Elegy* is seen to progress through a series of provisional stages culminating in a reunion of author and reader over the grave of the author's persona. Its purpose served, the poem finally calcifies into a monument to that outgrown (and now overgrown) persona. Hume himself suggests the basis for Gray's method. Having demonstrated the impossibility of establishing by deduction the existence of any continuing impression of personal identity, Hume concludes:

> the true idea of the human mind, is to consider it as a system of different perceptions or different existences, which are link'd together by the relation of cause and effect, and mutually produce, destroy, influence, and modify each other. . . . In this respect, I cannot compare the soul more properly to any thing than to a republic or commonwealth, in which the several members are united by the reciprocal ties of government and subordination, and give rise to other persons, who propagate the same republic in the incessant changes of its parts. [*THN*, p. 261]

Hume's idea of the mind as a differential system of existences mutually producing and modifying one another strikingly resembles the Saussurian view of language. Especially when he goes on to assert that "all the nice and subtile questions concerning personal identity can never possibly be decided, and are to be regarded rather as grammatical than as philosophical difficulties" (*THN*, p. 262), he can be taken as implying that in any given sentence "I" denotes not a particular actual person but only the linguistically determined speaker. Developing Hume's implication, Shelley adumbrates the modern theory of pronoun shifters: "The words, *I*, *you*, *they*, are not signs of any actual difference subsisting between the assemblage of thoughts thus indicated, but are merely marks employed to denote the different modifications of the one mind."[25] Metaphysically, Shelley's "one mind" corresponds to Hume's "system of different perceptions . . . which . . . mutually produce . . . and modify each other" without need of any substrate personal identity. Grammatically, "the one mind" corresponds to the consciousness of and in language, what Gray calls the shared "voice of [human] Nature" that speaks "ev'n from the Tomb."

I conclude this conspectus with a review of personal pronouns in the supreme Romantic elegy, Shelley's *Adonais*. The poem images its method in its portrayal of the author:

> Midst others of less note, came one frail Form,
> A phantom among men; companionless
> As the last cloud of an expiring storm
> Whose thunder is its knell; he, as I guess,
> Had gazed on Nature's naked loveliness,
> Actaeon-like, and now he fled astray
> With feeble steps o'er the world's wilderness,
> And his own thoughts, along that rugged way,
> Pursued, like raging hounds, their father and their prey.   [271–79]

The poet's plight reverses the traditional dualistic conception of the mind as an immutable preexisting subject from which thought is occasionally directed outward to external objects. Starting not with a hypothetical distinct impression of personal identity but with the immanent act of thinking, Shelley conceives the mind as the occasional object of continually inner-directed thoughts. In other words, for Shelley thought determines the existence of the thinker, not vice versa; we ourselves are the object intended by our initially unidentified thoughts. Having seen Nature "naked," without preconceptions, the poet is forced to confront the role of human thought in constituting her "loveliness." The result is a maddening, isolating self-consciousness. His experience of pure, objectless introspection induces the same "philosophical melancholy and delirium" as Hume's skepticism; yet because Shelley's idealist maxim "Nothing exists but as it is perceived" allows no escape from thought into a world of objects, the poet is denied the all-too-human Humean remedy of unselfconscious conviviality (dinner, backgammon, and company).

However, one must not underestimate the consistency of Shelley's skeptical idealism. If objects cannot be known in separation from our thoughts about them, then the preceding portrait of the author must itself exist as an actual thought in the reader's mind. Accordingly, the next stanza emphasizes the "pardlike" vitality of the "frail Form," calling him "a Power / Girt round with weakness . . . / . . . / It is a dying lamp, a falling shower, / A breaking billow;—even whilst we speak / Is it not broken?" (280–86). This makes it clear that we are not to take Shelley's objectification of himself within the poem as fixed and fully determined from without (by the immutable preexisting subject, "Shelley"). Since the persona's reality lies entirely in its power to affect the reader, it is, like the language of which it is composed, an absent presence that endures only so long as it is spoken, read, or thought. In demonstrating this, *Adonais* begins to transcend its initial speaker, the persona behind the opening pastoral section, so as to submit him to the uncontrollable intersubjective power of his own words: "The breath whose might I have invoked in song / Descends on me . . . / . . . / I am borne darkly, fearfully, afar" (487–92). The breath is that of the audience collectively speaking the poem, a larger consciousness into which the poet-speaker is subsumed. By thus navigating the strange seas of thought in his own poem, the reflexive experience of which will in turn reveal to him the audience's thoughts of him, the poet hopes to learn the answer to his earlier question, "Whence are we, and why are we? Of what scene / The actors or spectators?" (184–85). Instead of futilely seeking to observe his personal identity preexisting within the theater of his mind, the poet hopes to *achieve* such identity by objectifying himself on the stage of the reader's mind and then "reading" that mind through their shared consciousness of the poem.

The guide directing both poet and reader is, of course, Adonais. The latter's transformation during the poem from a very concretely, even gruesomely dead pastoral shepherd ("icy lips," "leprous corpse") to "a portion of the Eternal" that pervades Nature, "a presence to be felt and known / In darkness and in light, from herb and stone" (373–74), reflects the poet's evolving awareness of his own identity. Hence, for example, the term "Splendours," which first refers to Adonais's thoughts expressed enduringly in his poems (100, 111), is later applied to Adonais himself; *he* has become an enduring thought in *our* mind as we read those poems and so belongs among "The splendours of the firmament of time" (388). Inasmuch as Shelley's own poem insists we recognize this development, thereby "Welcoming him we lose with scarce extinguished breath" (450), the apparent suicidalism of its closing *invitation au voyage* is nothing more or less than a call for self-knowledge: "What Adonais is, why fear we to become?" (459). The poet's impassioned embarkation in the last lines is in this sense an exemplary allegory of the reader's completion of the poem:

> The massy earth and sphered skies are riven!
> I am borne darkly, fearfully, afar:
> Whilst burning through the inmost veil of Heaven,
> The soul of Adonais, like a star,
> Beacons from the abode where the Eternal are.   [491–95]

Adonais appears here not as a transitory flash within the fixed, timeless consciousness of the poet—as indeed he did appear from the earthbound perspective of the now-repudiated pastoral section: "th'intense atom glows / A moment, then is quenched in a most cold repose" (179–80)—but as a fixed star that eternally beacons, and beckons, the poet with powerful compulsion of its own. It is not the thought (Adonais) that belongs to the thinker (the poet) but the thinker that belongs to the thought. The poet's mind being at the moment wholly absorbed in thinking Adonais, Adonais constitutes his entire identity. Since he has "riven" the limiting materialist view of Adonais's death as something absolute and final, his glorification of death actually commends, as the pun on "borne" suggests, a dying into life—the eternal life of Adonais's poetry and of the language that animates it.

Hume having undermined the ground of all epistemological authority, Shelley's Romantic solution is for the poet to create his own authority— that is, create his own identity as author—by representing his very struggle to construct the poem as the key to its dramatic action. What prevents such self-conscious allegorical doubling from usurping on the dramatic action is the poet's urgent rhetorical appeal to the reader. The poet's progressive journey through the narrative, his quest for a completed poem, is seen as analogous to the reader's experience. Their relationship is reciprocal: the poet derives his authority from the reader, and conversely the reader would not be the particular reader he is without the poet. Through their mutual implication in the narrative, each becomes able to fashion and objectify an identity for the other.

Thus Romantic narrative poetry stands the insular neoclassical reader on his head. For in the last count, of course, the location of Hume's mental theater is obvious enough: it is in the body. Analogously, our reading takes place not at some vast remove from earthly life but within the self, which becomes altered as a result. Instead of confidently directing thought outward to a fixed universe of external objects, the poet and reader of Romantic narrative emerge, after much effort, as themselves the final object of an evolving universe of thoughts, namely the poem; and this process of crystallization is achieved, in open defiance of neoclassical decorum, through a progression of several poetic styles. In other words, the poet's developing awareness of the dramatic action turns out to constitute him *as* a poet. In a reversal of the customary relationship between poet and poem, the poet abdicates his priority as the hidden mastermind behind the poem and descends at great personal risk into the concrete human world within which the poem will eventually appear. Not only does the poet make the poem, the poem simultaneously makes the poet.

Wordsworth's explanation of his method in the preface to *Lyrical Ballads* can help clarify this dynamic. What "distinguishes these Poems from the popular Poetry of the day" is, he says, "that the feeling therein developed gives importance to the action and situation, and not the action and situation to the feeling."[26] In much the same way, the plot of the Romantic narrative poem climaxes not with the description of some ostensibly external event but in an awakening of the author himself. In fact, the author's discovery of the poem's underlying purpose *is* his awakening; for since his realization of the poem's latent unity implies the unity of his preceding experience in writing it, it is a self-realization as well. By thus returning him with heightened immediacy to the earthly particularities from which his writing initially provided seclusion, the poem offers the author, in A. N. Whitehead's phrase, "ultimate entry into the concrete," the affirmation of which is seen to be impervious to skeptical doubts because indeed it is presupposed by them. Having served its extrapoetic purpose, the poem at this stage ceases to exist as a formally contained art object and becomes self-consuming in the manner Shelley suggests: "Poetry is a sword of lightning, ever unsheathed, which consumes the scabbard that would contain it" (S, p. 491).

If the Romantic repudiation of dualism is consistent, everything I have just said about the poet also holds for his readers. The Romantic narrative poem's vortexlike interdependence of style and narrative can be seen to dramatize what Whitehead, in his own struggle with Hume in *Process and Reality*, calls "concrescence," the principle of efficient, and final, causation":

Concrescence is the name for the process in which the universe of many things acquires an individual unity in a determinate relegation of each item of the "many" to its subordination in the constitution of the novel "one." . . . Each instance of concrescence *is itself* the novel individual "thing" in question. There are not "the concrescence" *and* "the novel thing": when we analyze the novel thing we find nothing but the concrescence. "Actuality" means nothing else than this ultimate entry into the concrete, in abstraction from which there is mere nonentity. In other words, abstraction from the notion of "entry into the concrete" is a self-contradictory notion, since it asks us to conceive a thing as not a thing [for example, Blake's concept of Satanic Negation].[27]

To adapt the passage to our purposes, there are not the poem ("the instance of concrescence") *and* the reader ("the novel individual thing"— novel because transformed by his experience of the poem). The poem is not a hypostatized object causing change in the reader but a process of unification that includes the reader in phenomenological fashion. Thus "each item of the 'many' "—the stylistic variousness of the narrative— gradually achieves "subordination in the constitution of the novel 'one' "—namely ourselves, at last reintegrated as a unitary person, at least for a Blakean moment. Epistemologically, the reader of Romantic narrative is no longer an immutable pure subject-consciousness for whom each narrative object is a definite known quantity. Instead he becomes, in Whitehead's term, a "superject" immersed in a shifting, incompletely realized complex of preconscious thoughts and desires whose ultimate concrescence signifies his own momentary hard-won objectification as a human being here and now.

The reason such objectification is only provisional is that as soon as poet or reader reenters the empirical world, skepticism and its ironies return in a new way. The overcoming of doubt can never be final, the ending of Blake's *Milton* suggests, because if our individual identities are interdependent, then the poet's escape from self-isolation and the reintegration of his personal self cannot be fully real unless shared with the reader. And since the reader is an entity no less enigmatic than was the self that the poet was trying to know, it becomes necessary to doubt all over again. Yet this is not a vicious circle: a speculative uncertainty toward another's private thoughts and feelings is hardly the same as an anxious sense of self-loss. Indeed, the one is a remedy for the other; to transform self-doubt into doubt toward someone else is to see that it was precisely one's isolation that made the epistemological issue of personal identity seem an emotional crisis in the first place, rather than just an intellectual puzzle. In brief, it turns out that the anxiety for foundational certainty about the existence of one's identity, a certainty that would be independent of all other relationships both cognitive and emotional, is only an expression of self-loss. No wonder, then, that the foundational self proves impossible to find: the same desperation that motivates the search also directs it to the very place where the self is absent to itself.

The return of skepticism, aimed this time toward other minds rather than toward oneself, helps account for the peculiar ironies of the opening of *Jerusalem*. We've observed how the elusive but to all appearances supremely confident author of *The Marriage* seems to dismiss his audience while driving them to confront a mental freedom akin to his own. The reverse strategy emerges in *Jerusalem*'s prefatory address "To the Public" written at the opposite end of Blake's career but originating, as the accompanying verse passage makes clear, in the same fiery mental printing-house. Here the author appears in person as a private "Enthusiast" trying his limited best to exercise his God-given "talent" for art. Plainly, his language of Evangelical piety is intended to conciliate readers. And yet Satanic ironies still flicker beneath it: "After my three years slumber on the banks of the Ocean, I again display my Giant forms to the Public: My former Giants & Fairies having receiv'd the highest reward possible: the [love] and [friendship] of those with whom to be connected, is to be [blessed]: I cannot doubt that this more consolidated & extended Work, will be as kindly received" (E, p. 145). "Giants & Fairies" are the standard Spenserian terms by which an eighteenth-century mythographer like Joseph Spence would have referred to Blake's Prophetic Books. In view of the urgency Blake attaches to his poem's "theme"—"the awaking to Eternal Life" and opening of the seals of "the Human Imagination"—he evidently uses the phrase tongue in cheek, imparting just that air of amused condescension with which Augustans typically regarded the play of poetical fancy. The passage's satirical nature further appears from the fact that Blake deleted the words in brackets, presumably in order to replace them with their contraries "hatred," "enmity," and "damned," thus frankly avowing his bitterness at the public's neglect.[28] The question is whether such double-talk evinces self-control or ambivalence and evasiveness. Are the antinomian undertones of the final paragraph, where the author confesses his personal sinfulness in order to affirm the more emphatically his intimacy with Jesus, "the Friend of Sinners," an attempt to seduce polite readers into embracing a faith in desire, action, and energy which would appall them were they forced to acknowledge it more directly? Or does the passage rather show a resigned acceptance of Evangelicalism, "the Yea Nay Creeping Jesus," as the dominant religion of the day, whose cozy piety remains the best available way of communicating a belief in imagination? In short, is Blake craftily, sarcastically manipulating his audience, or is he humbly, glumly letting his audience, or his desire to win one, manipulate him?

The answer, the poem's opening shows, is a paradoxical yes to both questions, whose contrarious marriage, so far from tending to ironize the historical author, is seen to be "necessary" to his and our "human existence." I cite the first six paragraphs in consecutive order:

> Of the Sleep of Ulro! and of the passage through
> Eternal Death! and of the awaking to Eternal Life.
>
> This theme calls me in sleep night after night, & ev'ry morn
> Awakes me at sun-rise, then I see the Saviour over me
> Spreading his beams of love, & dictating the words of this mild song.
>
> Awake! awake O sleeper of the land of shadows, wake! expand!
> I am in you and you in me, mutual in love divine: . . .
>
> But the perturbed Man away turns down the valleys dark;
> [Saying. We are not One: we are Many, thou most simulative]
> Phantom of the over heated brain! . . .
>
> So spoke Albion in jealous fears, hiding his Emanation
> Upon the Thames and Medway, rivers of Beulah: . . .
>
> Trembling I sit day and night, my friends are astonish'd at me.
> Yet they forgive my wanderings, I rest not from my great task! [4:1–5:17]

The call to awaken is simultaneously addressed by the Savior to the inspired Blake about to begin his day, and by Blake to the reader likewise beginning the poem, for each is "in" the other. Yet the Savior wouldn't be calling Blake to awaken if Blake were not also present in the mistrustful dream-deluded Albion; and the same holds for Blake's call to the reader. Hence the surprise of the fourth verse-paragraph: the summons to rise and shine like the Son, which looks like an invocation preliminary to the narrative proper, is actually overheard and rejected by Albion, who thereby shows the narrative is already under way. Evidently the outside of this poem is also its inside; as Blake's myth is universal, he cannot stand above it but remains vulnerable to the very delusions he wants to expose. Indeed, the continued acknowledgment of this vulnerability turns out to be the only way of keeping fully awake. So in the sixth paragraph the author, who at first seemed coequal with Christ, suddenly resurfaces within the corrupted body of Albion. Even as he composes the poem from divine dictation with unpremeditated ease, it appears he must struggle against personal weakness to fulfill a revelation glimpsed but darkly. As a result, we can neither yea-say the poem as true writ guaranteed by an external God nor dismiss it as merely a fallen expression of the historical

author's anxieties. Forced in this manner to confront the authentic otherness of Albion, in whom we each dwell no less than does the enigmatic
author, we become exposed to the reciprocal nature of our skepticism.
Since our doubts toward the author apply equally to ourselves, they
cannot be solved through detached reasoning but only embraced through
the sympathetic realization that they are intrinsic to our own humanity.

Some such realization is invited by the poem's frontispiece, which
shows a pilgrim, lantern in hand, opening a vault and stepping into the
darkness within. Partly the image depicts confident Blake-Los's redemptive descent into the bosom of Albion to search out "the tempters" with
"his globe of fire" (45:3–5); from this viewpoint, "the Poets Work is
Done" (*Milton* 29:1; E, p. 127), and he has carefully arranged the frontispiece for maximum dramatic effect. Yet the image also depicts Blake and
the reader's commencement of the new poem, a nightmarish passage
through self-ignorance and doubt described in the accompanying inscrip-
tions (later deleted) as an exploration of the "Void, outside of Existence,
which if enterd into / Englobes itself & becomes a Womb" (1:1–2); from
this viewpoint, the poet has only just begun working with no end in sight.
As for the oddly whorled shape of the pilgrim's lanternlike "globe of fire,"
one suspects it represents *Milton*, the by now conglobed and superseded
vortex in light of which Blake is able to continue his life journey. Such
ironies demonstrate throughout *Jerusalem* how poet and reader are "in"
Albion, whose sundered parts scattered across time and place make up the
body of the poem. Our aim is to re-member this larger unity through the
self-annihilating, Christ-like act of identifying ourselves with his now-
fallen state.[29] That Albion appears a void of abstraction when seen from
without but a living womb when entered into is for Blake a merely
intellectual paradox that no more precludes experiencing one's humanity
than the paradox of the hermeneutic circle precludes actually reading and
understanding poems.

Blake's epistemology is aptly represented by Stanley Cavell's suggestion
that "the soul may be invisible to us the way something absolutely present
may be invisible to us."[30] What hides the soul or mind is not the body but
the mind itself, our *imagining* the body hides the mind, thereby separating
us from others. In reality, we are separate, but separate in body as well as
mind. And unlike the other sort, this double separateness need not entail
isolation. Since the mind does express itself, however inadequately, by
means of the body, indeed only by means of the body, some degree of
separateness becomes the necessary condition for any relationship, for it
supplies the difference that satisfies us the other person isn't just a projection. Thus the body is both a misery and a mercy. Blake recognizes this
ineluctable duality of the physical in his conception of the world as existing

William Blake, frontispiece for *Jerusalem*, ca. 1820. Relief etching, hand colored,
touched with pen and ink, white line engraving, touch of gold. From the collection
of Mr. and Mrs. Paul Mellon, Upperville, Virginia.

at the saving "Limit of Contraction and Opacity." Commenting on the illustrations to *Songs of Innocence and of Experience*, Coleridge accordingly notes "the ambiguity of the Drapery. Is it a garment—or the body incised and scored out?"[31] The ambiguity, which is productive of many ironies, reflects Blake's awareness that the body clothes the soul in the sense of expressing the soul as well as veiling it. "A Cradle Song" of *Innocence* emphasizes the former by its focus on spontaneous smiling: one does not "wear" a smile unless it is forced or hypocritical. On the other hand, "Infant Sorrow," "The Sick Rose" and "The Angel" of *Experience* consider how dissimulation practiced for its own sake—"infant wiles" and adolescent pleasure in sexual furtiveness—can perversely serve to assure a threatened self of its continuing privacy and free will. Coleridge makes explicit the paradox of such a fall: trapped in a world whose corruptness more and more upsets her, Christabel's sense of guilt eventually becomes for her the only proof of her intact innocence, becomes indeed the very ground of her self-knowledge. Her plight resembles that of Blake's Los, trapped by his awareness that "The Visions of Eternity, by reason of narrowed perceptions, / Are become . . . fix'd into furrows of death, / Till deep dissimulation is the only defence an honest man has left" (E, p. 198).

The body's double role of simultaneously revealing and reveiling the meanings of the soul is also played by language. At one extreme, language and the body are simply identical, as in the word made flesh. Thus the speaker of Blake's "The Lamb" actually becomes the answer to his own question, "Who made thee?" The poem tacitly develops a syllogism with Christ the middle term: the lamb is Christ, but Christ is a child just like the speaker, ergo the lamb is the speaker, who can conclude by affirming, "I a child & thou a lamb, / We are called by his name." Through Christ, the initial problem of verbal identification is resolved through an act of sympathetic identification wherein the original "making" of the lamb is recapitulated in the form of a conversion experience. One could say the poem is, in Coleridge's words, "A repetition in the finite mind of the eternal act of creation in the infinite I AM" (*BL* I, 304).

A similar but more dramatic resolution of doubts takes place in "A Dream." The speaker tells of a lost mother emmet separated from her family and goes on to remark:

> Pitying I drop'd a tear:
> But I saw a glow-worm near:
> Who replied. What wailing wight
> Calls the watchman of the night.

The glowworm then lights the emmet's way home. And yet the wailing wight to whom he is responding is not primarily the emmet but the dreamer himself. Elsewhere Blake amply explains his mistrust of dreams; what makes this one genuinely visionary is the act of sympathy by which the dreamer—like the poet at the beginning of *Jerusalem* whose dream tells him, "I am in you and you in me"—sees that the emmet's benighted wanderings symbolize his own unconscious activity in projecting the dream, which he is thus able to repossess and bring to a (self-)unified conclusion. Byron typically secularizes this process by reversing the priority of the two terms, showing not the word made flesh but the flesh made word, but the result is still incarnation. In the terrestrial paradise of Juan and Haidée's love, there is no gap between words and things because the lovers' own bodies articulate their meanings: "Though their speech / Was broken words, they *thought* a language there," so that when Haidée begins to "read . . . the lines Of [Juan's] fair face," she is also scanning the poetry of his soul.[32]

On the other hand, the "Introduction" to *Songs of Innocence* shows the relation between ordinary fallen language and the self to be considerably less immediate. Critics have noted how the opening series of repetitions suggests a fusion of subject and object in the vocal immediacy of music; we cannot tell the singer from the song. But by specifying the material technology of writing, Blake draws attention to the emerging gap between the piper and his original vision. Regardless of whether one hears the closing series of "ands" as expressing fatigue and tedium or as attesting a vigorously reductive effort of will, the piper's "staining" of the water and the "hollowness" of his reed—a parody of his pastoral pipe—indicate that expression in the Songs that follow will be neither direct nor unambiguous.

"Infant Joy" shows just how sinister fallen expression must be. "I happy am / Joy is my name": the infant incarnates its emotion absolutely, being the eternal human form divine or the universal idea of that experience (joy itself). Indeed, if joy is the *capacity* for experience, then in a reversal of ordinary begetting the infant can be seen as the ultimate Logos-like signifier through which all the rest of human life becomes possible. Yet its divine origins are fast disappearing: not newborn but "two days old," the child has already entered the temporal world. From this mundane perspective, it appears a mere vessel for passively receiving experience. Its eternal human identity is thus reduced to a proper name:[33]

> Pretty joy!
> Sweet joy but two days old.
> Sweet joy I call thee:
> Thou dost smile.
> I sing the while
> Sweet joy befall thee.

"Joy" here is no longer absolute but must be mediated by smiles, the language of the body; the smiling accordingly seems naive and temporary. Similarly, the mother in "A Cradle Song" regards her babe as a type of Christ—"Infant smiles are his own smiles. / Heaven & Earth to peace beguiles": the lines recall any number of Nativity odes and hymns—only to reveal an unexpectedly painful consequence. Like "befall," the ominous "beguiles" looks ahead to suffering and sacrifice that make the present peace seem merely the ease of dallying with false surmise. Both poems disclose the same bitter moral as *Christabel*'s closing cradle scene: he who cannot speak for himself in the ordinary language of experience gets spoken for by others, however well intentioned, and his meanings are appropriated by them.

Such dangerous ambiguities of expression render the problem of knowing other minds crucially different from that of knowing the material world. With respect to the latter problem the Keatsian question "Do I wake or sleep?" makes no practical difference. As Shelley says, "The relations of things remain unchanged by whatever system . . . and such is the material of our knowledge" (S, p. 478). We can always imagine the existence of another, deeper reality that would undercut the one previously deemed truest, and there is no limit to the number of concentric circles we can thus draw. If we awaken within a dream, we haven't really awakened. Coleridge was fond of observing how Berkeleyan idealists and Hartleyan materialists alike fall into an infinite regress:

> The formation of a copy is not solved by the mere pre-existence of an original. . . . It would be easy to explain a thought from the image on the retina, and that from the geometry of light, if this very light did not present the very same difficulty. We might as rationally chant the Brahmin creed of the tortoise that supported the bear, that supported the elephant, that supported the world, to the tune of "This is the house that Jack built." [*BL* I, 138]

Yet it isn't possible in this way to step outside of our relationship to other minds; our doubts about the other's reality or truthfulness inevitably form part of our relationship to her. As Robert Nozick argues, "tracking" the facts renders material-object skepticism trivial in most ordinary instances: "I believe this fact because it's true and if it weren't true I wouldn't believe it."[34] But this argument collapses with respect to skepticism toward other minds, which are always capable of self-concealment. To suspect the other of lying affects our thoughts and behavior toward her; indeed, if we refuse to express our doubts and persist in the unsuspecting role which we believe the liar intends for us, we may find ourselves constrained to playact our own genuine innocence no less than the liar is (or seems to be) playactii.g her false innocence. This is the insidious forfeiture of freedom that overtakes Christabel, whose self-fragmentation ensues from her unwillingness to admit that her doubts about Geraldine do make a difference.

For if the other can have feelings without necessarily expressing them, then her feelings can be separated from her outward behavior, personal history, and social station, which therefore become all that we know "for certain" about her. The other comes to be seen as a husk or shell surrounding a mysterious inner essence.[35] The result is ironic: what we do know about the other—all that constitutes our actual relationship with her—is devalued out of respect for that which we do not, perhaps cannot, know. We see her as withholding herself, which of course is how she must see us: our suspicion makes her suspicious. Hence our doubts become self-fulfilling, and indeed more self-revealing than we could have supposed.

Consider in this respect Keats's "La Belle Dame sans Merci," written early in 1819 at a time when hostile circumstances began to crowd in upon the poet (his brother's recent death, his continuing inability to secure his inheritance, ambivalence toward Fanny Brawne, possibly his realization of his impending illness) and often left him too irritable or distracted to compose verse. As Stuart Sperry points out, it appears Keats's poetic touchstone, the capacity for sympathetic identification, ironically only compounds his frustration by adding to these burdens still other sufferings not personally his own.[36] "His identity presses upon me so all day . . . that I live now in a continual fever," Keats writes of the sick Tom, and a few days later complains: "When I am in a room with People . . . the identity of every one in the room begins [so] to press upon me that, I am in a very little time annihilated."[37] In probing how a decent respect for the separateness of another person can slip into fear and pusillanimity, "La Belle Dame sans Merci" dramatizes this paradox whereby negative capability induces, by defensive reaction, a kind of misanthropy. The poem revolves about a problem similar to that of the Cretan Liar. Is the Belle Dame merely the knight's evil delusion, as the pale warriors warn in his dream; or is his love real, and the *dream* a delusion expressing his emotional insecurities? In other words, does the Belle Dame really have the knight in thrall, or is he merely enthralled by his belief that she has him in thrall? Posed this way, his dilemma is as insurmountable as the doubts, Do I wake or sleep? Is the external world real or illusory? Is the knight alive or dead, and if he lives, is it only the waking dream of life-in-death? Nevertheless these questions, like love itself, involve not the mind alone but also the body, as one can see by translating them into a form more easily verified. Am I breathing? Am I speaking? Am I indeed asking myself these questions? If so, then I am alive. Of course, it will be objected that I know only that these things *seem* to be taking place. But such an experience of "seeming" is precisely what was not acknowledged in the form of the original question, which was not "Do I seem to be awake?" much less "Does the seeming I seem to be awake?" The answer to *these* questions is a simple unhesitating yes. What makes "Do I wake or sleep?" so troublesome is that although the question concerns the body, it is tacitly framed so as to exclude all sense experience from the answer.[38]

Accordingly, we need only consider the knight's situation in pragmatic terms to see its irony. Looking tubercularly pale, he "loiters" on the cold hillside, his quest abandoned. What constitutes the evil spell, regardless of whether it has been devised by the Dame or inadvertently projected by the knight, is his inability to adopt a course of action; he is trapped in the life-in-death of paralyzing epistemological doubt. The knight's abstract uncertainties isolate him from both his visionary grotto of love and the realm of purposeful human activity represented by his initial quest; they place him on the border between the two, exactly nowhere. To the assertion that such a limbo constitutes, precisely, the Dame's spell, I would reply that *this* sort of spell has power over the knight only because he, like Christabel, chooses to believe in its potency. The poem thus demonstrates the necessity of living out our skepticism toward others. Since the knight has no way of determining the objective reality of his love apart from his actual feelings toward the Belle Dame, once he doubts those feelings he doubts himself no less than her. Indeed, his fading cheeks identify him with the (spellbound) warriors in his dream, so that he is literally becoming his own worst fears.

The knight's self-absorption indicates that our desire to know in an absolute sense reflects a deeper psychological need to *be known* (for Keats and Shelley, by one's lover; for Blake, ultimately by Christ). Although secretly we all share with Faust, the alchemists, and the Poet of *Alastor* the wish that knowledge would impose itself upon us with all the force and palpability of a material object, the Romantics show this desire, outwardly so altruistic, to be an abdication of moral responsibility in favor of a self-serving determinism. For there is no need to communicate with material objects; were knowledge such an object, we would have no need to grasp or interpret our knowledge, and consequently no need of that radical freedom to express our meanings which makes *us* more than animate objects. Questions about the nature of other minds form an inescapable part of our relationship to those minds, because the questions apply reciprocally to ourselves. In Stanley Cavell's phrase, "To the others, I am an other." In this context all doubt is, as Blake sees, self-doubt.

Keats's doubts tend to focus on the modern poet's inability to maintain this mutually objectifying relationship with his audience. In old times, *The*

Fall of Hyperion suggests, poet, priest, and king were one; now, however, the poet lacks an accepted social function and must become his own audience. Although "every man whose soul is not a clod / Hath visions" and "dreams" that he can "tell" so long as he "has been well nurtured in his mother tongue,"[39] it is the poet's special ability to reexperience his dreams imaginatively in the telling, so generating a "finer tone" or "intensity" by which they are not simply understood but cognitively shared by the audience. Such self-preoccupation is necessary, Keats realizes, because his poems are "things semireal which require a Greeting of the spirit to make them wholly exist" as public art objects (*Letters* I, 242), but at the same time he fears it may be turning him from a "true poet" into an obsessed "fanatic" (I, 1–18, 198–202) like the Ancient Mariner.

Indeed, in *Lamia* private poetic dream and commonsense reason are presented as mutually exclusive. Lycius wants both at once; yet so deep is their incompatibility, his crass desire to show off his dream-lover as an exotic object of envy only sets the stage for her disappearance. The proximate cause of death is the mere silent presence of the philosopher Apollonius, a material-object skeptic like the blinkered scientists Keats condemns for anatomizing rainbows. Apollonius, trusting only in Locke's solid and extended "substance," quite unempirically rejects Lamia's elusive beauty—a beauty manifestly real at some level, or why would Apollonius even deign to give her a thought? Thus the withering gaze with which he reduces Lamia to snakehood makes Apollonius, too, look distinctly reptilian: "possess'd, his lashless eyelids stretch / Around his demon eyes" (II, 288–89) as he becomes what he beholds. He is no more willing to "live" his skepticism toward this unverifiable "rainbow-sided" amalgam of subjective "secondary qualities"—color, shape, and texture, which together constitute her sole reality, as the kaleidoscopic descriptions of Part I, 47–58 and 146–70 go to show—than is the narcissistic Lycius willing conversely to acknowledge her as an ultimately unknowable other with an enigmatic identity of her own. Hence the irony of the poem's abrupt conclusion: like La Belle Dame—indeed, like poesy itself—the now-degenerate Lamia is presumably whisked back to her remote isle to await metamorphosis once again by the greeting spirit of the next victim. Apparently the cycle is inevitable because dream and reason eventually repel each other as negations rather than uniting as contraries. The hidden fear of self-delusion will always tempt us like Lycius to assert an impersonal objective reality for our imaginings, thereby abusing the delicate higher truth they actually do possess and falsifying our godlike ability to "smoothly pass / [Our] pleasures in a long immortal dream" (I, 127–28).

If a limited sample is any indication, people who meet demon-lovers seem unusually prone to self-absorption. Lycius discovers Lamia, the woman he has already been dreaming of, the moment "his phantasy was lost, where reason fades" (I, 234) at the limits of philosophical speculation. When Christabel meets Geraldine, she is confidently composed in solitary prayer "For the weal of her lover that's far away";[40] likewise, the *Alastor* Poet is sunk in ecstatic reverie during the encounter with his maiden, an idealized version of the Arab Maid whose attentions he earlier scorned. Inescapable their fate may be, but of course it is hardly external to them.[41] In their different ways, each character becomes vulnerable to falling in love with an illusion once he or she tries to cheat the normal economy of the emotions by getting something for nothing through unmediated wish fulfillment. For all its outward transcendentalism, such love recalls Hume's concept of religious faith as, ironically, a low-probability belief essentially no different, because no more verifiable, than belief in the external world. With nothing to lose but a world of disappointments and all of Truth to gain, what the transcendentalist seeks is to escape the complexity and mysteriousness of actual human relationships. Christabel, who would rather imagine her dream-lover Geraldine as a supernatural nightmare than admit her basically mixed nature, shows just how desperate the desire for such certainty can become.

Who's Afraid of the
Mastiff Bitch? Gothic Parody
and Original Sin in *Christabel*

In the establishment of principles and fundamental doctrines, I
must of necessity require the attention of my reader to become
my fellow-labourer. The primary facts essential to the
intelligibility of my principles I can prove to others only so far as
I can prevail on them to retire into themselves *and make their*
own minds the objects of their stedfast attention.

Coleridge, The Friend, *Essay iii.*

"The mastiff's howl is touched with a deathly horror," says G. Wilson
Knight, speaking for many others who have found *Christabel* a genuinely
chilling piece of gothic supernaturalism.[1]

> 'Tis the middle of night by the castle clock,
> And the owls have awakened the crowing cock;
> Tu-whit!—Tu-whoo!
> And hark, again! the crowing cock,
> How drowsily it crew.
> Sir Leoline, the Baron rich,
> Hath a toothless mastiff bitch;
> From her kennel beneath the rock
> She maketh answer to the clock,
> Four for the quarters, and twelve for the hour;
> Ever and aye, by shine and shower,
> Sixteen short howls, not over loud;
> Some say, she sees my lady's shroud.[2]

If we do a double take, however, the jocular reactions of contemporary
reviewers seem closer to the truth. As William Hazlitt put it, "Is she a sort
of Cerberus to fright away the critics? But—gentlemen, she is toothless."[3]
Indeed, there is comedy in the spectacle of so grotesquely dilapidated a
watchdog ("the picturesque old lady," commented another reviewer);[4] in
the weltering fricatives with which she is introduced in line 7, a tongue-
twister itself tending to induce momentary toothlessness; in the distinctly

uneerie cacophony she generates together with hooting owls, crowing cock, and tolling clock; in the narrator's somewhat disoriented identification of the bird song, suggesting his affinity with Wordsworth's Idiot Boy who likewise asserts, topsy-turvy, "The cocks did crow, to-whoo, to-whoo";[5] in the metronomic regularity of the dog's howling, heard all day every day and hence not a spooky special effect of this particular midnight; in the tedious precision with which the howls are computed, recalling the obtuse arithmetic of Wordsworth's narrator in "We Are Seven"; and in the contrasting vague portentousness with which the obligatory rumored ghost is abruptly brought forward in the last line. Coleridge's opening set piece accumulates in a short space so much paraphernalia of horror that the effect is less ominous than bathetic.

I

Unless, of course, we approach the dog full of the expectations gratified by popular gothic subliterature. "If the poem seems awkward," the reader tells himself, "surely this only reflects my own distance from the conventions of the genre." As Romantic gothic was deliberately archaic from its inception, moreover, contemporaries would have rationalized in the same way we do today. And yet Coleridge implies in four highly critical reviews of gothic fiction—one written in 1794, the others about the time of *Christabel*, Part I, in 1797 and 1798—that a too-willing suspension of disbelief is delusion, even hypocrisy. If his pathetic relic of a watchdog looks less fearfully symmetrical than Blake's Tyger (which in some versions also looks distinctly tame and toothless), that is only Coleridge's characteristically unintimidating way of dramatizing the same irony: our horror at the beast is sheer self-deception, its monstrosity just a projection of our own alienated energies. Coleridge aims to elicit the same realization as Jane Austen does at the end of *Northanger Abbey*, another gothic parody with almost the same twenty-year interval between commencement and publication (1798–1817 versus 1797–1816 for *Christabel*): "Nothing could shortly be clearer, than that it had been all a voluntary, self-created delusion, each trifling circumstance receiving importance from an imagination resolved on alarm, and every thing forced to bend to one purpose by a mind which . . . had been craving to be frightened."[6]

The reviewers for the most part admitted straight out that *Christabel* fails laughably if judged as ordinary gothic. By constantly provoking doubts about the plausibility of his narrative, Coleridge satirizes the number and artificiality of the conventions required by such literature. When the two ladies enter Christabel's chamber (190–225), for example, Geraldine's discomfort ensues so rapidly after talk of Christabel's guardian mother—spirit, the episode seems perfunctory. She acts as though she is fending off a persistent bee, thereby unluckily emphasizing the crassly tangible nature of the spirit: "Off, wandering mother! . . . Off, woman, off! . . . Though thou her guardian spirit be, / Off, woman, off!"[7] Since Geraldine twice declares the identity of her assailant, the narrator's puzzlement does not seem perspicacious: "what ails poor Geraldine? / Why stares she with unsettled eye? / Can she the bodiless dead espy?" The comedy increases when next Christabel intervenes with more wildflower wine: "Alas! said she, this ghastly ride— / Dear lady! It hath wildered you!" Christabel's charitable euphemism for what must appear a rather violent attack of insanity; her failure to put two and two together by connecting the attack with mention of her guardian mother just seconds before, or else the crude stylization whereby Geraldine's cries are supposed to be stage whispers unheard by Christabel; finally, Geraldine's double shot of the home-brewed wildflower medication to such "speedy" and "excellent effect," as the *Edinburgh* reviewer quipped, that her eyes begin to "glitter bright" and she arises from the floor invigorated[8]—all evince the humorous creakings of stage machinery.

Such lapses are attributable not to the author, however, but to his narrator. Humphrey House observes that the landscape of Part I is skewed inasmuch as all its details seem to be "behaving oddly and ominously," but he interprets this as Coleridge's attempt to "heighten the mystery by suggestions of slight distortions in ordinary behavior, . . . as if proportion is thrown out and normal vision perplexed."[9] Yet such oddness suggests not only danger, but that something funny is going on in both senses of the word. Although the narrator's perplexed vision does intimate that supernatural matters are afoot, it also reveals his utterly mundane difficulty in discerning the dramatic action at all. Dim-witted, nagging, sanctimonious, and overwrought, Coleridge's old duffer recalls the comically limited narrators of Wordsworth's "The Idiot Boy," "The Thorn," and "We Are Seven." He appears only partly in command of his story, so that his frequent querulous interpolations tend to break rather than heighten the suspense. Chiefly it is his frantic losing struggle to gratify the audience's sensational expectations—what the preface to *Lyrical Ballads* calls the "degrading thirst after outrageous stimulation" and "craving for extraordinary incident" (W, p. 449)—that produces the comedy.[10] The stock exaggeration in an outburst like "Hush, beating heart of Christabel!" (53) could have passed if muttered by the lady to herself; spoken by the narrator, however, the suspense is (in House's phrase) thrown out of proportion, for the reader thus infers a telltale heart no less audible than Geraldine's moaning out loud. The narrator's clumsy identification with his heroine is reemphasized when she next confronts Geraldine: "Mary mother, save me now! / (Said Christabel,) And who art thou?" (69–70). The embarrassed parentheses are necessary, of course, to distinguish Christabel's exclamation from the narrator's previous "Jesu, Maria, shield her well!" (54), likewise addressed to the mother of God.

Ultimately, the poem's proliferation of rhetoric so plainly devised for effect threatens to undermine the narrator altogether, blurring his distance from the dramatic action and exposing him as just another gothic gimmick no more credible than the rest. His gullibility is further suggested in lines like: "It moaned as near, as near can be" (39)—how near is *that*? "Is the night chilly and dark? / The night is chilly, but not dark" (14–15)—since this distinction remains, as House puts it, "perplexed," either the question must be superfluous or the answer banal. " 'Tis a month before the month of May" (21)—a pretentious circumlocution which, as the *British Review* pointed out, merely arouses "the strong suspicion . . . that it could not be, after all, any other than that month which a plain man would call April" (*CH*, p. 225), specifically, April Fool's Day. Coleridge's criticism of Ann Radcliffe applies above all to his own narrator: "Curiosity is raised oftener than it is gratified; or rather, it is raised so high that no adequate gratification can be given it."[11] At the same time, the many rhetorical questions and exclamations underscore his abhorrence of the gothic writer's implicit condescension in pretending horror at tales that really amount to mere bedtime stories for a childishly credulous audience. Through the same "tedious protraction of events" and "redundancy of description" as Coleridge denounces in Ann Radcliffe and the same "flat, flabby, unimaginative Bombast" as he condemns in Monk Lewis,[12] *Christabel*'s heavy-handed narrator serves to hasten a "satiety" which, the author trusted, "will soon banish what good sense should have prevented; and . . . the public will learn . . . with how little expense of thought or imagination this species of composition is manufactured" (Greever, pp. 186, 191).

As a "hireling in the Critical Review," Coleridge himself became sated soon enough. His letter to Thomas Bowles of March 16, 1797, complains, "I am almost weary of the Terrible. . . . I have been lately reviewing The Monk, the Italian, Hubert de Sevrac, & &c & &c—in all of which dungeons, and old castles, & solitary Houses by the Sea Side, & Caverns, & Woods, & extraordinary characters, & all the tribe of Horror & Mystery, have crowded on me—even to surfeiting" (*CL* 1:225). Only if we regard the supernaturalism of *Christabel*, Part I, as parody is the contradiction averted of Coleridge undertaking a major gothic narrative within months of declaring himself "surfeited" with such writing. Only thus is he saved from the shameless double standard imputed to him by any straight reading of the poem, which he commenced so shortly after proclaiming in print that "a romance is incapable of exemplifying a moral truth. . . . Tales of enchantment and witchcraft can never be *useful*," although they can be "*pernicious*" (Greever, pp. 192, 195). Even the philosophical plagiarisms of the *Biographia Literaria* assert ideas Coleridge shared and respected, and in large measure had already expressed in his own writing—as indeed he protested with guilty prolepsis in the *Biographia* itself.[13] Yet this would hardly be the case were *Christabel* intended to gratify his audience's detestable appetite for "the trite and the extravagant . . . the Scylla and Charybdis of writers who deal in fiction" (Greever, p. 169).

Recognizing that the "patent inconsistency" imputed of Coleridge's position puts an unusual burden of proof on the traditional reading of *Christabel*, Arthur Nethercot hedged. The poem was written, he argued fifty years ago, as a romance not of the supernatural but the "preter-natural": events highly improbable but not, like the gothic fiction Coleridge abhorred, "contrary to nature" and so incapable of serving a moral purpose.[14] When Nethercot wrote, Donald Tuttle had just revealed numerous parallels between *Christabel* and works of gothic romance, including M. G. Lewis's *The Monk*, and had concluded the poem was another such work.[15] But useful as Nethercot's distinction is for the wholly serious Part II, it fails to explain Part I's additional resemblances to passages of *The Monk* whose leering salacity, far from being typical of 1790's gothic, represents Lewis's special contribution and which Coleridge evidently imitates for a specific purpose. Compare Geraldine's disrobing and the Peeping Tom hypocrisy of the poem's narrator with the monk Ambrosio's prurient discovery that Matilda is not a fellow novitiate after all:

> Then drawing in her breath aloud,
> Like one that shuddered, she unbound
> The cincture from beneath her breast:
> Her silken robe, and inner vest,
> Dropt to her feet, and full in view,
> Behold! her bosom and half her side—
> A sight to dream of, not to tell!   [247–53]

> She had torn open her habit, and her bosom was half-exposed . . . and, oh! that was such a breast! The moonbeams darting full upon it enabled the monk to observe its dazzling whiteness: his eye dwelt with insatiable avidity upon the beauteous orb: a sensation till then unknown filled his heart with a mixture of anxiety and delight.[16]

The titillation of these episodes indeed does not run "contrary to nature." Yet contrary to Nethercot, Coleridge's February 1797 review excoriates *The Monk* for its "libidinous minuteness": "shameless harlotry . . . and trembling innocence . . . are seized . . . as vehicles of the most voluptuous images," making the book "a *mormo* [bugbear] for children, a poison for youth, and a provocative for the debauchee" (Greever, p. 195). One concludes that the implicit lesbianism of the poem's bedchamber scene deliberately burlesques the lubricious and implausible gender confusion at the heart of Lewis's tale. When Hazlitt spread the wicked rumor that Geraldine was really a man in disguise and Christabel's seduction there-fore boringly routine, he was closer to divining Coleridge's satire than he suspected.[17] In short, we must stand Tuttle's argument on its head: *Christabel* does not passively reflect the influence of popular gothic sub-literature; it reacts against that influence and the corruptions Coleridge saw therein. Less strenuously, his portrayal of the narrator reveals a tongue-in-cheek, essentially campy appreciation of the banality and melo-drama of a literary fad insufficiently aware of its cultural determinants to be considered serious art.

Why then has Coleridge's humor eluded so many sensitive and intel-ligent readers, including Byron, Shelley, and Walter Scott? I can only guess, of course, but one reason must be the tendency to compensate for the poem's fragmentary status by interpreting Part I in terms of the less conventionally gothic and utterly unfunny Part II. Perhaps another is that the immediate satire was passé by the time it was published in 1816, almost twenty years after the height of the gothic craze. One suspects the poem's reputation as a chiller resulted from the downplaying or omission of comic details during its prolonged underground existence through recitations themselves seemingly in the oral tradition of authentic balladry. Shelley's notorious panic at the bedchamber scene—"Shelley suddenly shrieking and putting his hands to his head, ran out of the room with a candle," Polidori reported[18]—came from hearing Byron recite a few verses from memory when at "twelve o-clock" the company "really began to talk ghostly": circumstances not exactly conducive to critical discernment (this was the meeting in which "The Vampyre" and *Frankenstein* originated). At any rate, parody of a genre that is itself based on another genre—as eighteenth-century gothic romance is based on certain preconceptions, however ahistorical or self-serving, about the manners and mores of medieval romance—possesses a confusing double artificiality whose cal-culated distortions are naturally liable to be confounded, by an audience already expecting artificiality, with the distortions present unwittingly in the object of parody. In fact, the gross carnage of Lewis and Maturin clearly involves an element of self-parody from the outset, an exuberant and unpretentious nihilism that is perhaps their chief appeal. When *Tales of Terror*, Lewis's collection of gothic ballads published in 1799, led by popular demand to *Tales of Wonder* a year later, the companion volume supplied not only more thrills but several satires directed at its presumed audience of young females.[19] Somewhat similarly, William Empson notes that *The Rime of the Ancient Mariner* originally included a stanza express-ing "the formula, '*fun* with corpse horror'"; and Leslie Brisman has recently elaborated Empson's proposal that the Mariner's experience is not, as he himself trusts, a type of Christ's redemption but "at best only a parody of it."[20] Not that the Mariner is a humorous figure, but his simplemindedness does yield a dramatic irony not unlike the black comedy of *Christabel*'s narrator.

Finally, if everyone was misreading *Christabel*, why didn't Coleridge set them straight? Mainly, I think, because he considered the imitative ac-curacy of Part I to reflect on his own integrity as an artist. As he later argued about, significantly, satires on "pretensions to the supernatural": "Whatever must be misrepresented in order to be ridiculed, is in fact not ridiculed; but the thing substituted for it. It is a satire on something else, coupled with a lie on the part of the satirist, who knowing, or having the means of knowing the truth, chose to call one thing by the name of another."[21] Thus an honest satire is self-evident, and either hits or misses. To explain the joke—a tedious task whose reward is not spontaneous shared amusement but only imposed intellectual understanding: my task in this essay—looks suspiciously like "calling one thing by the name of another." Since Coleridge believed the popularity of gothic to be a func-tion of supply and demand, ultimately his satire aims not to deride "the multitude of the manufacturers" (Greever, p. 191) but to open the eyes of consumers whose self-ignorance is what makes the stuff marketable in the first place. And, of course, the whole thrust of Coleridgean philosophy is that consciousness-raising is not much helped by rational demonstration, tending as it does to answer "delving & difficulty" with "a set of parrot words, quite satisfied, clear as a pike-staff, . . . a stupid piece of mock-knowledge."[22]

II

The poem's parody turns serious when we consider that Christabel's relation to Geraldine parallels that of the stereotypical gothic reader to the seductive gothic villain-hero. The most jaded horror addicts were gener-ally represented as well-bred young ladies like Jane Austen's Miss An-drews, "one of the sweetest creatures in the world, . . . an angel" who guarantees a book list of which the heroine Catherine anxiously inquires, "but are they all horrid, are you sure they are all horrid?" (pp. 34–35).[23] On the other hand, Geraldine's basilisk-eye, superb demeanor, and di-vided will, together with her momentary fits of compunction, manip-ulativeness based on uncanny insight into human nature, and apparent subordination to forces still more powerful than herself—all evoke such figures as Radcliffe's Schedoni, Lewis's Wandering Jew, or Joanna Baillie's de Monfort. Typical of these demons is their ambiguous identity, part human, part monster. Similarly, although critics have called Geraldine a vampire, witch, lamia, ghoul, metempsychosed spirit, and werewolf, nobody denies the equivocal nature of the evidence. Indeed, the real question is why we *prefer* that Geraldine be unequivocally supernatural, why (to munch an old critical chestnut) the evil in her seems more "interesting" than the good.

Coleridge's examination of this problem centers on Christabel's exaggerated notion of her own innocence. She scans the signature of Geraldine's wretchedness—"This mark of my shame, this seal of my sorrow"— but refuses to "declare" the human truth she thus "knows" "with open eyes" (270–92). For there is nothing necessarily supernatural about the spell with which Geraldine binds Christabel to silence. As Arthur Lovejoy points out, Coleridge's persistent concern was "that of vindicating philosophically man's moral freedom and accountability, and consequently the reality of genuinely moral evil—evil for which the individual is absolutely and alone responsible."[24] In his review of 1797, Coleridge accordingly objects that the victims of supernatural demons are made to beg the crucial question: why has this person been selected to encounter sin? "Human prudence can oppose no sufficient shield to the power and cunning of supernatural beings," Coleridge points out; therefore "let [the romance-writer] work *physical* wonders only, and we will be content to *dream* with him for a while; but the first *moral* miracle which he attempts, he disgusts and awakens us" (Greever, pp. 192, 194). Thus Geraldine no more commands Christabel's moral nature than one would expect in real life. It is hard to see how E. E. Bostetter's interpretation of "the helpless paralyzed good, invaded and violated without cause or warning" by an evil "imposed from without" constitutes anything but a mugging, much less "a nightmare vision of evil triumphant."[25] The critic's righteous assumption that Christabel's innocence should supply immunity from all earthly constraints reflects the same overidentification with the heroine as he proceeds to condemn in the poet. After all, her physical vulnerability does not necessarily entail moral capitulation.

Christabel's precursor, the Lady in Milton's *Comus*, is similarly liable to deception through her charity and, like Christabel, becomes paralyzed as a result, but upon discovering Comus's falsity she resolutely refuses to have anything more to do with him. She thus explicitly repudiates any personal guilt: "Thou canst not touch the freedom of the mind / With all thy charms, although this corporal rind / Thou hast immanacl'd."[26] In the same way, physical evil, no matter how supernatural its source, cannot touch Christabel's soul unless she consents to it, so forging manacles of the mind. Wrote Coleridge in a letter of March 10, 1795, "Almost all the physical Evil in the World depends on the existence of moral Evil" (*CL* 1:154)—not vice versa, as Bostetter's reading would suggest.[27] One could object that Coleridge here leaves room for the rare supernatural exception that proves the rule; but that the will was indeed susceptible to "forced unconscious sympathy" (409) with evil he reiterated throughout his life. "I believe most steadfastly in original sin," he wrote with ingratiating stern-ness to his older brother George, the reverend, exactly three years later, the probable date of Part I, "that from our mothers' womb our understand-ings are darkened; and even where our understandings are in the Light, that our organization is depraved, & our volitions imperfect" (*CL* 1:396).

So Christabel's innocence is not somehow exempt from human frailty. Yet she desperately desires to be perfect, and paradoxically this despera-tion corrupts her. Here lies the core dramatic irony that saves her character from the oversimplification alleged by Hazlitt and many others since. What makes Geraldine's spell insidious is that, in part at least, it is *not* supernatural but merely a lie or threat which Christabel embraces in order to keep believing in her own infallibility. The spell's power is psychologi-cal, based on Christabel's awareness that only forcible restraint can justify silence about her otherwise pardonable error in admitting evil into the castle (the poet thus analyzes his own growing self-enslavement to the spell of opium, a "*free-agency-annihilating* Poison" [*CL* 3:489] which he nev-ertheless chooses freely in the first place).[28] Hence Coleridge's well-known account of his poetic contributions to *Lyrical Ballads*:

> The incidents and agents were to be, in part at least, supernatural; and the excellence aimed at was to consist in the interesting of the affections by the dramatic truth of such emotions, as would naturally accompany such situations, supposing them real. And real in this sense they *have* been to every human being who, from whatever source of delusion, has at any time believed himself under supernatural agency.[29]

Thus Geraldine, who is not evil incarnate, only provides the opportunity for sinning; Christabel is free to stand or fall. But Christabel's fugitive and cloistered virtue is oblivious of the fine Miltonic distinction between feeling tempted and actually succumbing. She ignores her initial deception by Geraldine, thereby conniving at it.

As Bostetter aptly observes, Coleridge was much bemused at the way inadvertent sinful thoughts for which one bears no moral responsibility—his own nightmares being a major case in point—can elicit nonetheless an irrational sense of guilt and shame. This reaction would suggest that the thoughts are unconsciously perceived as deserved punishment for some previous unknown sin for which one does in fact bear responsibility. Coleridge attempts to explain the phenomenon through psychological association, as we'll see: sinful thoughts being in the final analysis products of the Fall, the mind associates them with that universal crime and the more appropriate guilt and shame which *it* elicits. Such identification with the aggressor forms the link connecting Christabel's latent sinfulness with Geraldine's actual evil. When Christabel awakens crying " 'Sure I have sinn'd!' " (381), her moral innocence remains intact; still in bed, she hasn't yet had occasion to withhold confessing the evil to her father downstairs. What her shocked little outburst therefore expresses is simply an awareness of her ordinary human fallibility, an awareness provoked by the sudden recollection, upon coming fully awake, of her mistaken assumptions about Geraldine's beauty and innocence the night before. But with her black-and-white morality, Christabel misinterprets her dismay. She assumes herself guilty of actually choosing sin in some hidden way and hence prays that God "Might wash away her sins *unknown*" (390; italics mine). Unwilling to incur the heavy guilt which she deludedly believes she has incurred through a moment's inattention, the girl thus rejects all responsibility whatsoever for Geraldine's presence in the castle. Trapped by her self-deception, she refuses to warn others of the evil which in reality she encountered only by accident. In sum, Christabel as the poem opens is perfect in all respects but one: she lacks the knowledge that she is not perfect. Put less paradoxically, she is ignorant of the one imperfection she cannot help, her *potential* for sin, a potential intrinsic to earthly life. And yet so pervasive are the corruptions of earthly life, Coleridge shows, this one imperfection ineluctably becomes a tragic flaw.

For Geraldine, like Milton's tempter, sees right through her victim. She tells the girl exactly what she wants to hear. To have caused the death of one's mother in childbirth, as Christabel says has befallen her, would seem prima facie ample grounds for supposing oneself inherently iniquitous. Recognizing that Christabel takes the opposite view—she optimistically believes the mother has become her guardian spirit—and that someone convinced that her every move is divinely protected might well consider herself invulnerable, Geraldine smooths the way toward the spell with mesmerizing flattery:

> All they who live in the upper sky,
> Do love you, holy Christabel!
> And you love them, and for their sake
> And for the good that me befell,
> Even I in my degree will try,
> Fair maiden, to requite you well.   [227–32]

Christabel is here lulled into regarding herself as the special friend of all the angels, the focus of heavenly concern. At which point the seducer gets down to business: "But now unrobe . . ." (233). Similarly, one suspects an ulterior motive behind Geraldine's histrionic account of her arrival at the oak tree in lines 79–103. Notes Nethercot:

> The traditional nature of such an episode is conclusively, though uncon-
> sciously, proved by Tuttle . . . when he cites passages from *The Mysteries*
> *of Udolpho, The Romance of the Forest,* and *Hubert de Sevrac,* all of
> which Coleridge had been reading and all of which concern the abduction
> of a young girl by a band (of between three and five in number) who are
> invariably described as either "villains" or "ruffians" (the latter being
> Coleridge's term in some manuscripts), who bind her to a horse and who,
> in the last case at least, deposit her at the foot of a tree. [p. 162*n*]

Most likely Geraldine has been lurking by the tree some time, appraising her victim; like original sin, she is always already there. She moans, allows herself to be discovered, and tosses off a melodramatic tale like those she surmises the girl has been reading, placing her in the desired (although pathetically inappropriate) role of rescuer. Hence Christabel's prompt compliance with Geraldine's request:

> Stretch forth thy hand (thus ended she),
> And help a wretched maid to flee.
>
> Then Christabel stretched forth her hand.   [102–04]

The suspect nature of her eagerness is further emphasized by the echo of Eve's temptation by Satan in *Paradise Lost*:

> Goddess humane, reach then, and freely taste.
> He ended . . .
>   . . . her rash hand in evil hour
> Forth reaching to the Fruit, she pluck'd she eat.   [IX:733–81][30]

So not only does Geraldine seem, in Hazlitt's words, "to act without power—Christabel to yield without resistance" (*CH*, p. 207); as critics have noticed, Coleridge further implies the girl is a willing victim. Her warning as they enter the castle, "But we will move as if in stealth" (120; "stealth," with its whiff of corruption, recurs twice in describing Christabel's movements); her "prudent precaution," as the *Anti-Jacobin* reviewer sneered (*CH*, p. 218), of taking the castle key, and her calculation in removing her slippers as they glide past the sleeping Baron; above all, the "hyperbole of courtesy," as Carl Woodring calls it,[31] whereby she offers to take the stranger to bed—all arouse our mistrust. Since Christabel's playacting ("as if in stealth") plainly conceals a real fear of discovery, one wonders if her charity isn't a cloak for sin.

Finally, of course, one wonders why she left her shrinelike chamber in the first place and made her prayers in the wood, sin's traditional playground outside the Christian pale. The narrator's trite rhetorical questions only cloud this enigma. Why does Christabel go to the tree? To pray for her lover. But why to that tree, the very spot where danger lurks? Perhaps, as "mistletoe" (34) implies, it is a lovers' rendezvous. But then why does she "steal" there, as though acting illicitly? So as not to disturb the sleeping Baron. But why must she make these prayers at all? And at this point the answer defies analysis: "She had dreams" (27). Whether they were nightmares or not, Christabel's baffling misfortune evidently reflects original sin, "the evil which has its ground or origin in the agent, and not in the compulsion of circumstances. . . . It is a mystery, that is, a fact, which we see, but cannot explain" (*AR*, pp. 245–46). Undeterred as usual, Coleridge does go on to explain the impossibility of an explanation: since "no natural thing or act" is known otherwise than as, in Hume's terms, "a mere link in a chain of effects," it follows "the moment we assume an origin in nature, a true beginning, an actual first—that moment we . . . are compelled to assume a supernatural power" (*AR*, p. 263). Thus the supernatural power of Geraldine's spell is a function of Christabel's desire to avoid facing the evil that originates in herself. Elsewhere Coleridge asserts that "the sensations which [objects appearing in dreams] seem to produce, are in truth the causes and occasions of the images. . . . The fact really is, as to apparitions, that the terror precedes the image instead of the contrary" (*LR* 1:202–03). Perhaps then it is Christabel's doubting anxiety toward her proper lover "far away" that leads her to his demonic surrogate.[32]

Once having awakened sin, the girl overestimates her ability to withstand it:

> They crossed the moat, and Christabel
> Took the key that fitted well;
> A little door she opened straight,
> All in the middle of the gate;
> The gate that was ironed within and without,
> Where an army in battle array had marched out.   [123–28]

Since "strait is the gate," it appears she anticipates a similarly deft entry into heaven. Seemingly an afterthought, the last two lines reveal that Christabel's is a hard, violent world. If the fortress is secure, the reason is its vigilance, not its invulnerability:[33]

> So free from danger, free from fear,
> They crossed the moat, right glad they were.   [135–36]

The inanity of the gladness, emphasized by the pseudoarchaic jocundity of the last phrase and the sloganlike repetition of the couplet ten lines later (the ridiculousness of which did not escape the *Edinburgh* reviewer [*CH*, pp. 228–29]), exposes Christabel's naive belief in her complete security (of course, Geraldine's gladness reflects even more damningly on her hostess). "The doctrine of Election," Coleridge's *Aids to Reflection* reminds us, "in relation to the believer is a hope, which . . . will become a lively and an assured hope, but which cannot in this life pass into knowledge, much less certainty of foreknowledge" (*AR*, p. 169). By contrast, Christabel "knows, in joys and woes, / That saints will aid if men will call: / For the blue sky bends over all!" (329–31). Such faith appears commendable, but in this imperfect world the sky is overcast (16–17) and Christabel, bound to silence, cannot call.

Late in life Coleridge came to perceive the confluence of two mighty opposites, necessitarianism and radical Calvinism, in undermining the will. The former tended to do so, he argued, by rationalizing human weakness through the assumption of an all-benevolent deity ever arranging things for the best—"All will yet be well!" Christabel helplessly reassures herself (472); the latter, by "swallowing up all the attributes of the Supreme Being in the one attribute of infinite power, and . . . exaggerating the diseased weakness of the will into an absolute privation of all freedom, thereby making moral responsibility, not a mystery above comprehension, but a direct contradiction" (*AR*, pp. 157–58)—hence Christabel's indiscriminate horror of any and all sin and her acceptance of moral enthrallment as the unalterable will of God: "Quoth Christabel, So let it be! / And as the lady [Geraldine] bade did she" (235–36). As early as 1795, however, Coleridge had identified the literary school responsible for fostering such hypocritically passive attitudes toward sin. His youthful attack on the slave trade warns: "Sensibility indeed we have to spare—what novel-reading Lady does not over flow with it . . . [but] Sensibility is not Benevolence. Nay, by making us tremblingly alive to trifling misfortunes, it frequently prevents it, and induces effeminate and cowardly selfishness."[34] Thirty years later *Aids to Reflection* repeats the message in a religious context, contrasting "excessive and unhealthy sensitiveness" with "prudence," the realistic grasp of life's common iniquities. Naturally, we must pursue our salvation by striving

> to avail ourselves of all the positive helps and furtherances which circumstances afford. But neither dare we, as Christians forget whose and under what dominion . . . is the world that constitutes our outward circumstances. . . . We are told to avoid its snares, to repel its attacks, to suspect its aids and succors, and even when compelled to receive them as allies

within our trenches, yet to commit the outworks alone to their charge, and to keep them at a jealous distance from the citadel. [*AR*, p. 77]

Christabel's lugging the suddenly limp Geraldine across the castle threshold, a patent allegory of sin gaining entrance to the soul, dramatizes Coleridge's hardheaded point here that the evils of fallen life, although unpleasant and saddening, are not irresistible. They have power to corrupt only when we take them to our bosom—as Christabel proceeds to take Geraldine. That "sensibility and all the amiable virtues may become . . . the pandars of vice, and the instruments of seduction" (*AR*, p. 89) is further illustrated by Christabel's picturesque worship "Amid the jagged shadows . . . , Kneeling in the moonlight, . . . Her slender palms together prest" (282–86). As Edward Dramin discerns, the scene is a veritable tableau.[35] With "eyes more bright than clear," it appears the girl has composed herself according to the moral chiaroscuro typical of Ann Radcliffe, where the heroine's unspotted purity is always set off by its dangerous proximity to darkness. Such unacknowledged attractions to the terrible demonstrate for Coleridge the deep-rooted persistence of sinfulness in spite of—even under cover of—the programmatic enlightened rationalism of his former heroes, Godwin, Paley, and Priestley.[36]

The superficiality of Christabel's saintliness can be seen through comparison with the Ancient Mariner. In blessing the spontaneously beautiful water snakes, he expresses an unconscious recognition that their previous deformity as "slimy things" was in some sense a projection of his own sinfulness. Christabel is similarly absorbed by Geraldine's dark glossy beauty—the latter's "richly clad" appearance in lines 58–68 recalls the snakes' "rich attire" in *The Rime* (272–81)—yet, spellbound, the girl withholds her blessing, refusing to countenance her own imperfection.[37] How then could Coleridge's son, Derwent, and physician, James Gillman, report independently that he envisioned a plot line of sacrifice by Christabel in her role as a St. Teresa? Although differing widely in details, both agree that, in Gillman's words, "the story of Christabel is founded on the notion, that the virtuous of this world save the wicked."[38] But this redemption need not be supernatural; indeed, Coleridge all his life repudiated the doctrine of vicarious atonement as inconsistent with individual moral responsibility. Thus Christabel saves Geraldine from simple physical distress easily enough at the poem's very beginning. Thereafter, she struggles inwardly to instigate Geraldine's moral rescue by the act of forgiveness that presumably would ease the "weight" (258) of Geraldine's remorse. The requisite sacrifice here is Christabel's renouncing her girlish self-image of absolute purity and accepting that "there but for the grace of God go I," so becoming a sadder and a wiser woman. Meantime, she is transfixed against the crossbeams of her cozy necessitarian certainty of her perfect innocence and her trembling Calvinistic horror of even the slightest signs of human frailty.

Coleridge's notes on St. Teresa's *Life* likewise focus on the spiritual complacency he believes to accompany her excessive protestations of sinfulness. In Teresa's "True it is, that I am both the most weak, and the most wicked of any living," he discerns a personality split that is due to falsely juxtaposed ideas of divine goodness and human evil:

> Can this . . . be other than madness or a lie? . . . That relatively to the command *Be ye perfect even as your Father in Heaven is perfect*, . . . the best of men may deem himself mere folly and imperfection, I can easily conceive; but this is not the case in question. It is here a comparison of one man [*sic*] with all others of whom he has known or heard;—*ergo*, a matter of experience; and in this sense it is impossible [to speak as Teresa does] without loss of memory and judgment on the one hand, or of veracity and simplicity on the other. Besides, of what use is it? . . . Will [other men's] sins lessen mine, though they were greater? Does not every man stand or fall to his own Maker according to his own being? [*LR* 4:67–68]

Hence the paradox whereby "this poor afflicted spotless innocent could be so pierced through with fanatic pre-conceptions" about her unworthiness as almost to imagine herself "possessed by the Devil" at the very time of receiving the Sacrament. Coleridge's interest is not in the blatant "medical" aspects of Teresa's case—that is, her hysterical confusing of physical and spiritual rapture—but more sympathetically in Teresa's self-victimization, her half-conscious schizoid suspicion that the only lover of whom she could possibly be worthy is Satan and not God.[39]

Derwent Coleridge and Gillman both projected fairy-tale happy endings for the poem. But alongside the familiar sort of fairy tale showing, as in "The Beauty and the Beast," that love conquers all stands its parodic counterpart wherein the Beast really is evil.[40] The characters have no foolproof way of determining which of the two plots will develop. Early on Christabel herself projects a happily-ever-after conclusion to Geraldine's story:

> O well, bright dame! may you command
> The service of Sir Leoline;
> And gladly our stout chivalry
> Will he send forth and friends withal
> To guide and guard you safe and free
> Home to your noble father's hall. [106–11]

But the increasing complexity of life at Langdale Hall makes this look facile. If in the parodic tales the victim's fate seems unmerited, nevertheless it usually turns out to be no accident but a mechanistic Newtonian version of Sophoclean justice. As in Coleridge's original version of "The Raven," or his famous profession to Mrs. Barbauld of the *The Rime*'s ultimately amoral purpose, the individual's misfortune serves within the vast impersonal scheme of things to right a past injustice or fulfill a necessary prophecy (thus Geraldine is the reluctant instrument of some higher agency). Moreover, upon scrutiny the evil is revealed to be overdetermined: the heroine has abundant unconscious reasons for favoring it. Accordingly, Christabel's seduction entails a crossover from the land of simple gothic fairy tales, where evil is physical and imposed from without, to the genuinely terrifying daylight realm of Part II, where moral evil is chosen freely "with open eyes."

III

Part II shows Christabel living down a lie, hating it all the while she compounds it, thereby becoming the horror she beholds. Coleridge himself was about to live down the plagiarisms of the *Biographia Literaria*, published a year after the poem finally appeared; but of course his concern with neurotic vice was long-standing. Involving as it does subversion of the will, he finds habitual immorality, although in any single act less reprehensible than a crime, to be nevertheless "more hopeless and therefore of deeper Evil than any single Crime, however great" (*CL* 4:553). Christabel's continued silence is worse than the Ancient Mariner's criminal but merely momentary loss of control because it entails making herself over in the image of evil. As Laurence Lockridge remarks, Coleridge "comes to identify the origin and nature of evil with something more basic and frightening than fallibility, and yet, like fallibility, near at hand."[41] Speech, or the affirmation of moral identity sustained and tempered by a coherent community of relationships, would give consciousness back its waking dominance, anxiously incomplete but at least hopeful and meliorable, over the isolate unconscious will, as, for example, the Mariner's retelling of his tale helps to do. Christabel's muteness, on the other hand, involves not only acquiescence in her seduction but a despondent hardening of conscience at the further seduction of her father, in which she thus becomes Geraldine's accomplice.

Like daughter, like father: as with Christabel, Geraldine manipulates the Baron's eagerness to believe himself the rescuing hero of a gothic romance.[42] Her stagy behavior first provokes him to a blustering show of chivalry ill suited to one so "aged" (431–46) and then to infatuation masked—from himself although not from the ladies—by high-minded concern for his former friend Lord Roland. Plainly, when Geraldine "meets" and "prolongs" his gratuitous second embrace, the spell that ostensibly lies "in the touch of this bosom" (267) is not operating in any *super*natural fashion. Finally the Baron, like Christabel, is led to choose evil: piqued, he rejects his daughter in favor of the beautiful stranger, thereby repeating the rashness of her own earlier rescue effort. Not that he hasn't good cause to doubt Christabel. Her stammering entreaty, "this woman send away!" (617), says the right thing but not necessarily for the right reason. Through procrastination, Christabel's stand upon conscience has become tainted by the complexities of other people's wills, so that the Baron's charge of jealousy seems likely enough.[43]

That actions can ramify in this fallen manner creates an uncertainty principle precluding foresight into their full consequences. Says Jeremy Taylor, the seventeenth-century divine quoted throughout *Aids to Reflection*, "then is it that every man dashes against another, and one relation requires what another denies; and when one speaks another will contradict him; and that which is well spoken is sometimes innocently mistaken" (*AR*, p. 245). In the same way, Christabel's charitable aid of Geraldine hurts herself and perhaps also the Baron; the Baron's chivalrous aid of Geraldine hurts Christabel and perhaps also himself; and Christabel's attempted filial aid of the Baron would perhaps deprive him of rejuvenating affections long overdue—affections for Lord Roland as well as for Geraldine—and so only perpetuate his death-in-life endured since his wife's demise (332–44). For these reasons Coleridge rejected Paley's necessitarianism as shallowly behaviorist: it "draws away the attention from the *will*, that is, from the inward motives and impulses which constitute the essence of *morality*, to the outward act,"[44] so divorcing the agent from his acts and, by extension, from any reassuringly concrete involvement with reality.

Christabel's self-alienation in Part II likewise discloses, on one hand, a delusive acceptance of responsibility for any and all misfortunes resulting from her initial act of charity, no matter how unpredictable, as though they reflected a necessarily evil motive, and on the other hand, a disavowal of all responsibility, even for conniving at the spell. Whether or not it is a demonic possession, her horrified hissing gasp at the Baron's courtship of Geraldine attests a divided self. Partly it shows Christabel's startled recognition of her own fallibility based on recollection of her experience the previous night, and partly it recalls the prudish voyeurism of the Part I narrator ("a sight to dream of, *not to tell*"), thus implying overreaction to the sight of ordinary lechery (454–59). Having gained awareness of sexuality through the sight of Geraldine's naked body, Christabel is now evidently reading sexual meaning into Geraldine's embrace of the Baron. The abruptness of the metamorphosis suggests a schizophrenic antinomianism much like that of James Hogg's Justified Sinner:[45] when the Baron twice turns at the sound, he "nothing saw, but his own sweet maid / With eyes upraised, as one that prayed" (461–62). If Christabel here can "imitate" Geraldine's snake eyes with "all her features" (602–05) while outwardly acting the saint, then plainly a snake must be how she pictures herself. The reader, on the contrary, sees such envy as only too human. At the same time, Geraldine is by her own admission a very sinful woman, so she may really look reptilian; in which case the doting Baron, as fascinated by Geraldine's eyes as Christabel is, but rather inclined to see them as "large bright eyes divine," is an unreliable judge of either woman's face. What this baffling, wordless exchange of glances demonstrates is the impossibility of deducing who saw what first. Geraldine's snaky iridescence making her all things to all people evidently comprises the mystery of original sin, which originates in the agent but becomes activated by the ambiguities of human relationships.[46]

The Baron's diagnosis of jealousy is therefore only partly correct. Christabel's reactions evince what Coleridge, in a long notebook entry of 1803 describing Wordsworth's "*up*, askance, pig look" and his own ensuing "little ugly Touchlets of Pain & little Shrinkings Back at the Heart"—an episode that duplicates Geraldine's "look askance" and Christabel's "shrinking" at "the touch and pain"—deems "a vice of personal Uncharitableness, not Envy" although very like it (*N* 1, entry 1606).[47] Envy Coleridge considers merely a secondary effect of "the instinct of all fine minds to *totalize*—to make a *perfectly congruous whole* of every character—& a pain at the being obliged to admit incongruities." Specifically, the pain results from disruption of one's "representative" or "phantom image" of the other based on the coalescence of accustomed impressions.[48] Confronting the inadequacy of that image produces a sense of "Self-degradation," leading to invidious comparison of oneself with the other such as Coleridge finds so pitiable in St. Teresa.

Christabel's "forced unconscious sympathy" with Geraldine's spiteful glance attests a repetition compulsion of which the spell is merely a neurotic symbol. In order to master it, the girl repeats her traumatic confrontation of evil, an experience the more painful, and hence the more inescapably repetitive, for being so alien to her self-image. Doomed to a similar vicious circle, the Ancient Mariner at least obtains temporary relief by attempting to *tell* his experience. Coleridge's analysis of the incident with Wordsworth shows him "deeplier than ever . . . the necessity of understanding the whole complex mixed character of our Friend." Similarly, Geraldine and the Baron—even Bard Bracy, whose subservience to his patron violates his poetic vow to purify Langdale Wood—are all what Jane Austen likewise calls "mixed characters" containing "a general though unequal mixture of good and bad." Apparently Christabel has yet to realize, as the heroine of *Northanger Abbey* finally sees, that indeed "in Mrs Radcliff's works, and . . . the works of all her imitators, . . . such as were not as spotless as an angel, might have the dispositions of a fiend. . . . But in England it was not so" (p. 177). From Part I to Part II Christabel's view of Geraldine plunges between these simple extremes, and with the same paralyzing abstraction of good and bad from the complexities of real human relationships as Austen and Coleridge both condemn in the School of Sensibility.

Accordingly, the increasing fortitude of Coleridge's Christian faith leads him, beginning in late 1801, to a critique of his earlier associationism, a moral critique rooted in the staunch Miltonic premise that "good and evil we know in the field of this world grow up together almost inseparably. . . . And perhaps this is that doom which Adam fell into of knowing good and evil, that is to say, of knowing good by evil" (Hughes, p. 728). The perfectibilist Hartley believed the process of association to spiritualize the "sensible Pleasures and Pains" into "intellectual" ones, thus tending to "reduce the State of those who have eaten of the Tree of Knowledge of Good and Evil, back again to a paradisiacal one."[49] But Coleridge, who dedicated a youthful poem to Hartley's thesis, no longer envisions such a utopia. At the source of association he locates mankind's depraved will— that is, our animal apprehension of pain and pleasure as simple stimuli able indeed to be quantified and equated in behaviorist fashion, but for that reason all the more liable to be sadomasochistically confounded together to the detriment of the more complexly organized personality. A notebook jotting from this period offers a preview of *Christabel*'s tailpiece: "Laughter of Parents & Grandames at little children's motions, is Laughter in its original state—a little convulsive motion to get rid of a pleasure rising into pain" (*N* 1, entry 1533).[50] Hence arises "the Origin of moral Evil from the *streamy* Nature of Association" (*N* 1, entry 1770): although association supplies the basis for sympathetic identification with others, its "height, & ideal" is "Delirium," continuous self-enclosed reverie hostile to the higher-order moral distinctions that define the self's relation to the outer world. So whereas the youthful Coleridge developed his philosophy of organic unity in reaction to the soullessness of Newtonian mechanism, he later sees the enemy to be "this anti monadic feeling" itself, the selfish desire to unify, or "totalize," associations actually discrete and incompatible: "That deep intuition of *oneness*—is it not at the bottom of many of our faults as well as Virtues / the dislike that a bad man should have any virtues, a good man any faults / & yet something noble and incentive in this" (*N* 1, entry 2471).

The Conclusion to Part II explicitly confronts this paradox. "A very

metaphysical account of Fathers calling their children rogues, rascals, &
little varlets" (CL 2:729), the poet and recent father described it in the
letter to Southey in which it first appeared. The passage doesn't only
recapitulate the peculiar violence with which the Baron rebukes his beloved daughter, as commentators tend to point out.[51] By exposing the
corruptness of our interest in gothic horror, it further offers a psycho-
religious gloss on the parody of Part I, so bringing the poem full circle. "A
little child," writes Coleridge,

> Makes such a vision to the sight
> As fills a father's eyes with light;
> And pleasures flow in so thick and fast
> Upon his heart, that he at last
> Must needs express his love's excess
> With words of unmeant bitterness.
> Perhaps 'tis pretty to force together
> Thoughts so all unlike each other;
> To mutter and mock a broken charm,
> To dally with wrong that does no harm.
> Perhaps 'tis tender too and pretty
> At each wild word to feel within
> A sweet recoil of love and pity.
> And what, if in a world of sin
> (O sorrow and shame should this be true!)
> Such giddiness of heart and brain
> Comes seldom save from rage and pain,
> So talks as it's most used to do.   [660–77]

The father tenderly abusing his own child images the reader's relation to
his own purest feelings as embodied by Christabel. To feel "a sweet
recoil . . . at each wild word" refers in this sense to the sadistic relish with
which we peruse Christabel's seduction. The recoil involves "giddiness"
because her innocence seems truly excessive; it disrupts our necessary
familiarity with imperfections typical of "this world of sin," thrusting us
back into the "streaminess" of associations not yet comfortably organized
into a "representative image" of the other person.[52] For Coleridge, then,
the great "sorrow and shame" of man's fallen estate is his inability to love
deeply without selfish ambivalence. "To mutter and mock a broken
charm" is to profess and imitate beliefs that are belied by one's conduct.[53]
Similarly, Christabel's guardian mother, her superstitious charm against
Geraldine's evil eye, is ineffectual so long as she hypocritically embraces
the spell (this affords a perfectly naturalistic view of the mother, whose
assault on Geraldine seems in any case to be an expression of the latter's

remorse). Yet the reader, too, is guilty of "dallying with wrong." The speciousness of Geraldine's spell represents the falseness of gothic sub-literature, of which Coleridge remarks that "the reader, when he is got to the end of the work, looks about in vain for the spell which had bound him so strongly to it" (Greever, pp. 169–70). Thus the Conclusion to Part II insists we recognize that the evils, which at the beginning of the poem we assumed to exist "out there" in the safely impersonal form of monsters, are in fact trivial compared to our own fascination with them. In a reversal of accustomed causality, it isn't so much the monsters that elicit our fascination; rather, our prior fascination with sin itself produces the monsters in order to enjoy the mixed pain and pleasure of a catharsis. "Words of unmeant bitterness" therefore characterize gothic authors unaware that their supernaturalism, seemingly so inventive and exotic, is only specious embellishment of an all-too-common sinfulness that simply "talks as it's most used to do," making the authors its mouthpiece.

In sum, the Conclusion reveals a forcing together of unlike thoughts on two levels. At the narrative level, such forcing occurs in Christabel's not-quite-innocuous visit to the midnight woods, in the Baron's somewhat lecherous chivalry, and in Geraldine's calculated but reluctant deceptions. At the thematic level, it occurs in the mind of the reader: since the idea of innocence (Christabel) inevitably tempts the idea of its corruption (Geraldine), the reader is led to face squarely the "mixed," fallen nature of his own mind. As Coleridge declares again and again in the notebooks, "Extremes meet."

IV

Accordingly, *Christabel* is itself "mixed": the poem comprises three distinct narrative styles. Whereas the setting of Part I is archaic, dim, and fictitious, and the action is witnessed with difficulty over the shoulder of a narrator who obstructs the view as much as he reveals it, Part II discloses the familiar Lake District landscape that evidently has been standing behind the gothic darkness all along. Consider, for example, Bracy's account of the matin bell's echo:

> Saith Bracy the Bard, So let it knell!
> And let the drowsy sacristan
> Still count as slowly as he can!
> There is no lack of such, I ween,
> As well fill up the space between.
> In Langdale Pike and Witch's Lair,
> And Dungeon-ghyll so foully rent,
> With ropes of rock and bells of air

> Three sinful sextons' ghosts are pent,
> Who all give back, one after t'other,
> The death-note to their living brother;
> And oft, too, by the knell offended,
> Just as their one! two! three! is ended,
> The devil mocks the doleful tale
> With a merry peal from Borodale.   [345–59]

The passage looks back on the self-enclosed dream world of Part I from the outside, satirizing its horrors in a tone of gruff, rise-and-shine joviality. Bracy's tale of his nightmare, an allegory of Christabel's entrapment by Geraldine, works in a similar manner: "I woke; it was the midnight hour, / The clock was tolling in the tower" (555–56). In other words, Bracy woke at the very moment the poem itself begins: " 'Tis midnight by the castle clock" (1). So, events that at the poem's outset seemed supernatural reappear in Part II as explicitly psychological disturbances. In turn, the Conclusion to Part II examines more minutely and frankly the source of these disturbances in our diseased will. In the end, then, the poem reaffirms the same principle of verisimilitude—"observance of real life" (Greever 185)—that Coleridge's reviews proclaim the measure of success or failure in fiction.

Christabel's stylistic development reveals a unified method. The poem progresses from supernaturalism overladen with gothic conventions to a more naturalistic presentation of the claustrally intense little society at Langdale Hall, an English country house very like Southey's Greta Hall where the Wordsworth circle tended to congregate. Thence the Part II Conclusion proceeds self-consciously to analyze the reader's experience of the first two parts. The poem's mounting intimacy, corresponding to its three main phases of composition and the increasingly autobiographical nature of its material, dramatizes the process of self-realization discussed in the essay "On Method" (1817–18):

> Finding nowhere a representative of that free agency which yet is a fact of immediate consciousness . . . , [man] at once discovers and recoils from the discovery, that the *reality*, the *objective* truth, of the objects he has been adoring, derives its whole and sole evidence from an obscure sensation, which he is alike unable to resist or to comprehend, which compels him to contemplate as without and independent of himself what yet he could not contemplate at all, were it not a modification of his own being.
> [*Friend* 1:509]

By linking the reader's conscious preoccupation with horror to the deeper, less articulate forces of the unconscious will, the poem fulfills its initial parodic goal of putting gothic sensationalism to moral use. "Deep feelings" are accompanied by "obscure ideas," writes Coleridge; hence "one should reserve these feelings . . . for objects, which their very sublimity renders indefinite, no less than their indefiniteness renders them sublime" (*Friend* 1:106). Original sin is the ultimate such object; raising it into view as *Christabel* does is not to define it—an impossibility—but on the contrary to render its mysteriousness the more sublimely apparent, making darkness visible.[54] The poem thus supplants the fetishistic feelings aroused by the murkiness of Part I with more durable and profound "feelings of dimness from *growth* . . . yearnings & strivings of obscurity from *growing*" (*N* 2, entry 2509).[55]

Considered in this light, *Christabel*'s incompleteness seems less an accident of Coleridge's personal debilities than an unavoidable consequence of his theme, man's universal fallenness. Bard Bracy's time-serving compromise of his poetic autonomy hints that the author is no less fallible and weak than his characters. Indeed, inasmuch as original sin defies causal analysis, it is also bound to thwart all attempts at ordinary narrative resolution. Whereas *The Rime of the Ancient Mariner*, Coleridge's one finished narrative of any length, simply posits an irrational act of will which it then uses (as Empson puts it) "to make the story go," *Christabel*'s very story centers on the irrational will—hence the frequent complaint that the poem doesn't really go anyplace. Nevertheless, as in "Kubla Khan," another acknowledged fragment whose subplot most critics nowadays take to be complete, Coleridge managed finally to satisfy thematic and stylistic, if not narrative, criteria for bringing *Christabel* to a unified close.[56] As an observation of 1796 suggests—"Poetry—excites us to artificial feelings—makes us callous to real ones" (*N* 1, entry 87)—he was willing to sacrifice the poem's formal unity and his own deep "intuition of oneness" as a poet, for the sake of discriminating without totalization certain real and irreducible incongruities of human feeling. Spiraling more and more deeply toward its central mystery of evil, *Christabel* in the end conducts the reader to the main region of its song, Coleridge's skeptically religious version of the Wordsworthian internalized sublime: "such fear and awe / As fall upon us often when we look / Into our Minds, into the Mind of Man" (W, p. 45).

Shipwreck and Skepticism:
Don Juan, Canto II

Life is, in itself and forever, shipwreck. To be shipwrecked is not to drown. . . . Consciousness of shipwreck, being the truth of life, constitutes salvation.

Ortega y Gasset, *"In Search of Goethe from Within"*

It is Christabel's refusal to acknowledge contingency that leads her into self-doubt. The desire to inhabit a fully intelligible universe drives her to rationalize her misfortunes as having a supernatural cause and then to wonder why she of all people should deserve such a fate. Rather than living out her doubts toward Geraldine, doubts ultimately about herself, Christabel desires to know her life definitively, as if it were already over; thus she takes personal responsibility for her chance but unconsciously overdetermined encounter. Her error is also committed by the Ancient Mariner whose compulsive garrulity, although outwardly the opposite of Christabel's muteness, attests a similar self-entrapment and paralysis. For it seems clear that the Mariner's sense of guilt stems in some measure from his supposition that somehow he must have intended to cause the deaths of his shipmates by shooting the albatross, and so becalming the ship and bringing on the killing drought. Indeed, one suspects the reason he shot the bird was to validate, even justify in a parody of Miltonic theodicy, a *prior* awareness of guilt reflecting a similarly prior sinfulness.[1] Of course, the irony of such atonement is that it is based so conspicuously on an assertion of individual autonomy, not to say prideful defiance, which only repeats the original sin. One can see the same masochistic confusion of cause and effect in the author's fitful attempts to curtail his laudanum addiction. Since it appears Coleridge consistently mistook the ensuing withdrawal symptoms for the already partly psychosomatic ailments he was trying to relieve, he naturally had every excuse to renew the dependency, thereby achieving a method of self-torture far more exquisite than if he had simply maintained a steady dosage. The ensuing cycle of pain and guilt much resembles the Mariner's periodic unexamined need to retell his tale. Although the retelling involves reexperiencing the torturous voyage—this presumably constitutes the Mariner's penance—by the same token it leads him to reenact the sin for which he believes penance is required.

Noticing the grandiosity of the Mariner's guilt allows us to reconcile Coleridge's Christian beliefs with William Empson's and E. E. Bostetter's skeptical views of the Mariner as a victim of religious delusion.[2] The Mariner's closing message of God's love for all things great and small is to be taken both literally and ironically. On one hand, we see the Mariner doesn't practice what he preaches, since his exaggerated, egotistic guilt prevents him from finding redemption through love; he actually prevents the Wedding Guest from joining the very Christian community he extols in the closing stanzas. On the other hand, those stanzas do affirm the author's oft-declared belief in salvation through the sanctified community of "the One Life"; the pious moral only reemphasizes the contrast between the Mariner's naive enthusiasm and the reductive moralizings of the glossator. Wantonly killing the albatross is indeed "the violation of a great sanctity," as Robert Penn Warren claimed,[3] but the bird is a "symbol" of that sanctity only in the Coleridgean sense: "It always partakes of the Reality which it renders intelligible; and while it enunciates the whole, abides itself as a living part in that Unity, of which it is the representative."[4] Although the occasion of the albatross distinctly resembles that of the biblical dove of peace, its symbolic significance is not predetermined and absolute (Christ, innocence, goodness) but contingent upon time and place (as Byron implicitly recognizes in *Don Juan*, Canto II): the bird is the only living creature, beautiful, rare, and yet hospitable, amid an alien world of ice. In this sense it is not *essentially* different from the ungainly "charm"-bearing rook that flies over the solitary poet at the end of "This Lime-Tree Bower My Prison."

A phenomenological rationale for *The Rime*'s method can be seen in Coleridge's religious disquisition to Thomas Clarkson of October 13, 1806:

> What the Spirit of God *is*, and what the Soul *is*, I dare not suppose myself capable of *conceiving*: according to my religious and philosophical creed they are *known* by those, to whom they are revealed, even (tho' in a higher and deeper degree) as . . . the difference between the Spirals of the Hop-plant and the Scarlet Bean. *Datur*, non intelligitur. They can only be explained by images, that themselves require the same explanation, as in the latter Instance, that the one turns to the right, the other to the Left, the one is with, the other against the Sun, i.e. by relative and dependent, not positive and fundamental, notions. The only reasonable form of the question appears to me to be, under what connection of ideas we may conceive and express ourselves concerning them, as that there shall be no inconsistency to be detected in our definitions, and no falsehood felt during their enunciation, which might war with our internal sense of their actuality. [*CL* 2:633–34]

This explains why Coleridge goes out of his way to expose the literally fair-weather friendship of the crew. Their oscillating condemnation and approval of the shooting, based on no moral code but mere Paleyan calculation of the "general consequences" for themselves,[5] is really no more superstitious than Warren's ostensibly Christian interpretation of the shooting as an allegory of fall and redemption, based likewise on a symbology in which the good or bad significance of an act is determined by its effects. When Warren argues that the drought comes *because* the Mariner shot the bird, or that the rain shower arrives *because* he blessed the water snakes, he is committing the same fallacy of *post hoc, ergo propter hoc* as the crew.[6] The gloss writer, a scholarly rationalist whose language is at once more superstitious *and* more Christian than the crew, is in this respect a proleptic parody of Warren.

Just as *The Rime* repudiates a fixed symbology, it also repudiates the confident Blakean view that "every Natural Effect has a Spiritual Cause, and Not / A Natural: for a Natural Cause only Seems, it is a Delusion / Of Ulro: & a ratio of the perishing Vegetable Memory."[7] The poem thus eschews a *Milton*-like fortunate fall—or even a *Christabel*-like unfortunate fall—presented by a progressive series of narrative styles, each repeating the same basic "spiritual" plot on a more accessibly naturalistic level. In keeping with the author's conviction that ultimate spiritual things are not explicable without solecism ("*Datur,* non intelligitur"), the plot of *The Rime* never takes shape. The Mariner's voyage is simply juxtaposed with his tale to the reluctant Wedding Guest and the glossator's comments.[8] As against the redemptive closure offered by the cozy, childlike Christian community depicted at the poem's beginning and end, Coleridge upholds the autonomy of the exile who would painfully fashion his own salvation from the tracts of history. If that sounds existentialist, it is also deeply Protestant. Although the Mariner contends that the sexless family of simple Christabels all joined in prayer—"Old men, and babes, and loving friends, / And youths and maidens gay"—is "sweeter far" to him than the marriage feast,[9] in fact he rejects all such established forms of worship (the bizarre nuptial overtones of Christabel's night with Geraldine show that she likewise has embarked, although with much greater reluctance, upon this process of moral self-definition). Having blessed the water snakes inwardly and "unawares," the Mariner is compelled to choose the rigors of a more introspective, if also more dangerously self-centered, pilgrim's progress whose final outcome can be known only to himself.[10]

Both the Mariner and Christabel, in taking responsibility for physical accidents stubbornly alien to man's moral life (the weather, chance encounters with strangers), reveal a distinctly hubristic self-importance. Yet the deeds which they believe have rendered them the focus of universal attention—the shooting of the albatross, the midnight prayers in the wood—are striking for their capriciousness. So it appears that contingency, denied in the external world, reemerges within the characters themselves. Ironically, the Coleridgean universe proves to be organic in an unintended sense. Instead of humanizing nature in accordance with its own desire for unity, the self becomes "thingified" by subsuming the very randomness in nature that it feared.

This process collapses the distance needed for viewing nature as a repository of translucent symbols of the divine. Coleridge turns toward nature in order to see through it to God, but instead he tends to become absorbed into it, much as the Blakean pilgrim mistakes the vegetative solace of Beulah for the more passionate delights of eternity, his true goal. His lifelong forced unconscious sympathy for pantheism attests nature's uncanny power over him. Similarly, the indistinct, even viscous physical settings of *The Rime*, Parts I–IV, and *Christabel*, Part I, reveal the protagonists' confused identification with the material objects of perception. The undulating water snakes first appear as mere undifferentiated "slimy things . . . with legs / Upon the slimy sea" (125–26); and Geraldine seems to coalesce animistically out of the old oak tree, whose "broad-breasted" trunk (42) resembles her own prominent "heaving breasts" (380). But the ensuing countermovement away from nature, which the essay "On Method" portrays as man's discovery of his free agency and supernatural origin, and hence as the basis for all religious idealism, remains problematic in both poems.

Nature's tendency to short-circuit the dynamics of symbolic perception is most glaring, because least elaborately concealed by revisionary glosses or prefaces, in Coleridge's first major lyric, "The Eolian Harp." The poem begins with twilight thickening around the languorous poet. As he savors the seductive scents and sounds that increasingly pervade the scene, his musings exfoliate sympathetically into a pantheistic monism, blurring the neat moral perspective by which the jasmine and myrtle that have "o'er-grown" his cottage were safely reduced, in the opening lines, to "Meet emblems . . . of Innocence and Love" (3–5). Commentators tend to note the violent interruption of the last verse paragraph, where Sara's disapproving eye causes the poet guiltily to repudiate "these shapings of the unregenerate mind . . . vain Philosophy's aye-babbling spring" (55–57) in favor of simple Christian faith.[11] Yet the tone of pious self-condemnation enters the poem as early as the third verse paragraph:

> And thus, my Love! as on the midway slope
> Of yonder hill I stretch my limbs at noon,
> Whilst through my half-clos'd eye-lids I behold

The sunbeams dance, like diamonds on the main,
And tranquil muse upon tranquillity;
Full many a thought uncall'd and undetain'd,
And many idle flitting phantasies,
Traverse my indolent and passive brain,
As wild and various as the random gales
That swell and flutter on this subject Lute!   [34–43]

Here Coleridge leaves off philosophizing and returns to the descriptive mode of the poem's opening lines, where he appeared as an objectified figure within a landscape allegorical of higher truths such as Innocence, Love, and Wisdom. But so inexorable is the poem's dialectic, such self-objectification paradoxically works only to extend the pantheistic merging of mind and nature in "the one Life" (26). For the above passage depicts not his immediate situation together with Sara by the cottage at twilight but another, unspecified time alone on "yonder hill" at noon; far from objectifying the poet, the passage displaces him. A similar reversal occurs when the wind-harp, which earlier was treated as an object of the poet's thought (12–20), is discovered to be the poet himself, a "subject lute" whose response to nature's caresses is evidently the preceding verses. In this way the lute comes to be both subject and object. Accordingly, the next verse paragraph beginning "And what if all of animated nature / Be but organic Harps diversely fram'd" (44–48) doesn't just codify the poet's previous intuition of nature's unity; it actually realizes that intuition, inasmuch as the lute is now mind and nature together. It turns out the antisubjective moral perspective of the third verse paragraph, instead of leading beyond nature to God, has merely played a provisional antithetical role within a larger dialectic leading deeper into nature. And thus the poet is driven, in the vehement final verse paragraph, to discard dialectic altogether in favor of a priori "Faith that inly *feels*" (60)—a repudiation of not only pantheism but the poem itself.[12]

The Romantic who discerns most clearly how the organicist teleology tends to assimilate mind to nature, so inhibiting man's freedom to create his own destiny by boldly countenancing the force of circumstance in all its savage indifference, is, of course, Byron, above all in the shipwreck and cannibalism of *Don Juan,* Canto II. Nor is the author himself exempt from circumstantiality. Indeed, the poem as a whole evinces his gradual coming to grips with the implications of Canto II. As the narrator's digressions increasingly edge out the story of Juan, the poem's thematics of contingency apparently begin to encompass its own actual, fitful mode of composition. At the same time, Byron's freewheeling Oriental exoticism gives way, in the later English cantos, to subtle, almost Jamesian depictions of a constricted social class little different from the narrator's own (its manipulativeness calls to mind the Wordsworth clique as portrayed in *Christabel*, Part II). As Juan grows more and more "gaté and blasé,"[13] the narrator conversely gives frequent signs of recognizing the limitations of his own worldliness, so that the two characters begin to approach each other. During the banquet at Lord Henry Amundeville's described in the last completed canto, they even dine at the same table, although without meeting (XVI, lxxxi). One surmises from these developments that subsequent cantos would have had Juan and the narrator draw still closer and eventually merge, thereby eliminating any remnants of a planned story and turning the poem into a prolonged extemporaneous meditation by the author. Having rejected all pretensions to an external narrative, Byron would have finally stepped out from behind the now-superfluous narrator and spoken forth directly as himself, much as Blake does at the end of *Milton* or Coleridge at the end of *Christabel*. Such (admittedly hypothetical) poetry would resemble the sudden first-person address to the ocean with which *Childe Harold's Pilgrimage* daringly concludes. The difference is that one can imagine *Don Juan* continuing—quite unlike *Childe Harold* but rather in the manner, oddly enough, of *Jerusalem*—as a fluid interchange of realistic contemporary narrative and candid skeptical commentary, as in short an explicitly personal mythologizing of the author's world-historical experience. But I am getting ahead of myself.

I

Mazeppa, composed simultaneously with *Don Juan*, Canto I, during the late summer of 1818, is in several respects a preliminary version of the shipwreck episode in Canto II. In both poems, a youthful adulterer undergoes a kind of descent into Hell, finally awakens before a Nausicaa, and thereafter remains exiled from his homeland. More important, Byron's active juxtaposing of different historical contexts in *Mazeppa* sheds light on his considerably subtler manipulations of ottava rima in *Don Juan*. *Mazeppa*'s opening stanza, alluding to the recent fall of Napoleon, introduces the poem as contemporaneous. The narrative, however, takes place immediately following the Battle of Pultowa in 1709; and within that narrative, the old hetman tracks his "seventy years of memory back" to his "twentieth spring," 1660.[14] The time frames distance the reader from the events of Mazeppa's story; yet by forming a continuum they implicitly connect us at the far end. The effect is of a progressive historicism, as the intensely private experience standing at the core of the narrative (virtually a nonexperience, since Mazeppa loses consciousness at the nadir of his journey) is gradually subsumed into a public context, becoming transformed from, first, the original, near-solipsistic event itself to the long-stored-up memory of a single individual to a beguiling story intended for a small "band of chiefs" (44) to, finally, a poem whose audience includes ourselves.

Mazeppa thus appears less a formal poetic object crafted by an author than a naturally evolved artifact inseparable from the surrounding contours of European history. Furthermore, those contours are seen to be limned largely by chance. Contra William Marshall, who ingeniously makes Mazeppa a parody of Charles's common sense, the narrator's position is not "clearly anti-providential," nor does Mazeppa express by contrast an "organized moral view of the universe" according to which his rescue by the Cossack maid constitutes a "providential intervention."[15] Quite the opposite—the moral of Mazeppa's tale is that he was saved by an unforeseeable stroke of luck, the same luck that will perhaps save Charles now. In devising a clever torture for Mazeppa, the Count Palatine unintentionally raised him to power and so ensured his own defeat; by the same token, the defeated Charles may also live to destroy his enemies.[16] The narrator's remark about "the hazard of the die" (15) therefore tends to support Mazeppa's affirmation of chance as a positive force. If you have hit bottom, if "the foe" are "ten to one at least" (114), then even random chance can only help. This capacity to sustain ups and downs is what makes man more than merely animal, despite his untamed passions which the wild horse plainly represents. Whereas the horse's unrelenting instinct for its homeland proves self-destructive, Mazeppa, whose home is simply wherever he happens to find himself (as shown in stanzas 3 and 4), survives his ride to love again. Similarly, the reason "Danger levels man and brute" (115) is that it brutalizes man; but danger needn't be the sole condition of human existence—hence Mazeppa ridicules Charles for constantly making war to the exclusion of love (126–42). Indeed, the satirical thrust of his tale is its tacit advice that, since we all must suffer defeat sooner or later, it is better to have loved and lost than never to have loved at all and still to have lost.

Yet even random change has its limits: the dice may be fickle but their permutations repeat. The constant recurrence within the poem of rivers (the Borysthenes, the dark unnamed stream of fifty years past), horses (Gieta's, Mazeppa's Bucephalus, and the wild Tartarian courser), and an assortment of personal and military defeats suggests that, although meaningful causal connections between the individual occasions of experience may be impossible to determine, nevertheless life's various circumstances do unmistakably embody distinct, often ironic patterns of contrast and resemblance. So the top and bottom of man's universe—paradise and death, love and brutalization—emerge from the narrative as fixed lineaments of experience without which it would lose all self-differentiation and simply dissolve into the general flux. As random as an individual's life may be, it can never trespass those bounds beyond which lies the merely unimaginable: gods and dust.

II

Far more than even *Mazeppa*, *Don Juan* abounds with chance surprises, above all in the shipwreck episode of Canto II, where the narrative seems to be propelled by no human motive or desire but simply by raw forces of nature. Subjugated by storms from without and starvation from within, man appears throughout the episode as a cipher lacking effective power to resist. A total newcomer to the larger world in which henceforth *Don Juan* takes place, Juan is here less a protagonist than just another sufferer scarcely to be distinguished from everybody else aboard ship. One recalls only his heroic stance, pistols drawn, before the rum room (II, xxx-xxxvi) and his tacit refusal to eat Pedrillo (II, lxxviii). The shipwreck, then, is Juan's rite of passage into "our nautical existence" (II, xii) on the sea of adventitious circumstance, the deluge which precludes any direct return to Spain and Donna Inez. It serves to define the Stygian bottom of his new-found universe, much as the subsequent Haideé idyll defines its paradisiacal apex.

For Byron himself, moreover, it seems the decision to continue the poem beyond Canto I, which apparently was first designed as a separate poem like *Beppo*, involved an embarkation similar to his hero's.[17] The two famous stanzas he added to the already completed draft of Canto I make the parallel almost explicit:

> No more—no more—Oh! never more on me
>   The freshness of the heart can fall like dew,
> Which out of all the lovely things we see
>   Extracts emotions beautiful and new;
> Hived in our bosoms like the bag o' the bee.
>   Think'st thou the honey with those objects grew?
> Alas! 'twas not in them, but in thy power
> To double even the sweetness of a flower.   [I, ccxiv]

"Thou" evidently refers to Byron's reader. Assuming our ignorance of the melancholy truth he wishes to convey, the poet rejects the earlier first-person plural and addresses us directly. Yet the continuing second person of the next stanza reveals that Byron is really addressing his own heart and perhaps has been all along:

> No more—no more—Oh! never more, my heart,
>   Canst thou be my sole world, my universe!

Once all in all, but now a thing apart,
  Thou canst not be my blessing or my curse:
The illusion's gone for ever. . . .   [I, ccxv]

Ultimately, however, such distinctions fail, for Byron's heart and his
implied readers are one and the same. His heart can no longer be his
universe because it now must take account of the larger world existing
beyond poetry and encompassing ourselves as actual readers. Hence *we*
become the objects out of which the disillusioned poet will extract new
emotional sustenance. The series of contexts that *Mazeppa* deployed as
framing devices, then, *Don Juan*, Canto II, actively incorporates as a
method of composition. The consequent relationships between Juan's
occasion of shipwreck, the narrator's collateral expressions of skepticism,
and finally the reader's subsuming experience of both supply the subject of
this chapter.

Unexpected as it is, the shipwreck episode starts out open-ended.
Anything might happen. Yet it is almost completely closed off at the other
end, and Juan seems to escape through an orifice. This development stems
from the way the law of attrition at sea logically works itself out: "Fam-
ine—despair, cold, thirst and heat, had done / Their work on them by
turns" (II, cii), to which one might add drowning, bad meat and delirium,
exposure and sharks. If the one doesn't get you, the others will. The form
of the episode is therefore a vortex of diminishing possibilities. Juan's
situation grows progressively more cramped and isolated as he moves
from the Seville aristocracy to a ship carrying approximately 250 people to
a longboat containing 30. Within the longboat, Juan's refusal to devour
Pedrillo distinguishes him from all "save three or four" (II, lxxviii) who die
anyway, leaving Juan the sole survivor. As the allusion to Dante's Ugolino
suggests (II, lxxxiii), cannibalism is the innermost ring of this Hell; Juan's
struggle with Ocean's "insatiate grave" (II, cviii) is the nadir; like Dante,
he squeezes through it and emerges into a new world, Haideé's island.

Byron articulates the descent as a series of small mishaps in which hopes
are raised only to be dashed. The episode begins in full expectation of a
safe passage; but "at one o'clock" the ship is suddenly about to sink (II,
xxvii). Then it appears the pumps will save them; but they almost capsize
in a squall (II, xxx). Then there comes "a flash of hope once more" as the
wind lulls with "a glimpse of sunshine" (II, xxxviii); but the storm renews
and the lifeboats must get out (II, xlv). Then we learn that "people in an
open boat . . . live upon the love of life" and " 'T is very certain the desire
of life / Prolongs it" (II, lxiv–lxvi); but we also learn this desire will not
suffice them indefinitely because "man is a carnivorous production, / . . . /
He cannot live, like woodcocks, upon suction" (II, lxvii). Then arrives a

sleep-inducing calm that restores the survivors' strength; but on awaken-ing they eat all their provisions (II, lxviii). And so forth. The sequence implies that events trick us into hope in order that we may be doubly defeated when they subsequently turn more dangerous yet. For the failure of each new promise of deliverance leaves the men not the same as before but worse, because they have irrevocably used up one more chance for survival. " 'T is best to struggle to the last," advises the narrator, " 'T is never too late to be wholly wreck'd" (II, xxxix). Good advice, surely—and yet three stanzas later one discovers its terrific irony, as the pumps give out and the dismasted ship rolls "a wreck complete" (II, xlii). It is as though the struggle to keep it afloat only led to a greater devastation, and indeed we are told they deliberately cut away the masts to avoid broaching (II, xxxii). This almost systematic way in which various saving possibilities yield only fresh defeats distinctly conveys the impression of an impersonal, casually malignant power of circumstance gradually disclosing itself in the course of the episode.

Yet as their situation worsens, the men hope all the more intensely. From the cannibalism to Juan's final arrival on the beach, the poem presents a series of auguries: the shower of rain, the rainbow, the white bird, the turtle. The episode begins with an objective narrative of suspense-ful action telling with considerable show of authority exactly what the ocean did to the ship and what the crew is doing to save it (II, xxvii). The reality of the world "out there" is assumed; it may be inhuman and destructive, but one can still be confident of knowing how to handle an emergency. Later, however, the objective narrative virtually disappears—appropriately so, for no longer is anything taking place out there; inert, the survivors are not engaged in any visible activity. The poem therefore shifts to a phenomenalistic presentation of their experience of reality, a realm in which belief, illusions, and symbolism play a vital part. Causality stands in abeyance; as the boat drifts, events seem to transpire without what Hume calls "necessary connexion," comprising instead simply an observed suc-cession of independent phenomena (a rainbow, a bird, a turtle). In such a world, as in Coleridge's Ancient Mariner's, there is no reason for rational, purposive action because no likelihood exists that it will produce its intended effect. Mental activity such as hope appears at least as effective.

This is not to imply that the phenomenal world of the lifeboat survivors is experienced directly by the reader the way the Ancient Mariner's is. "We" are not in the longboat; "they" are: we see them through the narrative presentation. But this is just what we were *not* conscious of doing at the outset of the episode, when the narrative appeared objective. Now it is emphatically a presentation and furthermore a skeptical one. Says Byron of the rainbow: "Our shipwreck'd seamen thought it a good omen— / It is as well to think so now and then / . . . / And may become of great advantage when / Folks are discouraged" (II, xciii). In their helplessness the survivors have made a possibly useful interpretation, no more or less. Their hope, which interprets natural phenomena as evidences of things unseen, is a tentative form of faith. Moreover, the comparison of the rainbow to "Quite a celestial kaleidoscope (II, xciii) suggests that such faith is inevitable under the circumstances. Like a kaleidoscope, a rainbow is not simply seen, but seen *into*, for it is an optical illusion existing as a unitary object entirely in the eye of the beholder. Being all appearance, as it were, the rainbow is thus whatever the half-dead men in the lifeboat perceive it to be.

If we prefer the narrator's skepticism here, it is with the awareness that he stands outside the lifeboat and can afford to be rational. Standing in "their" shoes (which anyway they have already eaten), we might well find skepticism to be just one more discouragement. Byron's point about the survivors' providential attitude is that it is more pragmatic than rationalist. They shrewdly anticipate a twofold benefit from the turtle and sacred-seeming white bird: the animals are regarded as both auguries and meat, and the two viewpoints do not conflict. After all, given a boatload of starving men, how else is a turtle evidence of a heavenly concern but that it may serve to sustain life? Similarly, what makes the bird a "bird of promise" is partly its promise of becoming food (II, xcv). Had the Ancient Mariner done the natural thing with *his* white bird—eaten it—he might have spared himself much grief, for the killing in that case would not have been wanton.

Such pragmatism gets its force from the way we experience *Don Juan's* ottava rima. Much has been said on this score, with attention usually directed toward the closing couplet rhyme. Alvin Kernan has emphasized the "but then" movement of the poem, its vital unpredictability. For him, the wavelike "onward rush of life" that the poem imitates, "upward to a pause, and then a sweep away, is most consistently present in the stanza form. . . . The first six lines stagger forward, like the life they contain, toward the resting place of the concluding couplet and the security of its rhyme—and a very shaky resting place it most often is."[18] Edward Bostetter replies that the reader's expectations are not simply thwarted but renewed as curiosity; he proposes a complementary movement, "what next?" which "puts the emphasis on the anticipatory suspense."[19] What perusal of the poem's individual stanzas shows is that these two movements coalesce so as to deny readers an accustomed complacency. We are drawn into and then thrust out of each stanza, which thus forms a miniature vortex. We end where we began, but meanwhile have become consciously aware of experiencing a fiction. Then we suspend that consciousness and proceed to repeat the process by moving on to the ever-imminent next stanza. The vortex form of the *Don Juan* stanza is not, however, simply a stylistic version of the thematic "falling" first discerned in the poem by George Ridenour.[20] It is less the characteristic Romantic fall into reality or experience—as exemplified, say, in Blake's passage through the vortex of *Milton*—than it is a freely willed descent into what Peter Manning, borrowing a phrase from Wallace Stevens, terms "the fictions of reality." "The actions of the poem complete themselves in [the reader's] consciousness," says Manning;[21] yes, and they do so by directly exercising our moral imagination. The questions Byron raises entail active examination of ourselves as social individuals. In Canto II he is not asking, "What would you do if stuck in a lifeboat with thirty others without any food?"—as though unshipwrecked readers could give any answer that were not merest fantasy. The inevitable reply, "*I* would heroically save them all (just don't press me for details)" reflects the question's lack of ballast. Instead Byron asks, "Exactly what *does* one do, having arrived at such a situation through force of circumstance?"—and what one does is, as usual in life, no one particular thing: not everybody eats Pedrillo. To repeat myself, "we" are not in the same boat as "they," but it is conceivable we could be because clearly their world much resembles ours. This consciousness of sharing the same context of possibilities as the shipwrecked men, without sharing even vicariously in their experience, is clarified by scrutinizing the individual stanzas themselves.

First consider stanza xxvii, the beginning of the end for all but Juan:

> At one o'clock the wind with sudden shift
> > Threw the ship right into the trough of the sea,
> Which struck her aft, and made an awkward rift,
> > Started the stern-post, also shattered the
> Whole of her stern-frame, and, ere she could lift
> > Herself from out her present jeopardy,
> The rudder tore away: 't was time to sound
> The pumps, and there were four feet water found.

In poetry, the prototype for such a nautical tour de force was William Falconer's *The Shipwreck* (1762), an exciting firsthand account in which numerous professional-sounding marine terms are casually retailed in rhyming couplets. But Byron's stanza is effective as much by what it does not do as by what it does. It is all objective narrative, a sudden accumulation of events without any real development. The wind shifts, and then no less than six violently active verbs happen to the ship one after the other; even the syntax, perfectly unextraordinary in itself, appears jerked about to fit the ottava rima. One realizes the helplessness of the ship, and the immense arbitrary power of the ocean that has evidently cuffed it. Appropriately, therefore, we find that the birthday-snapper in the couplet rhyme is too damp to explode except matter-of-factly. Events have so overwhelmed the crew, it isn't until line 7 that the men manage to take defensive action; but even then, all they do is discover still another way in which Ocean has anticipated them. So by forcibly failing to meet our expectations, this unusual stanza serves to reveal what, in fact, we expect of the usual *Don Juan* stanza: namely, that it should begin with an objective narrative of events leading to description of an active human response, leading in turn to commentary by the narrator himself. Not coincidentally, this is the same pattern of development we saw take place within the episode as a whole: Canto II progresses from an impersonal narrative of the sinking ship, implying confidence in the reality of the world "out there," to a presentation of the survivors' subjective construing of that world, to the narrator's clear-minded but sympathetic statements of skepticism.

Stanza 1 I take to be the ottava rima model on which Byron elsewhere plays changes. It is a manipulation of narrative, but not to make any particular point. The manipulation, however, involves several distinct shifts of perspective which we can enumerate:

> Some trial had been making at a raft,
> > With little hope in such a rolling sea,
> A sort of thing at which one would have laugh'd,
> > If any laughter at such times could be,
> Unless with people who too much have quaff'd,
> > And have a kind of wild and horrid glee,
> Half epileptical, and half hysterical:—
> Their preservation would have been a miracle.

Lines 1–2: objectively speaking, the raft is a futile effort; line 3: so futile, the reader might find it ridiculous; line 4: now, however, we are grimly reminded that under the circumstances a raft is better than nothing; lines 5–7: and yet there is room for compromise between the two points of view—if you want to laugh, laugh with them, the hideous despairing drunks; line 8: this line cuts off the lurid description of the laughter, itself slightly hysterical, by giving a blunt assessment of the raftsmen's chances. It thus repeats lines 1–2, only now it is the colloquial narrator speaking, not the impersonal narrative ("a miracle," not "little hope"). The stanza bends into the reader, challenging us directly with the "If" of line 4. Then, with the concessional "Unless," it turns back toward the fictive scene, which, however, now seems real inasmuch as it ironically subsumes our own response to it; with the introduction of "wild and horrid glee," the reader is forced to recognize that, under pressure of actual shipwreck, his armchair amusement at the raft could well become something less pleasant. The intervention of the narrator in line 8 completes the proof that we are not entitled to judge these people, only their chances for survival.

In the previous stanza, xlix, the same pattern is used first to insinuate the existence of an evil deity hidden in matter and then skeptically to show that people aboard a storm-beaten ship at least have good reason to believe so:

> 'T was twilight, and the sunless day went down
>   Over the waste of waters; like a veil,
> Which, if withdrawn, would but disclose the frown
>   Of one whose hate is mask'd but to assail.
> Thus to their hopeless eyes the night was shown,
>   And grimly darkled o'er the faces pale,
> And the dim desolate deep: twelve days had Fear
> Been their familiar, and now Death was here.

The first four lines, with their hint of a reversed Genesis, present the uncreating God of Byron's "Darkness." (What makes the last line of stanza l so potent is partly its suggestion that the raftsmen need *two* miracles, one to save them, plus one to create the good God who might bother to do so.) But then this vision is attributed to "hopeless eyes" looking only at "the night." Yet there is no cynicism here, for it next appears that the night these people saw really did "grimly darkle o'er the faces pale, / And the dim desolate deep." The horror they imagined therefore wasn't *all* illusion, a point the narrator reinforces by affirming that "now Death was here." The skepticism cuts too deep to be cynical.

Too deep, perhaps, for those who see in stanza lv only a failure of good taste. Even Andrew Rutherford, author of a tough-minded chapter entitled "*Don Juan*: War and Realism," hits upon this stanza as "the only one . . . in which Byron lapses into a flippant derisive tone which would have been perfectly appropriate in *Beppo* but which constitutes a blemish, a breach of decorum, in his wonderful description of the wreck."[22]

> All the rest perish'd; near two hundred souls
>   Had left their bodies; and what's worse, alas!
> When over Catholics the Ocean rolls,
>   They must wait several weeks before a mass
> Takes off one peck of purgatorial coals,
>   Because, till people know what's come to pass,
> They won't lay out their money on the dead—
> It costs three francs for every mass that's said.

Certainly the lapse is there, yet in a sense it belongs as much to the reader as to Byron. For consider the context. As early as stanza xxxiv, the ship presents the spectacle of a Walpurgisnacht: "Some plunder'd, some drank spirits, some sung psalms / . . . / Strange sounds of wailing, blasphemy, devotion, / Clamour'd in chorus to the roaring Ocean." The spectacle intensifies once the sinking commences. We now become witnesses to a microcosm revealing the various ways men prepare to meet death: "Some went to prayers again . . . / . . . / . . . and some look'd o'er the bow; / Some hoisted out the boats," "Some lash'd them in their hammocks; some put on / Their best clothes, as if going to a fair; / Some cursed the day on which they saw the Sun, / And gnash'd their teeth," "Some trial had been making at a raft . . ." (II, xliv–l). The ship sinks in a virtual apocalypse: "the sea yawn'd round her like a hell," "And first one universal shriek there rush'd, / Louder than the loud Ocean . . . / . . . and then all was hush'd" (II, lii–liii). Or almost all: wind and ocean continue, and "at intervals there gush'd, / Accompanied with a convulsive splash, / A solitary shriek, the bubbling cry / Of some strong swimmer in his agony." In retrospect, instant and utter apocalypse would have been a relief. Instead of anything so final, one ship went down. The point of Byron's bringing in the agonized drowning castaway of William Cowper's poem here is to provide some distance from this disaster, which is absolute in itself but limited; he shifts our perspective to the survivors in the lifeboat.

To read the limpid elegiac opening of stanza lv, then, is to prepare for a eulogy: "All the rest perish'd; near two hundred souls / Had left their bodies." The second phrase is taken as a pathetic restatement of the first, recalling as it does the Ancient Mariner's "Four times fifty living men" whose "souls did from their bodies fly . . . / Like the whizz of my cross-bow." But it becomes a trick, for Byron proceeds, in a travesty of Coleridge's literalism, to belabor theological assumptions hidden in the phrase. The result is a satire of the eulogy we expected. For plainly the leave-taking of these men's souls was not the graceful affair such a formula implies. After so horrific a spectacle, what remains to say? Only cant. If we realize this, then the circumspection with which we read that "Nine souls more went" in the cutter will steady us to accept lines otherwise unacceptable:

> They grieved for those who perish'd with the cutter,
> And also for the biscuit-casks and butter.   [II, lxi]

"High thought / Link'd to a servile mass of matter" is Lucifer's Hamlet-like description of man in *Cain* (II, i, 50–51). Here the couplet performs the linkage.

We began this perusal with stanza xxvii, an objective account telling precisely what happened to the ship the moment the wind shifted. We end with the evocative stanza lxxxiv:

> And that same night there fell a shower of rain,
>   For which their mouths gaped, like the cracks of earth

When dried to summer dust; till taught by pain,
  Men really know not what good water's worth;
If you had been in Turkey or in Spain,
  Or with a famish'd boat's-crew had your berth,
Or in the desert heard the camel's bell,
You'd wish yourself where Truth is—in a well.

By contrast with meat, which must be hunted and killed—for "Man . . .
like the shark and tiger, must have prey" (II, lxvii)—the rain shower comes
spontaneously as a gift. Like Truth, water is valuable essentially; it is free,
yet under the circumstances it makes these men "rich" (II, lxxxvi). Chiefly,
though, it is the hallowed biblical tone that makes the rain so much
resemble grace or manna. Lines 2–3 echo with the thought that man is
dust of the earth, his life a summer day; there is deep, melancholy sympathy for this dust so fiery with thirst. Almost immediately, however, this
developing awareness of the boat crew's universality begins to become
rationalized by the philosophy of suffering introduced in lines 3–4. Line 5
goes a step further and addresses us directly; taking us outside the narrative, it establishes a global context for thirst in which "a famish'd boat's-
crew" is but a local instance. Their predicament is not fundamentally
different from that of others whose thirst we find small difficulty in
imagining. The joke at the end becomes effective by our recognizing that it
is our universal experience of water's preciousness that makes us identify it
with Truth in the first place. This is the same pragmatism we met earlier in
the providential turtle. The allusiveness that functions as pathos in lines 1–
3 is thus made an explicit intellectual point in line 8—almost, but not
quite, the butt of a joke. The rain shower *has* really seemed like grace; but
it is no wonder that it should.

   Clearly, Byron's skepticism is less a definite philosophic rationalism
than a perpetual process of pragmatic adjustment. Hence it completes
itself only in the reader's mind—not the narrator's, whose thought, however various, remains determined by what Byron actually wrote—as over
and over we are made to confront, examine, and revise our own prior
responses to the poem. To a skepticism so paradoxically thoroughgoing in
its tentativeness, an affirmation any less indirect is bound to appear merely
self-approving. As Peter Manning points out,

> *Don Juan* baffled contemporaries and incurred accusations of cynicism
> because its first readers did not realize that Byron had transferred the
> locus of meaning from within the poem outside to them. Pope draws his
> audience into a compact of solidarity against the fools he presents—the
> Dunces, the Timons, the Sir Balaams. In Byron, however, the object of
> satire is not a fictive, representative character, but the false assumptions in

the individual reader that his reactions to the poem bring to the surface.
[p. 260]

So with regard to the shipwreck episode, what is most striking about first readers' reactions is not their horror but specifically their mortification, as though they felt Byron had somehow personally duped them. All protest their excruciated "consciousness of the insulting deceit which has been practised upon us. . . . Every high thought that was ever kindled in our hearts by the muse of Byron . . . every remembered moment of admiration and enthusiasm is up in arms against him"—thus the *Blackwood's* reviewer.[23] Keats—whom *Blackwood's* held as anathema—less prissily expressed the same sense of betrayal; Joseph Severn reported that he flung the book down, exclaiming that Byron had evidently grown so jaded "that there was nothing left for him but to laugh & gloat over the most solemn & heart-rending scenes of human misery; this storm of his is one of the most diabolical attempts ever made upon our sympathies" (*CH*, p. 163). Such reactions are quite accurate in their way. Most of the stanzas we have just examined contain a development whose challenge to the reader could easily be construed as mockery or betrayal. As stanza l shows no less than lxxxiv, *Don Juan* elicits pathos not for the sake of pathos alone but in order that we may consider its appropriateness within a particular context. Normally, this entails the intervention of the narrator whose irony, as in the stanza Rutherford singled out, can seem even to unmoralizing readers like the devilish laughing and gloating Keats imagined. Among contemporaries it seems only Shelley, applying the arguments of *Areopagitica*, was able to grasp how the poem locates its meanings within the individual reader, thereby making his response a directly moral act. "You unveil & present in its true deformity what is worst in human nature," he wrote Byron, "& it is this what the witlings of the age murmur at, conscious of their want of power to endure the scrutiny of such a light."[24]

Byron's implicit rejection of the cannibalism, the portion of the shipwreck that remains to be explored, follows from the premium *Don Juan* places upon the socialized individual. That the cannibalism is indeed to be regarded as a moral issue appears from the fact that somebody is killed to facilitate it. Nevertheless the reader is not allowed to pass judgment, and the narrator judges the event only in utilitarian fashion—by its consequences:

> 'T was not to be expected that [Juan] should,
> Even in extremity of their disaster,
> Dine with them on his pastor and his master.
>
> 'T was better that he did not; for, in fact,
> The consequence was awful in the extreme;

For they, who were most ravenous in the act,
　　Went raging mad—Lord! how they did blaspheme!
And foam, and roll, with strange convulsions rack'd,
　　Drinking salt-water like a mountain stream,
Tearing, and grinning, howling, screeching, swearing,
And, with hyaena-laughter, died despairing.　　　　　[II, lxxviii–lxxix]

The "extremity" to which they resort is repaid in kind by the consequence being "awful in the extreme" but holier-than-thou readers, convinced the cannibals got what they deserved, must immediately confront a mock-serious distortion of themselves: "Lord! how they did blaspheme!" The narrator here is holier than anybody, and as a result is merely hypocritical: "Kill people and eat them is you must, but swearing like that is an affront to society." Cannibalism thus appears as "man's worst—his second fall," the fall of civilized man into barbarism:[25] the last two lines describe primarily the behavior of monkeys. This is Byron's societal version of Coleridge's death-in-life. Yet the Ancient Mariner sucked only his own blood, whereas Byron's boat crew in much the same situation—compare the calm at stanza lxxii with that in the *Rime*, Part II—choose to sacrifice a victim to their vampiric surgeon.[26]

Leading as it does to madness and "a species of self-slaughter" (II, cii), the cannibalism is seen to be a socialized form of suicide. Unlike hope, "the desire of life [that] Prolongs it" by binding "people in an open boat" into a hardy community (II, lxvi), the killing and eating of Pedrillo is an act of cynicism. It is the individual's capitulation to his instinct for self-preservation at any cost, a desire of life murderous in the event. In the boat the men "lay like carcasses; and hope was none, / . . . / They glared upon each other . . . / . . . and you might see / The longings of the cannibal arise / (Although they spoke not) in their wolfish eyes" (II, lxxii). Like original sin, the longings arise and intensify from within. As their speechlessness indicates, the men are visibly lapsing into barbarism; "like carcasses" is how they perceive one another. It appears that Byron's survivors see only the low half of what Lucifer saw, the "servile [and serviceable] mass of matter." Moreover, having consumed Pedrillo, "as if not warned sufficiently," the men next dispense with democratic lottery and like a wolf pack fix upon the master's mate "As fattest" (II, lxxx–lxxxi). Their dehumanization emerges vividly in the next stanza: "At length they caught two Boobies and a Noddy, / And then they left off eating the dead body" (II, lxxxii). Previously the feast possessed a certain macabre gusto (II, lxxvii); now it seems genuinely necrophilic, an impression heightened by the ensuing reference to Dante's Ugolino. With the reappearance of normal food sources, normal standards of edibility resurface, and the other meat is recognized with horror as a damaged human corpse.

Cannibalism, then, represents the furthest reach from Spanish society, the barbaric inner ring of Hell below which lies the merely animal, Juan's struggle with Ocean. In a parody of the Genesis God's fecundity, Byron shows the survivors' day-by-day exhausting of their provisions; finally on "the seventh day" (II, lxxii), the day God breathed life into man and placed him in the Garden, the boat crew kills the Christly Pedrillo and consumes him. Yet this Hell opens up within a group of ordinary, civilized Westerners. The reader looks down into it from the circle of his own values, which are the same—hence the encapsulated quality of the whole episode. The cannibalism is barbarism localized as an unlikely but genuine possibility occurring within a broader social context that, although it usually escapes barbarism, nevertheless cannot control the force of circumstance that makes barbarism always a danger. Pedrillo's skillful euthanasia by a doctor we may regard as Byron's reductio of a runaway principle of enlightened rational self-interest, his own Modest Proposal to the Malthusians in the audience.

III

Juan's heroism in the shipwreck is his Promethean persistence in adhering to civilized values that he knows, implicitly, to be greater than his own personal annihilation or suffering. "No! / 'T is true that death awaits both you and me. / But let us die like men, not sink / Below like brutes' " (II, xxxvi), he tells the whiskey-craving crew, and then silently proves his credo in the nasty crucible of the longboat. Unlike the others, he resists "the savage hunger which demanded, / Like the Promethean vulture" (II, lxxv), the sacrifice of Pedrillo. For Byron, civilized man is a Prometheus who internalizes the vulture that gnaws him. Barbarism occurs when the individual looses his vulture to gnaw upon others; inside and outside thus collapsed, the individual actually becomes his vulture. The cannibalism is Byron's literalizing of this myth of the modern Prometheus, and the bestial deaths that result, simply the natural penalty for so uncivil a "pollution" (II, lxxv; the word translates the Aeschylean *miasma*, or blood-guilt, which as E. R. Dodds remarks "is the automatic consequence of an action, belongs to the world of external events, and operates with the same ruthless indifference to motive as a typhoid germ).[27] No matter then that "None in particular had sought or plann'd it" (II, lxxv); cannibalism is inevitably self-defeating.

Admittedly, Juan's persistence may be naive, but it reflects in any case a vigilant sensitivity to the possibilities for true, unspecious survival—that is, for Byron, survival "like a gentleman," without compromise. The change of mind whereby Juan finally decides to eat his favorite spaniel not only shows that his forbearance of Pedrillo is something more than fastidiousness; it attests his moral continence under even the most trying conditions. When it comes to the crunch, we see, the profligate Juan is able to make the crucial discriminations between the moral and the sentimental, the human and the merely animal, seeing which of them is inessential and expendable and which not. It is no coincidence that Byron's manipulation of his readers through the ottava rima involves us in discriminations of the same kind. Not that Juan is therefore a directly exemplary figure, but his behavior during the shipwreck does illustrate the same resolute pragmatism we discovered in stanzas l–lxxxiv. This we may summarize as follows: hope for the best, and act accordingly, but do not expect this or that consequence to follow or you will soon despair. To doubt something, on the other hand, is to believe not that it is impossible but only unlikely; far from necessarily conducing to despair, every doubt thus contains the hopeful seed of a possibility. Or as bold Mazeppa puts it, the battle lost, his forces routed, and himself surrounded by an enemy "ten to one at least": "What mortal his own doom may guess? / Let none despond, let none despair" (853–54). The shipwreck episode of *Don Juan* represents Byron's exploration of the ellipsis between these two statements, the first skeptical, the second affirmative, and his laying bare the moral fabric that connects them.

"Nothing Exists but As It Is Perceived"

> I am sometimes so very sceptical as to think Poetry itself a mere
> Jack a lanthern to amuse whoever may chance to be struck with
> its brilliance—As Tradesmen say every thing takes its worth from
> what it will fetch, so probably every mental pursuit takes its
> reality and worth from the ardour of the pursuer—being in itself
> a nothing.
>
> Keats, letter to Bailey of March 13, 1818

Milton's repetition of a single plot sequence in a series of different styles reflecting a mounting self-awareness closely resembles the double-track model of "method" outlined by Coleridge in his essay on the subject. On one hand, "method implies a *progressive transition*," an organic spontaneous evolving that resists analysis by dissection. On the other hand, the man who coined the words *self-realization* and *existential* fully recognized the chicken-and-egg paradox that the self must already exist *in potentio* in order for it to desire a greater actuality for itself. Instead of being unrestricted, therefore, any methodized development is shaped and guided at every step by a "prior purpose" or "pre-cogitation" that determines the outcome. For "as, without continuous transition, there can be no Method, so without a preconception ["the initiative" or "leading thought"] there can be no transition with continuity."[1] Insofar as the preconception is fulfilled, the beginning of the whole process becomes established retroactively as an epistemological ground; for how can the beginning be known as a true origin until the idea implicit in it attains completion? As Hegel argues in *The Science of Logic*, "Each step of the *advance* in the process of further determination, while getting further away from the indeterminate beginning is also *getting back nearer* to it, and therefore . . . the retrogressive grounding of the beginning, and the *progressive further determining* of it, coincide and are the same."[2]

Consider Coleridge's gradual mastering of contingency in "This Lime-Tree Bower My Prison," written, as he explains in the introductory note, when "some long-expected friends [Lamb and the Wordsworths] paid a visit to the author's cottage; and on the morning of their arrival, he met with an accident, which disabled him from walking during the whole time of their stay."[3] Although the note circumspectly goes on to say that the author composed the poem while these friends "had left him for a few hours," from the more immediate perspective of the poem itself their departure looks to be permanent: "Well, they are gone . . . / Friends, whom I never more may meet again" (1–6). The poet's aim is to surmount this separation anxiety by transforming the solitary act of writing into a form of companionship. As the friends walk, he writes, all the while seeing in his mind's eye the same familiar rural scenes and experiencing in his heart the same "delight." Moreover, as the opening of the second verse paragraph makes clear—"Now my friends emerge / Beneath the wide wide Heaven . . . / Yes! they wander on" (20–26), leaving behind the roaring dell just described—the poet's composing proceeds at exactly the same pace as his friends' walk, so that his "beauties and feelings" are correlated with theirs.

Still, this correlation is at best vicarious and is possibly delusive, for although the poet clearly knows the surrounding countryside in detail, he doesn't claim to know by telepathy where *exactly* the friends "perchance" (8) have gone. This limitation he surmounts in the long closing verse paragraph by acknowledging a spatial continuum wherein he can observe directly, without mediation by memory, the same glowing sunset hues as they. Regarded now as a paradisiacal microcosm of processes occurring throughout nature, the lime-tree bower, so far from confining the poet, stimulates him to survey the day's events from a perspective of omniscience. "A delight / Comes sudden on my heart, and I am glad / As I myself were there!" (43–45): in a naturalized descent of grace, images of the bower remembered from earlier in the afternoon, present perceptions of the deepening twilight, and moral resolutions for the future combined with a proleptic blessing of the absent Lamb all merge in meditative appreciation of the ubiquitous "Almighty Spirit," the one life within us and abroad. Yet although the bard sees present, past, and future, he remains emphatically earthbound: the final image of the rook "creeking" homeward past "the mighty Orb's dilated glory" (72) clinches the poet's mastery of his fears in solitude precisely because it symbolizes his visceral sense of a shared locale connecting him with a larger human community.[4] The point is that he has done more than simply recognize that he participates in the same organic processes as his absent guests. Such recognition is essential but does not in itself constitute participation in the community, inasmuch as nature's workings are cyclical and pervasive, and their experience correspondingly general and unintimate. What matters is that the poet's projected union with the absent guests occurs through an irreducibly personal act of spatiotemporal sense perception—a minor and ordinary act of which they themselves are not even aware, but one that is by the same token absolutely particularized, historically unique, and unrepeatable.

The governing "law" of "Lime-Tree Bower," as of *Milton*, is not deductive cause and effect but self-evidence. Much like Blake's discovery in *Milton* of the renovating "Moment in each Day that Satan cannot find / . . . but the Industrious find / This Moment & it multiply,"[5] "Lime-Tree Bower" shows how "the man of methodical industry and honorable pursuits . . . organizes the hours and gives them a soul; and that, the very essence of which is to fleet away, . . . he takes up into his own permanence" (*Friend* 1:450), so performing his Christian duty to help redeem the time. Since victory over the contingencies of the poem's inception is achieved by internalizing and symbolically reprojecting them through imagination, "the germinal power that craves no knowledge but what it can take up into itself and reproduce in fruits of its own" (*Friend* 1:473), the reader must not "attempt to master by the reflex [that is, reflective] acts of the Understanding what we can only *know* by the act of *becoming*."[6] But if the process of becoming what we behold supplies knowledge of the world—"Never could the eye have beheld the sun, had not its own essence been soliform" (*BL* 1:115)—then it must also supply self-knowledge or "self-intuition." As Shelley puts it, "Neither the eye nor the mind can see itself, unless reflected upon that which it resembles."[7] Thus the action of the methodized poem reflexively implicates the reader even as it pursues a representational form of its own. The reader who attempts to master the poem through rational reflection is appropriating and reifying a reflexivity already built into the poem.

Especially for Shelley, reflexivity works to reveal the deep truth as a matter not of sight but of insight, for it is found to reside neither in subject nor in object but in the act of perception by which the two become contradistinguished.[8] In "To a Sky-Lark," for example, the characteristically breathless speed of the verse creates an effect of photomontage that empties the images of depth and substantiality, reducing them to a series of phenomenal appearances. The similes proliferate so rapidly one is forced to recognize their fictiveness, hence their inadequacy to represent the transcendent freedom which the poet imagines for the bird. At the same time, though, their negligent profusion shows the poet's imaginative identification with the bird: he, too, "sings and soars." So whereas the images fall short when considered singly—as similes, their likeness to the bird only emphasizes a fundamental unlikeness—taken together they do intimate the source of the bird's freedom. All four stanzas depict a central object whose light or music or odor paradoxically conceals it, thereby enabling us to bathe in its emanations as though we had projected them ourselves. The stanza on the poet portrays him as "hidden In the light of thought" (36–37); thus decentered and dispossessed, the thought irradiates the audience, which thinks it with one mind. Such creative participation in the bird's singing is the reason Shelley rejects the crassly audible music of "Chorus Hymeneal / Or triumphal chaunt" and dismisses the restless question of Keats's "sole self" about the similarly transcendent song of the nightingale, "Do I wake or sleep?" "Waking or asleep"—the distinction is unimportant—our "sympathy" with the skylark, that obscure object of desire, makes us the object of one another's desires. Since "we hardly see [the bird]—we feel that it is there," its song subverts the dividedness of ordinary subject-object relationships and reveals the imageless deep truth to be a matter of shared personal experience. As in "Ode to the West Wind," where the poet's internalization of the cold impersonal wind enables him to breathe it forth as renovating prophecy, Shelley here becomes a mouthpiece for the bird's song, humanizing it in the process. In the final moment of attentive silence when he exhorts "the world" to "listen then—as I am listening now," the audience is invited to apprehend prophetically its own potential, thereby realizing the earlier image of the poet as "Singing hymns unbidden, / Till the world is wrought / To sympathy with hopes and fears it heeded not" (38–40).

This would suggest that for Shelley the audience enables the poet to achieve self-realization, no less than the poet creates the audience in his own image. The preface to *Prometheus Unbound* asserts explicitly that "a Poet, is the combined product of such internal powers as modify the nature of others, and of such external influences as excite and sustain these powers; he is not one, but both. . . . Poets . . . are in one sense the creators and in another the creations of their age" (S, p. 135). For if "*external* and *internal* . . . is merely an affair of words" and "it imports little to inquire whether thought be distinct from the objects of thought,"[9] then the distinction between poet and audience breaks down. The result is a self-conscious ironic doubling that illustrates Schlegel's gnomic dictum: "In all its descriptions, this poetry should describe itself, and always be simultaneously poetry and the poetry of poetry."[10] In *Prometheus Unbound*, for example, the union of Asia, the ideal, with Prometheus, the universal mind, produces intellectual beauty or vision, much like Ololon's union with Los-Milton-Blake in *Milton*. Hence the imagery used to portray the visionary dream of Panthea, Asia's child, shows poetry gradually coming into existence as inspiration is attained. Asia rebukes Panthea for oversleeping: "my heart was sick with hope, before / The printless air felt thy belated plumes." Then, looking into Panthea's eyes in order to "read" her dream of Prometheus' "written soul," she sees "two circles underneath / Their long, fine lashes . . . / Orb within orb, and line through line inwoven" (II, ii, 33–117). These crystal balls are not only Panthea's eyes but the mirror images of Asia's, now concentrically "reflected upon that which they resemble." Asia therefore gains insight into herself; the orbs and lines she reads are the hitherto invisible script of her own soul. Appropriately, her subsequent lovemaking with Prometheus is presented as social rather than sexual intercourse, a conversation expressive of the same "beautiful idealisms of moral excellence" as the preface says the poem itself is. To read of this reunion is thus in large measure to enact it, thereby fulfilling the plot.

Such a process of enactment is almost inevitable if "nothing exists but as it is perceived" (S, p. 477). Nevertheless, Shelley's maxim is an extremely unsteady basis for poetry. The meaning of the pivotal "but as" is prone to slacken from the tensely confrontational "except insofar as," which still provides for varying intensities of perception and hence different degrees of reality, to the feebly solipsistic "but only so long as." Once this happens, Shelley finds himself asserting a monistic conformity between subject and object more conducive to withdrawn self-sameness than energetic self-realization. The danger is inherent in the radical reader responsiveness of later Romantic poetics, which strives to reinterpret "the body" not only as the ground of individual personal identity but as imaginative form more generally. The earlier view is represented by Blake, whose repudiation of skeptical sensationalism in the name of the prophetic conscience still accepts the individualist premises of the sensationalist position. The later view is epitomized by Shelley, for whom the embodied self is constituted not only by the individual's perceptions but also by others' perceptions of him, so that the body becomes an intersubjective concept able to mitigate the Romantic prophet's potential egotism and isolation. The problem is that since the body isn't a concept in the Blakean view but a determinant of the very nature and content of perception, the Shelleyan position tends to confound embodied consciousness with reflexive self-consciousness, thus denying the body all over again.

In the next chapter I shall explore Shelley's reflexive imagery—that is, imagery that compares a unitary object to an aspect of itself, as happens, for example, when the *Alastor* Poet gazes into the well in a delusive parody of Asia's self-discovery: "*His eyes beheld / Their own wan light* through the reflected lines / Of his thin hair, distinct in the dark depth / Of that still fountain" (469–73; my italics)—and we shall see how such imagery implies the underlying presence of a consciousness that perceives all narrative objects and events in terms of their interrelationships. Whose consciousness? Evidently the poet's and reader's combined, that of "the one mind" which transcends the specious distinctions of "*external* and *internal*" (CW 7:65) and "*I, you, they*" (S, p. 477) because it is essentially self-referential, being the enlarged consciousness of the text. The progression of "To a Sky-Lark" beyond the dualities of simile suggests the utopian possibilities of such unity. In Shelley's more skeptical poems, however, reflexiveness, instead of allaying doubt as it does for the logocentric Coleridge, only announces a return of solipsism.

Hence the bewildering sense of dislocation throughout *The Triumph of Life*, whose entire prologue functions as an extended reflexive image. As the entranced poet describes his immediate surroundings, he begins inadvertently to compare the scene to itself, and his responses to the scene to themselves. The result is the sort of "delirium" that Coleridge saw to be the logical consequence of Hartley's associationism:

> . . . and I knew
> That I had felt the freshness of that dawn,
> Bathed in the same cold dew my brow and hair
> And sate as thus upon that slope of lawn
>
> Under the self same bough, and heard as there
> The birds, the fountains and the Ocean hold
> Sweet talk in music through the enamoured air.   [33–39]

"I knew that I had felt the freshness of that dawn *before*," one assumes the poet is going to say. That he does not say it suggests an experience considerably more schizoid than déjà vu, for one is forced to ask where exactly the self is that thus "knows" omnisciently the surroundings it is still in the process of perceiving. The "transparent shade" (30–31) of the poet's trance shows the intervention of any uneasy self-consciousness which by doubling everything in the scene tends to undermine the scene's reality, making it a mere simile of itself. Such, indeed, is the main action of the poem, which shows repeatedly how figures of expression take on a life of their own and become "figures" in the Blakean sense of specters, projected dark doubles that escape the speaker's control and define him in spite of what he meant, or thought he meant, to say. Ultimately, then, the question of whether the poet's "waking dream" (42) presents the truth or merely re-presents it yields before the sickening discovery that these are one and the same, truth being itself a matter of representation and there being no truth "behind" its representations.

Through the infinite evasions of *as* which he deploys ambiguously to denote both likeness and duration, Shelley shows how the poet's demystifying rhetoric of temporality, or in Coleridgean terms his progressive "method," can be assimilated to the synchronic, a priori structure of language. In a Shelleyan narrative, moving onward means moving into or out of the mind, and hence lifting or lowering the veils of comparisons through which the world is perceived. Thus Rousseau tells the narrator of *The Triumph of Life* how the visionary "shape all light"

> . . . waned in the coming light
> *As* veil by veil the silent splendour drops
>   From Lucifer, amid the chrysolite

> Of sunrise ere it strike the mountain tops—
>   And *as* the presence of that fairest planet
> Although unseen is felt by one who hopes

> That his day's path may end as he began it.   [412–18; italics mine]

These lines do not simply describe an experience in Rousseau's life whose ironic outcome the reader has already witnessed (Rousseau, the natural man, has withered to a tree stump). They signal ominously that the consciousness of the narrator, whose story likewise began at dawn, is undergoing the same waning right now as a result of listening to Rousseau's story. Such doubling indeed creates an effect of distancing and postponement, as most readers agree, but it does so in order to generate an overriding sense of impotency and frustration in the face of crisis. After all, the narrator in his role of listener directly resembles the complacent reader, who more than anybody is the "one who hopes / That his day's path may end as he began it." If narratologists are correct in holding that the essence of narrative is to keep separate and independent "the time sequence of plot events, the time of the *histoire* ('story-time') and the time of the presentation of those events in the text, which we call 'discourse-time,' "[11] then what the little word *as* does is conflate "story-time" with "discourse-time," providing glimpses of the plot's ending as immanent within the dramatic action. Since the narrative thus appears to be continually re-beginning, the basis for any culminating realization or anagnorisis is undermined.

Such poetic doubling undermines even the rough-hewn sincerities of Wordsworth and is largely responsible for the ineffable "symbolic" quality of his seemingly unvarnished descriptions of scenes in nature.[12] Coleridge, attempting in *Biographia Literaria* to define the *un*naturally translucent "freshness" of Wordsworth's poetry, its visionary gleam "like the moisture or the polish on a pebble," says it is due to the poet's distinctive mood of "meditative pathos." He thus recognizes that the imagery, even as it "brings out many a vein and many a tint, which escapes the common eye of observation," so raising the pebble "to the rank of gems," has been internalized by the poet in memory: "Like a green field reflected in a calm and perfectly transparent lake, the image is distinguished from the reality only by its greater softness and lustre" (*BL* 2:148). For Coleridge, then, the freshness of the imagery springs from Wordsworth's "coadunating" or "modifying power" to project his meditative "reflections" back onto the remembered objects of experience. The paradox in this, Shelley shows in the Wordsworthian Narrator of *Alastor*, is that the naturalistic imagination may usurp on what it represents, thereby using up the raw materials it needs in order to work its metamorphoses.[13] Such a usurpation subverts the affirmations of Coleridge's progressive "method," turning self-realization into self-estrangement.

Coleridge himself testifies to a similar collapse of method in a morose letter to James Gillman of October 9, 1825, surveying his poetic career from "The Eolian Harp" to the Dejection Ode:

> In Youth and early Manhood the Mind and Nature are, as it were, two rival Artists, . . . each having for it's object to turn the other into Canvas to paint on, Clay to mould, or Cabinet to contain. For a while the Mind seems to have the better in the contest, and makes of Nature what it likes . . . ; transforms her Summer Gales into Harps and Harpers, Lovers' Sighs and sighing Lovers, and her Winter Blasts into Pindaric Odes, Christabels & Ancient Mariners set to music by Beethoven. . . . But alas! alas! that Nature is a wary wily long-breathed old Witch. . . . She is sure to get the better of Lady MIND in the long run, and to take her revenge too—. . . not alone turns the mimic Mind, the ci-devant Sculptress with all her kaleidoscopic freaks and symmetries! into clay, but *leaves* it such a *clay*, to cast dumps or bullets in; and lastly (to end with that which suggested the beginning—) she mocks the mind with it's own metaphors, metamorphosing the Memory into a lignum vitae Escrutoire to keep unpaid Bills & Dun's Letters in.[14]

This contest between the youthful romantic Mind and the hoary old witch Nature accurately defines the autobiographical aspect of Christabel's losing struggle against Geraldine. Unlike Coleridge, Wordsworth persisted in believing Nature never did betray the heart that loved her, but increasingly he had to admit the imagination might.[15] The evangelical-sounding "Ode to Duty" shows an exhausted Wordsworth falling back on the "control" of social custom and Newtonian law for relief from the "unchartered freedom" of "being to myself a guide."[16] "I long for a repose that ever is the same" (40), he sighs, knowingly pronouncing a death wish upon his imagination. The poignancy of his condition emerges when one considers the poem's epigraph from Seneca: "Now at last I am not consciously good, but so trained by habit that I not only can act rightly but cannot act otherwise than rightly." Plainly what Wordsworth desires is to become as "insensibly subdued" and un-self-conscious as his Cumberland Beggar who, in the passage Wordsworth detached from the poem and entitled "Animal Tranquillity and Decay," "is by nature led / To peace so perfect that the young behold / With envy what the Old Man hardly feels."

Arguably, the impetus for Wordsworth's greatest poetry is his fear that by internalizing nature, his supposed source of inspiration, he is generating an opaque self-consciousness that only screens him from her. It is ostensibly the actual process of composing the poem that remarries the poet with nature and allays his fear of separation, at least for the nonce. The question Shelley poses is: since Wordsworth's doubts concern the tendency of poetry to appropriate the external world, trapping the poet in a self-enclosed realm of surrogate representations, how can he expect to solve this problem by writing yet more poetry?[17] Assuming the new poem supplies the poet a means of self-transformation, how can he be sure it is a positive one? If the poet *is* altered by his writing, then his perception will also be altered; where then is the guarantee that the inspiration he thinks he has recovered isn't really a delusion? The question gains force from the fact that so many of the epiphanies in *The Prelude* spring from relatively banal cognitive confusions, such as the boy's failure to take parallax into account when noticing a crag's apparent change in position as he moves away from it (the rowboat episode in Book I, 373–85), or his dizziness from playfully spinning in circles (the end of the ice-skating episode eighty lines later). The successful poem itself guarantees the authenticity of the poet's inspiration, Wordsworth might plausibly reply. And yet Wordsworth's much-honored later career as a Burkean spokesman for the Establishment was a standing example to Shelley of how inferior verse can "succeed" in the world by succumbing to the same mundane criteria it ought to transform.

"Tintern Abbey" explores these problems. The poet begins by depicting a scene whose actual referent turns out to be his own mind immediately engaged in contemplation:

> Five years have past; five summers, with the length
> Of five long winters! and again I hear
> These waters, rolling from their mountain-springs
> With a soft inland murmur.—Once again
> Do I behold these steep and lofty cliffs,
> That on a wild secluded scene impress
> Thoughts of more deep seclusion; and connect
> The landscape with the quiet of the sky.   [1–8]

Even if the mountain springs are not a domestic version of the Nile, compared in *The Prelude* to the imagination "Poured from his fount of Abyssinian clouds / To fertilize the whole Egyptian plain" (VI, 615–16), clearly we are invited to see the poet's sense of refreshment as arising from a renewed flow of inspiration after five years of urban drought. The ensuing image of cliffs that "impress / *Thoughts* of more deep seclusion," gentling the wild sublimity of the landscape and harmonizing it with the quiet sky, shows that Wordsworth is recomposing the scene like a painter. The "blending, fusing power" (*BL* 2:150) of his imagination emerges more forcibly in the "plots of cottage-ground . . . Which . . . *lose themselves* 'Mid groves and copses," and in the "hedge-rows, *hardly hedge-rows*, little lines / Of sportive wood run wild"—signs of habitation no sooner discerned than they dissolve before our eyes, merging with the surrounding greenery. These authorial interventions reach their climax, ending all possibility of objective description, with the picturesque vision of

> wreaths of smoke
> Sent up, in silence, from among the trees!
> With some uncertain notice, as might seem
> Of vagrant dwellers in the houseless woods,
> Or of some Hermit's cave, where by his fire
> The Hermit sits alone.   [17–22]

As the full stop of the exclamation mark indicates, the "notice" is the poet's own, grown "uncertain" because he has taken his eye off the actual external scene in order to reimagine it through his description. Poetry's usurpation of that scene becomes explicit with the image of the Hermit, a patent fiction whose sole reason for appearing in the well-populated valley is, as Richard J. Onorato and others have pointed out,[18] that he personifies the poet's now fully objectified "thoughts of more deep seclusion."

Moreover, the closing address to Dorothy, intended to resolve the doubt that such imaginative projection might be deluded, in fact only reawakens it. Wordsworth's argument is that, since the younger Dorothy views the scene the same way as he did five years ago, his present realization of "something far more deeply interfused" will be repeated in her when she likewise revisits the scene, perhaps sometime after he is dead. Nevertheless, if Dorothy upon her return will experience the same problematic self-consciousness as Wordsworth now does, one wonders whether he has solved his present difficulties or merely fobbed them off on her (and Dorothy, unlike Wordsworth, has no younger sibling whom she can address in turn). This disquieting possibility reflects a basic contradiction in Wordsworth's argument. He is implying that Dorothy's present experience includes him standing beside her as a part of the landscape, analogously to the way his own present experience contains an objectified image of himself during *his* first visit, namely the factitious Hermit; yet such fraternal companionship is precisely what makes Dorothy's experience *unlike* Wordsworth's first visit, which, as the image of the Hermit goes to show, he made alone. The basis for Wordsworth's assertion of their identity is that he can catch in her voice "The language of my former heart, and read / My former pleasures in . . . thy wild eyes" (116–19). His knowledge depends, in other words, on his interpreting Dorothy's responses in terms of his youthful self—a process of representation no less usurping of its object than was his perplexed survey of the valley which needed to be resolved in the first place.

The cause of Wordsworth's difficulty is of course that writing, instead of transcribing thought, can displace it by generating an immediacy of its own. Observes Coleridge:

> If one thought leads to another, so often does it blot out another. This I
> find when having lain musing on my sofa, a number of interesting
> thoughts having suggested themselves, I conquer my bodily indolence,
> and rise to record them in these books, alas! my only confidants. The first
> thought leads me on indeed to new ones; but nothing but the faint mem-
> ory of having had these remains of the other, which had been even more
> interesting to me. . . . my thoughts crowd each other to death.[19]

Contrary to Wordsworth's confident assumptions, writing here produces not self-unity but a dreamlike, schizoid split between Coleridge the indolent but alert freethinker and Coleridge the writer, whose dutiful effort at the physical activity of composition only adds to his inertia by stymieing him mentally. Elsewhere Coleridge finds it utterly "opposite to nature and the fact to talk of the 'one moment' of Hume, of our whole being an aggregate of successive single sensations";[20] but the above passage suggests just such a discontinuity. The flux of associative thought being too rapid and turbulent for cogent representation, the self, swept forward within a narrow envelope of recent recollections, remains forever incomplete because it is unable to objectify its private musings within the concrete world of action.

From this viewpoint, even so massively resolute an object as the Cumberland Beggar seems to exist for Wordsworth solely in order to be versified:

> Bow-bent, his eyes for ever on the ground,
> He plies his weary journey; seeing still
> And seldom knowing that he sees, some straw,
> Some scattered leaf, or marks which, in one track,
> The nails of cart or chariot-wheel have left
> Impressed on the white road,—in the same line,
> At distance still the same. Poor Traveller!

His staff trails with him; scarcely do his feet
Disturb the summer dust; . . .

. . .

                     . . . all pass him by:
Him even the slow-paced waggon leaves behind.   [52–66]

The onrushing chariot of Shelley's *Triumph of Life*, which actually runs
over people, presents with grander severity the same image. In Shelley's
reduction, there is no reliable memory present to organize the mind's
successive impressions into an enduring self. Compared to lovers heedless
of tomorrow, the impressions therefore vanish beneath the chariot of life,
"nor other trace I find / But as of foam after the Ocean's wrath / Is spent
upon the shore" (161–64). Wordsworth's aged Beggar suffers much the
same plight. It is hard to escape the suspicion that the "line" of "marks"
"impressed" upon the Cumberland road depicts the train of sense-impressions continually imprinting themselves upon the tabula of the Lockean
mind. Moreover, the Beggar's mind has become, we are told, so worn with
repeated impressions that now he "hardly feels" them; his mental palimp-
sest is on the verge of reverting to its original blankness. This makes the
Beggar himself into another of the road's near-obliterated ciphers, just like
the Shelleyan lovers; Wordsworth differs from Shelley only in portraying
such senility as special and somehow privileged, rather than as the deplor-
able and universal condition of human existence. Why would Wordsworth want to mentalize the Beggar's traveling in this way? Because by
doing so he could make his own mind blank so as to record through minute
introspection the whole scene's impressions on *him*. On this level, the
road's tabula becomes an image of Wordsworth's mind gradually absorb-
ing the Beggar to itself. The notion gains force from the similarity of the
"white road" imprinted with a "line" of regularly spaced marks to the
poet's versifying on the blank page. Paradoxically, therefore, Wordsworth's attempt to observe the Beggar in objective detail, without sentimental preconceptions, leads him to appropriate what little autonomy the
man still possesses. Like Dorothy in "Tintern Abbey," the Beggar becomes
transformed into an image of writing.

The solipsistic underside of Wordsworth's endeavor "at all times . . . to
look steadily at my subject" (W, p. 450) is explored with poignant wit in
John Ashbery's "The Skaters." Here the skating episode depicted in the
first book of *The Prelude* is viewed as a form of writing or troping
("figure" skating). Wordsworth himself intimates that his skating is a
mimetic usurpation on nature when he tells of racing "To cut across the
reflex of a star / That fled" (I, 450–51). More self-consciously, Ashbery
sees such poetry's perspectival illusion of physical and emotional depth as

constantly tending to collapse into lines of verse that are "flat" in both senses of the word:

> Forgotten as the words fly briskly across, each time
> Bringing down meaning as snow from a low sky, or rabbits flushed from
> a wood.
> How strange that the narrow perspective lines
> Always seem to meet, although parallel, and that an insane ghost could
> do this,
> Could make the house seem so much further in the distance, as
> It seemed to the horse, dragging the sledge of a perspective line.[21]

And yet no sooner do the Wordsworthian skated figures turn into parallel lines of poetic figures than the poetry, lacking anything "out there" to be about, turns into an embarrassingly literal portrait of the artist looking back on his work in progress in the best tradition of Romantic "conversation" poetry:

> So much has passed through my mind this morning
> That I can give you but a dim account of it:
> It is already after lunch, the men are returning to their positions around
> the cement mixer
> And I try to sort out what has happened to me.

This constitutes a return to representationalism, but of a much more constricted sort than the Wordsworthian children's impulsive skating in a refreshingly inhuman world that echoes their shouts with "an alien sound / Of melancholy not unnoticed" (I, 438–43). Thus does Ashbery confront the inescapably imprisoning "magic lantern" of Romantic self-projection.[22] Through a poetry of collage and Shelleyan anticlimax, Ashbery thwarts—one could even say he deconstructs—our assumption of psychological depth. Insistently forcing our attention back to the shifting surfaces of his language, he struggles to maintain verbal immediacy and undermine Romantic confessionalism. But since surfaces are the cause of such confessional self-projection in the first place—the glassy ice, the white page, in both of which the poet is only too liable to see himself reflected—verbal immediacy proves to be a goal just as deceptive as the discredited Wordsworthian goal of "sincerity" was.

His much-touted "gusto" and tactility notwithstanding, a similar paradox emerges in the mature Keats's verse as he struggles to achieve negative capability, his declared alternative to "the wordsworthian or egotistical sublime,"[23] through ironic self-concealment. The problem is that for becoming a nightingale to be something more than escapism, the self must consciously savor the process of its extinction; only if some remnant of the ego persists can the transcendent experience become humanly meaningful. Keats therefore opens the ode by implying that full union with the bird has already occurred "one minute past."[24] Evidently poetry begins, as Shelley says, when "inspiration is already on the decline" (S, p. 504). However, by dramatizing his belatedness through the failure of a series of increasingly drastic proposals for reunion—wine, poesy, death—the poet does briefly succeed in glimpsing an alien realm beyond the bourn of ordinary life. And yet it is not the nightingale's realm. In the penultimate stanza, the bird's song not only transcends Keats's lifetime, it has sounded throughout human history and perhaps transcends that as well, being

> The same that oft-times hath
> Charm'd magic casements, opening on the foam
> Of perilous seas, in faery lands forlorn.

Obviously, this spontaneous overflow of powerful feeling quite exceeds its avian object. Inasmuch as the passage refers to no place outside the poem, it shows that Keats finds inspiration in the process of composition itself, thereby becoming his own nightingale and finally matching the bird's song with his poem, now grown (in Milton's words) most musical, most melancholy. Apparently Keats has discovered the same perilous seas of self-referentiality that Shelley embarks upon at the end of *Adonais*.

Poesy's "faery lands" are always already forlorn (even for Spenser) because, imbued as they are with an ironic self-consciousness verging on suicide and madness, it is impossible to inhabit them longer than a moment and still return to tell the tale (as Shelley also sees: *Adonais* ends as soon as the poet abandons himself to the tempest). Once Keats moves in the above stanza from representing the bird's song as a "voice" (63) not unlike his own to staging that voice's effects upon himself, he begins to hear his own music as external, thus raising the issue of its reference: "Forlorn! the very word is like a bell / To toll me back from thee to my sole self!" And so the poem returns in its closing questions to the epistemological doubts of the empirical "sole self" whose "irritable reaching after fact & reason" (*Letters* 1:193) is the very antithesis of negative capability. My point is that the egotism behind such doubting is inherent in the self-transcendence of the preceding stanza, which is therefore necessarily provisional. The focus of the poet's attention being a bird, not a person (not even a Cumberland Beggar), it cannot reciprocate or in any way validate his experience. Moreover, this is not the enigmatic woodland creature of the earlier sonnet "What the Thrush Said." Invisible among the leafy boughs, the actual individual nightingale is supplanted almost immediately by the symbolic nexus of poetry and romance traditionally associated with the species from the medieval troubadours through Milton to Coleridge. From the very outset, then, the poet is already implicit within the object of his sympathy, which in retrospect is bound to appear solipsistic.

Indeed, if the most widely accepted ordering of the major odes is correct—Nightingale, Urn, Melancholy, Autumn—it would seem Keats increasingly rejected the impersonality and disinterestedness of negative capability. Embracing the "melancholy" realization that opposites interpenetrate ("Ay, in the very temple of Delight / Veil'd Melancholy has her sovran shrine"), he proceeds to close the distance, now seen to be delusive, between subject and object. A Grecian urn is a more patently human construction than a nightingale, whatever the latter's poetic associations; and melancholy, the central term in an influential Renaissance aesthetic which Keats would have known from reading Shakespeare and Milton if nobody else, isn't an external object at all but in the course of the poem turns out to be inspiration itself. "To Autumn" goes a step further by reintroducing the poet into the daily physical world, which, however, he now finds to be intrinsically subjective because it is constituted in part by his own responses. The awareness of interpenetrating opposites, which in "Melancholy" seemed rare and ephemeral, thus becomes a constant human season wherein he can calmly survey all of life.[25]

To sum up: if as Shelley says, "Nothing exists but as it is perceived," so that all commonly perceived phenomena are collective representations correlative to human consciousness, then there can be no absolute distinction between words and things. What we term "objects" are representations, no less than the words that represent *them*. Only the unrepresented is, by definition, independent of consciousness and language. To conceive of knowledge as a union with the represented "behind" the representation is therefore a fallacy, in this view. Rather, knowledge is the self-consciousness with which we participate in the activity of representation: ignorance, the unawareness of such activity. In Shelley's *Alastor*, to which I now turn, the dramatization of the protagonist's ignorance proves to be the reader's means to knowledge.

"Things Not As They Were":
The Phenomenology of *Alastor*

> *Formerly philosophers were afraid of the senses. . . . We today are*
> *inclined to make the opposite judgment (which actually could be*
> *equally wrong), namely that ideas are worse seductresses than our*
> *senses. . . . they have always lived on the "blood" of the*
> *philosopher, they always consumed his senses and even, if you*
> *will believe us, his "heart." These old philosophers were heartless;*
> *philosophizing was always a kind of vampirism. . . . In sum: All*
> *philosophical idealism to date was something like a disease,*
> *unless it was, as it was in Plato's case, the caution of an over-rich*
> *and dangerous health, the fear of over-powerful senses, the*
> *prudence of a prudent Socratic.—Perhaps we moderns are merely*
> *not healthy enough to be in need of Plato's idealism?*
>
> Nietzsche, The Gay Science, *sec. 372.*

Like *Alastor*'s protagonist, the history of *Alastor* criticism appears curiously self-defeating. Ever since Raymond Havens almost sixty years ago pronounced the poem "not a unity,"[1] commentary on Shelley's first major narrative has revolved about a single question. If the hero Poet is so overwhelmed "by the furies of an irresistible passion," as the preface says,[2] that from the very outset he eagerly pursues his own destruction, then where is the moral drama and basic narrative suspense of his quest? Havens confessed he couldn't tell ("morally he was a suicide" [p. 1102]), and ended by suggesting the poem is an expressive rather than a representational autobiography: " 'A Portrait of the Artist as a Young Man' may indeed be discovered in *Alastor*, but we shall find it, not by scanning the vague features of the wandering poet, . . . [but] by seeking in the poem for the *mind* of its author, for his idealism, his immaturity, his yearnings, his melancholy" (p. 1108). Subsequent readers accordingly viewed the poem not as an indulgence of Shelley's youthful yearning after the unconditioned so much as his struggle to measure a tolerable distance from it. Attention shifted from the lone Poet to his relationship with the Narrator, now regarded increasingly as a character in his own right. Albert Gérard strengthened the case for authorial self-exploration by finding the Poet's quest to be "a demonstration *a contrario*" of excessive idealism which contrasts with the Wordsworthian Narrator's unstable nature worship, itself tending at times to topple into immaterialism.[3] More recently, Earl Wasserman's compendious *Shelley: A Critical Reading* is predicated on treating *Alastor* as a formal heterocosm that pits visionary Poet and worldly Narrator against each other without endorsing either, thereby avoiding decision on the ethical dilemma set forth in the preface: namely, how to uphold the ideal in life without either destroying it through compromises or destroying oneself by refusing them.[4] In this manner *Alastor*, considered by all these critics to be a key to Shelley's poetic development inasmuch as it introduces in stark form so many characteristic features of his work—reflexive imagery, suicidal idealism, a mystical solitary voyage—has reverted to being the same enclosed hall of mirrors the key was supposed to unlock.

Alastor is indeed a threshold work, but by intrinsic design. One reason it is so difficult to put the poem in perspective and see it whole is that it portrays neither the lone Poet nor, somewhat less simply, the philosophical ambivalence of the author as expressed in the opposition of Poet and Narrator, but by undermining these merely provisional fictions it enables the reader actively to repossess and confront the hopes and doubts he and the author have projected into them. In a sense, Shelley deliberately dramatizes the process of sympathetic identification by which reading takes place. The basis for the poem's method is explained in the essay "On Life." Here Shelley accepts Hume's finding that "mankind . . . are nothing but a bundle or collection of different perceptions,"[5] but he suspends Hume's devastating conclusion that personal identity is therefore nonexistent by bracketing the different perceptions within a monistic "one mind": "The words, *I*, *you*, *they*, are not signs of any actual difference subsisting between the assemblage of thoughts thus indicated, but are merely marks employed to denote the different modifications of the one mind" (S, pp. 477–78). The Shelleyan "one mind" can be seen as the consciousness simultaneously of and in the text, through which author and reader mutually realize each other's identities *as* author and reader of this particular poem at this particular place and time. Hence the essay goes on emphatically to repudiate solipsism, "the monstrous presumption that I, the person who now write and think, am that one mind. I am but a portion of it." *Alastor* compels the reader to become what he beholds not in the Urizenic sensationalist sense of impressing upon him its hegemonic authority as a fixed, immutable art object but by gradually revealing a reciprocal otherness—the objectified figure of the author—which the reader can see to be his own figure as viewed from the author's perspective.

Thus *Alastor* both holds the mirror up to nature—nobody denies the Poet is, at some level, a portrait of the young artist, regardless how much he contains of the historical Shelley—*and* it functions as a self-referring heterocosm. For what the poem finally reflects is the interlocking of Poet and Narrator, of self-conscious subjectivity and the unself-conscious awareness of external physical nature, of solitary introspection and objectified experience—an interlocking that constitutes "Life, and the world, or whatever we call that which we are and feel, . . . that which includes all" (S, pp. 474–75). The grim final "vacancy" of the Poet's quest demonstrates the same antimetaphysical pragmatism as Shelley's cold-eyed successor Yeats, who in the late "Meru" asserts: "man's life is thought, / And he, despite his terror, cannot cease / . . . / Ravening, raging, and uprooting that he may come / Into the desolation of reality."[6] At the same time, *Alastor* thereby provides a means to the very "sympathy" the Poet rejects. The poem works to arouse a desire for love attainable only in the world of concrete human life beyond poetry, a desire whose mimetic gratification within the narrative Shelley perceives to be an insidiously narcissistic surrogate for the real thing. In contrast to the Poet's suicidal striving for unmediated union with his dream-maiden, we are led to acknowledge the necessity of a vigorous but unanxious skepticism toward the contents of other minds.

Indeed, such skepticism is, we see, the sole guarantee of our own identity. As Shelley's "Speculations on Metaphysics" put it, "We are ourselves then depositories of the evidence of the subject which we consider" (*CW* 7:63). *Alastor* subverts the customary dualism by which the text, regarded as a formal object of contemplation, gently "broadens" the mind of the retired reader. Instead, *Alastor* directly makes the reader *its* object, driving him to recognize the narrative action as ultimately a displacement of his own immediate activity of reading, the cessation of which is thus the first step toward achieving self-unity. The poem progresses toward an explicit allegory of reading which it no sooner discloses than it concludes. It could hardly do otherwise, having by the end of this process completely undermined the dramatic narrative. As a "self-consuming" work that repudiates its own mimesis in order to reveal to the reader in a final flash of insight his immediate ground of identity, *Alastor* illustrates the dictum of the *Defence of Poetry*: "Poetry is a sword of lightning . . . which consumes the scabbard that would contain it" (S, p. 491).

I

Alastor can therefore be considered a "sympathetic" narrative in the epistemological sense of the word developed by Hume and later Adam Smith.[7] Sympathy, argues Hume in the constructive second and third books of *A Treatise of Human Nature*, reverses the normal course of association whereby sense-impressions are converted through memory into ideas, "the faint images" of impressions. As other people more closely resemble ourselves than any other objects, "the ideas of the impressions of others, [which] appear at first in *our* mind as mere ideas, and are conceiv'd to belong to another person, as we conceive any matter of fact, . . . are converted into the very impressions they represent" (*THN*, pp. 319–20). And so an imitative relationship between two different components of an individual mind—ideas and impressions—becomes superseded by an identificatory relationship between impressions in two different minds altogether. A corresponding development occurs in philosophical metaphors. The Lockean blank slate of private sense-impressions is refined by Hume and especially Smith into a mirror capable of imaging other people's impressions. By thus shifting focus in Book II of the *Treatise* from epistemology to morals, from the isolated individual to the individual in society, Hume mitigates his crushing discovery in Book I that we cannot establish by introspection the existence of personal identity. For if "the minds of men are as mirrors to one another" (*THN*, p. 365), so that they reflect one another's thoughts, then perhaps each can know himself through knowing others.

Indeed, Smith claims sympathy alone "is capable of counteracting the strongest impulses of self-love" arising from Lockean individualism: "it is reason, principle, conscience, the inhabitant of the breast, the man within, the great judge and arbiter of our conduct."[8] Since this "abstract and ideal spectator of our sentiments" not only personifies our private self-image as moral agents but subsumes a whole nexus of social relationships without which that image wouldn't exist—the motive passions of the agent, the reaction of his object, and the judgment of a hypothetical witness to their interchange—the turning inward to our better self becomes a turning outward. In Shelley's words, "Each is at once the centre and the circumference; the point to which all things are referred, and the line in which all things are contained" (S, p. 476).

And yet Smith begins by positing the Humean caveat that we cannot actually know what another person feels; we can only represent to ourselves in imagination what we *think* he is feeling. It would appear that his argument is contradictory: as spectators we stand at a distance from the other in order to observe him and stage his supposed feelings within our private mental theater, but at the same time this process erases distance by making us actors able to lose our identity in the role that we have thus imagined. "The dream of sympathy, the fiction of sympathy," says David Marshall,

> is that an interplay and interchange of places, positions, persons, sentiments, and points of view could cancel out the theatricality of the most

theatrical of situations. According to Smith, we desire and depend on
spectators, but we can tolerate them only if we can believe in the fiction
that they can transport themselves from their distant position and become
us. . . . *The Theory of Moral Sentiments*, then, must describe what it is
like to want to believe in the fiction of sympathy, and what it is like to
live in a world where sympathy is perhaps impossible.[9]

But the fiction has a compelling logic of its own, for the moral theorist is
himself included in this society of interlocking circles or mutually reflecting mirrors or spectators turned actors. The resulting forfeiture of authorial privilege is well compensated by a gain in dramatic immediacy, as
Robert Cumming suggests: "The operation of sympathy explains the role
of the theorist as a scientific observer as well as the role the moral spectator
plays within that theory. Indeed the scientific observer plays essentially the
same rhetorical role as the moral spectator—he leads and directs the
judgement and conduct of men."[10] Hence the analytical effort at constructing a theory of sympathy merges with the rhetorical effort at communicating the theory persuasively. The sweeping periodic style of Smith's
Theory of Moral Sentiments and his impassioned elaboration of so many
vignettes either noble or dastardly in the extreme serve to win a specifically
sentimental assent from the audience on the assumption that the moral
theory remains moot without it. Hostile as it is to mankind's most cher-
ished beliefs, Hume's epistemological skepticism bows before the same
need. Having just demolished any ground of personal identity, the philosopher allays our horror in the Conclusion to Book One of the *Treatise* by
stepping forth in propria persona as a poor forked creature, living proof of
the undesirability of such extreme doubt:

> I am first affrighted and confounded with that forelorn solitude, in which
> I am plac'd in my philosophy, and fancy myself some strange uncouth
> monster, who not being able to mingle and unite in society, has been ex-
> pell'd all human commerce, and left utterly abandon'd and disconso-
> late. . . . I call upon others to join me, in order to make a company apart;
> but no one will hearken to me. Every one keeps at a distance, and dreads
> that storm, which beats upon me from every side. . . . All the world con-
> spires to oppose and contradict me; tho' such is my weakness, that I feel
> all my opinions loosen and fall of themselves, when unsupported by the
> approbation of others. [*THN*, pp. 264–65][11]

Forced to decide between reason and society, Hume demonstrates his
overriding need to choose the latter, thereby legitimizing his authority to
treat the larger subject named in his title.

The opening paragraph of Shelley's brief essay "On Love," to all
appearances a ripe specimen of immedicable narcissism, distinctly resem-

bles Hume's self-description and evinces a similarly calculating fusion of argument and performance. As well as explaining the nature of love via the standard imagery of sympathy ("We dimly see within our intellectual being a miniature as it were of our entire self, . . . a mirror"), the essay aims actually to awaken desire, so inviting us, as Shelley says elsewhere, "to feel that which we perceive, to imagine that which we know, . . . to act that which we imagine" (S, pp. 505, 502). The author begins by posturing as a wounded lover, addressing his audience as would-be intimates:

> I know not the internal constitution of other men, or even of thine whom I now address. I see that in some external attributes they resemble me, but when misled by that appearance I have thought to appeal to something in common and unburthen my inmost soul to them, I have found my language misunderstood like one in a distant and savage land. The more opportunities they have afforded me for experience, the wider has appeared the interval between us, and to a greater distance have the points of sympathy been withdrawn. With a spirit ill fitted to sustain such proof, trembling and feeble through its tenderness, I have every where sought, and have found only repulse and disappointment. [S, p. 473][12]

To find the passage self-indulgent only reveals one's own complacency. Shelley's Cain-like ostracism is ironic—"other men" are the murderers of fraternal love, not he—and it implies a challenge. If in the past the author has been misunderstood, will we understand him now? To take up the gauntlet is to validate the essay's unillusioned thesis that mature love can develop only when, after repeated narcissistic defeats, youth accepts the necessary loss of its "prototype" self-image and makes "the discovery of its antitype: the meeting with an understanding" *like* one's own but not identical because belonging to another person. The reason Shelley dramatizes this process is simple consistency; since the thesis holds that love is known only through the vulnerabilities of immediate lived experience, plainly Shelley requires a different sort of reader than the comfortably withdrawn spectator-judge of ordinary discursive prose. Being "an attraction . . . beyond ourselves," love is generated by the very failure of detached self-observation, "when we find within our own thoughts the chasm of an insufficient void" (S, p. 474).

The mental void that drives us to seek love distinctly resembles the lacunae that Hume discovers from his failure to deduce any "necessary connexion" existing between the mind's successive perceptions. "The mind is a kind of theatre," says Hume, "where several perceptions successively make their appearance; pass, re-pass, glide away, and mingle in an infinite variety of postures and situations" (*THN*, p. 253). Gazing into this private camera obscura, the Humean individual doesn't "have" perceptions in any active visceral sense; he simply witnesses them; alone and disconnected, he lacks even "the most distant notion of the place, where these scenes are represented." Such is the self-alienation of *Alastor*'s Poet at the conclusion of his quest when he resigns himself "To images of the majestic past, / That paused within his passive being now" (628–30). But in contrast to both Hume and the Poet, Shelley himself affirms that in love we seek not a direct perception of self-identity, "the prototype" of our self-image or ego ideal, but the sympathetic realization of that image in another. The Poet's delusion is clarified by the comparison of emotional and celestial attraction in "On Love." As a bright "mirror . . . that describes a circle around its proper Paradise," the "soul within our soul"— that is, the beloved—resembles the moon orbiting Earth. Accordingly, "the invisible and unattainable point to which Love tends" is mathematical infinity, the focus of any centripetal force. The reason "pain and sorrow and evil dare not overleap" the circle is that this paradise dwells not in the two bodies, however "heavenly" they may be, but in the differential space between them. It thus resists the depredations of ordinary fallen experience, quite unlike Milton's Satan who disdained "due entrance" to Eden and "At one slight bound high overleap'd all bound."[13] Insofar as the Poet of *Alastor* believes he can consciously reexperience his paradisiacal dream, he becomes like Satan a reductive sensationalist and merits the same phrase: "He eagerly pursues / Beyond the realms of dream that fleeting shade; / He overleaps the bounds. Alas! Alas!" (205–07).

Luther Scales is therefore not quite correct in seeing the Poet as a Miltonic Adam.[14] That indeed is how the deluded Poet sees himself, but the similarities only underscore a basic difference: unlike Adam's dream, the Poet's takes place in a fallen world. Shelley reinforces his point by depicting the Poet's early travels in terms of the bituminous sublime of the Miltonic Satan's journey through Hell and Chaos (81–94). For clearly the maiden's destructive power reflects nothing but the "intensity and passion" (preface) of the Poet's own mind. In other words, she is his muse, demonized. As far as the Poet is concerned, his quest is for inspiration. The irony is that he *is* inspired, but as we shall see he is prevented from realizing it by the negativistic view of poetry inherent in his radical idealism. Much like the meditative-Miltonizing poets of Sensibility whose Penseroso-like streamside musical reveries he shares, the Poet of *Alastor* does not travel forward to actual authorship in the world at large; rather he eddies entropically back into the diffusive "solemn vision, and bright silver dream" (67) of his infancy.

This suggests that *Alastor* could have served to mediate Shelley's own tendencies toward a dangerous self-absorption. It does so, I believe, partly through the characteristic device of "reflexive imagery" that compares a unitary object to a differentiated aspect of itself.[15] To take an example from Byron's *Childe Harold's Pilgrimage*, whose relationship to *Alastor* appears curiously symbiotic, we may say the Poet is like Harold "The wandering outlaw of *his own* dark mind" (italics mine).[16] Such imagery tends to shift the ordinary duality of subject and object onto the object itself, so making the duality explicit and pointing back to the troping presence of the author. In the same way, the many similarities between *Alastor*'s Poet and Narrator—compare lines 20–23 with 469–74, 23–29 with 121–29, 29–37 with 151–91 passim, and 37–49 with 666–68— show they are related not as opposites but as mirror images that contain each other. In this sense, *Alastor*'s very structure is reflexive and reveals, as Havens said, not "a portrait of the artist" but "the mind of its author." Unfortunately, no mind yet, not even God's, has ever articulated itself without some form of temporal mediation, "so told to earthly sense." Likewise, *Alastor*'s reflexive structure is narrativized by Shelley's sympathetic method. By causing the Poet's dream to usurp the dramatic action, Shelley converts the reader's secondhand "idea" of that dream into a direct "impression." Since this process gradually derealizes the Poet as a dramatic character, ownership of the dream passes to the reader, who leaves the poem ready to commence his own equally intense search "to awaken in all things that are, a community with what we experience within ourselves" (S, p. 473). And yet the reader's quest is crucially different from the Poet's, for it has become tempered by the lesson of the Poet's defeat, the lesson that we cannot in actuality possess the woman of our dreams except through her real-life "antitype." As the distinctly moralistic preface implies, to reject the fallen human world is to deny the very stuff of imagination, thereby dooming one's sympathy to consume itself in solitude.

Section III of the "Speculations on Metaphysics," "Difficulty of Analyzing the Human Mind," explores the dangers of self-absorption in epistemological terms. Can detached introspection provide self-knowledge? Shelley begins by surmising that if "a person should give a faithful history of his being, from the earliest epochs of his recollection, . . . a mirror would be held up to all men in which they might behold their own recollections." *Alastor* can be considered the experimental testing of this hypothesis; the figure of the Poet inscribes the history of one such attempt at total recall. Shelley goes on to examine why the attempt is unlikely to succeed:

> But thought can [only] with difficulty visit the intricate and winding chambers which it inhabits. It is like a river whose rapid and perpetual stream flows outwards;—like one in dread who speeds through the recesses of some haunted pile, and dares not look behind. The caverns of the mind are obscure, and shadowy; or pervaded with a lustre, beautifully

bright indeed, but shining not beyond their portals. If it were possible to
be where we have been, vitally and indeed—if, at the moment of our
presence, we could define the results of our experience,—if the passage
from sensation to reflection—from a state of passive perception to voluntary contemplation, were not so dizzying and so tumultuous, this attempt
would be less difficult. [CW 7:64]

Whereas the natural flow of ideas, says Hume, "carries forward the
thought in a corresponding course to that . . . established among external
objects,"[17] the preoccupied Poet of *Alastor* travels upstream against the
flow, finally expiring "on that verge where words abandon us, . . . the dark
abyss of—how little we know" (S, p. 478). Or to change metaphors in
midstream: since the Poet repudiates the Humean "pre-established harmony between the course of nature and the succession of our ideas," and
hence the emotional attunement with another person which his musical
dream announces—"the meeting . . . with a frame whose nerves, like the
chords of two exquisite lyres . . . , vibrate with the vibrations of our own"
(S, p. 473)—his deprived body can only "Scatter its music on the unfeeling
storm" (597). It becomes a defrauded harp, the standard associationist
image for thought grown indolent and passive.

As the above passage implies, the Poet's journey to the source of
association is doomed to defeat simply because by the time thought returns
to its flashlike origin in the caverns of the mind, its luster is already
confined to the portals of memory. The imagery suggests self-estrangement is a necessary consequence of self-observation. For Shelley, the
immediate empirical report of introspection is that perceptions possess an
inescapably alien quality; he describes it as an irrational feeling of "shadowy hopes and fears," anticipation of the future mingled with anxiety to
preserve the past. Paradoxically, however, the habitual self no sooner
experiences this uncanny awareness than it begins to extinguish it by
process of assimilation. This elusive sense of the self-life or sheer otherness
of perception reflects the basic presence, within the percipient, of the so-
called external world. Remarks Alfred North Whitehead of our immediate
past, roughly defined as a split second ago:

It is our indubitable self, the foundation of our present existence. Yet the
present occasion while claiming self-identity, while sharing the very nature of the bygone occasion in all its living activities, nevertheless is engaged in modifying it, in adjusting it to other influences, in completing it
with other values, in deflecting it to other purposes. The present moment
is constituted by the influx of the other.[18]

It follows that we can never achieve epistemological certainty through
ostensibly detached introspection. Only by arresting time in a durationless

Newtonian instant could we "be where we have been, vitally and indeed." In Shelley's gothic melodrama of alter egos, the self that knows always chases the self that becomes, the dreading other who speeds ahead of consciousness and "dares not look behind," since to stop fleeing one's immediate past is death.[19]

II

Alastor can thus be seen to initiate Shelley's lifelong struggle to reach a stance of skeptical idealism. In the words of C. E. Pulos, Shelley was fundamentally "a sceptic who pursued a non-dogmatic idealism compatible with scepticism."[20] Despite their symmetrical forty-nine-line length, the Narrator's prologue and epilogue do not serve, as Earl Wasserman claims, to frame the Poet's idealist quest within a patently inferior "limited, worldly view" and "earth-bound perspective" (pp. 35–36). For Wasserman, *Alastor* reflects the author's blasted utopianism and mounting philosophical ambivalence: "Shelley was repeatedly to be a poet of two parallel realities, often related as an image is related to its watery reflection: one that seems and one that is; one finite, the other infinite; one perceived by the senses, the other apprehended by imagination; one existent in life, the other in death" (p. 31). Nonetheless, if by skepticism we mean the reasoned denial of the possibility of knowing reality, the assertion that the human mind by its very constitution cannot grasp the ultimate nature of things, then clearly we must disqualify anyone convinced he has grasped even one reality, much less two. Although such a person might feel the same hesitation as a skeptic, the feeling reflects no genuinely epistemological doubt, only vacillation. Indeed, Wasserman's Shelley believes too much, not too little. In distinguishing appearance and reality, he does not suspend judgment; rather he has already judged. The result is predictable: wisely preferring the "real" reality presupposed by so specious a dualism, Shelley is found to valorize the Poet's quest and scorn the straw-man Narrator. Such a reading leads back, of course, to the autobiographical "portrait of the artist" perspective which Havens discommended. More to the point, it tends to dissolve the very ambiguity and tension that in Wasserman's view is all that binds the poem's conflicting attitudes together.

Pace Wasserman, *Alastor* proceeds by deconstructing the dualism initially established between idealist Poet and skeptical Narrator and reformulating it as a dualism within each of them. Poet and Narrator gradually forfeit their identities as distinct dramatic characters and interpenetrate. For as he pursues his visionary ideal, the Poet doubts increasingly if it exists anywhere on earth. His obstinate questing thus comes to include the "obstinate questionings" (26) formerly avowed by the Wordsworthian Narrator. Commencing as it does after the Poet's Baconian craving for the wisdom of the ancients ("all of great . . . which the sacred past / In truth or fable consecrates" [72–74]) has led him through past civilizations to the limits of empirical knowledge ("he saw / The thrilling secrets of the birth of time" [127–28]), the pursuit of the dream-maiden develops into a skeptical search for epistemological knowledge through ascetic introspection—hence his questions of "doubt" and "despair" that immediately follow the dream (196–98, 208–09, 211–29, and 285–90). At the same time, the Poet's experiences are found to duplicate those of the Narrator described in the invocation, as I pointed out. Thus when the Narrator returns in the epilogue, he sounds less like a skeptic than an injured idealist; no fewer than three times he declares his wish that the imagination's dream, the elixir of life, were true (672–86).[21]

In the end, then, the Poet's increasingly dogmatic skepticism is confronted by a further doubt that Pyrrhonistically questions the goals of dogmatic skepticism itself. In Shelley's pragmatic revaluation, skepticism is not an abstract logic whose truth is "discovered" but an exploratory, speculative activity that takes its worth from actual concrete experience. If "life, and the world, or whatever we call that which we are and feel, is an astonishing thing," the most constructive philosophizing may be that which refrains from system, generating only awareness of our own ignorance. If mankind's central problem is that "the mist of familiarity obscures from us the wonder of our being" (S, pp. 474–75), such philosophizing could expose at least the mist, if not what lies beneath it. Hume himself recognizes that systematic skepticism conduces only to nihilism and paralysis: "All discourse, all action would immediately cease, and men remain in a total lethargy until the necessities of nature, unsatisfied, put an end to their miserable existence" (*ICHU*, p. 67).[22] This, of course, is the fate of the Poet, who evidently dies of starvation and exposure. His radical idealism merely swings round to its opposite, undermining both positions and leading to "vacancy."[23]

One might therefore infer that Shelley supports the more balanced skepticism of the Narrator, who ends where he begins, with "Nature's vast frame, the web of human things, / Birth and the grave" (719–20). And yet the Narrator admits these familiar realities have somehow become altered by the Poet's example and "are not as they were" (720). In seeming conformity with the preface, the Narrator sees the Poet's story as illustrating the transient nature of all transcendence:

> . . . mighty Earth
> Lifts still its solemn voice:—but thou art fled—
> Thou canst no longer know or love the shapes

> Of this phantasmal scene, who have to thee
> Been purest ministers, who are, alas!
> Now thou art not.   [694–99]

What the Narrator fails to see is the necessary provisionality of his own wise passiveness. Recent criticism has noted that the prologue and epilogue give ample grounds for supposing the Poet to be a passionate youthful version of the Narrator now recollected in tranquillity, somewhat in the manner of Wordsworth's Immortality Ode and "Tintern Abbey," or his lines on the Boy of Winander (the one quoted, the others echoed repeatedly in the poem).[24] Evidently from the Narrator's standpoint, composing *Alastor* enables him in typical Wordsworthian fashion to objectify a coherent self comfortably wedded to Nature and no longer prey to transcendental restlessness. And yet, everything we've been saying about the poem suggests it glaringly rejects the organic unity and spiral shape of what M. H. Abrams terms "the Greater Romantic Lyric," epitomized for him by "Tintern Abbey."[25] It would appear *Alastor* questions the underlying fiction by which such poetry pretends to forgo intentionality and make the actual process of writing a means of spontaneously integrating the poet's past and present selves. In the figure of the Narrator, then, the Wordsworthian internalized sublime is exposed as an egocentric deception whose falsity is inseparable from its persuasiveness. For Shelley, Wordsworth renounces sincerity precisely to the extent that he makes it a rhetorical effect.[26]

Consider, for example, the ironies of the closing elegy. Here the Narrator repudiates cold pastoral, implying that his own verse speaks with the true voice of feeling:

> Nor, when those hues
> Are gone, and those divinest lineaments,
> Worn by the senseless wind, shall live alone
> In the frail pauses of this simple strain,
> Let not high verse, mourning the memory
> Of that which is no more, or painting's woe
> Or sculpture, speak in feeble imagery
> Their own cold powers.   [703–10]

The elaborate double negative, imitating Wordsworth imitating Milton imitating Latin, bathetically undermines the Narrator's stated scorn of artifice. If Wordsworth's narrators speak with such compelling self-assurance, apparently the reason is their textuality. Only because they are personas distinct from the historical author can they safely avoid the radical discontinuities of identity which they so often verbalize (for example, "obstinate questionings," what Shelley elsewhere calls "the vanishing apparitions which haunt the interlunations of life" [S, p. 505]). The thrust of Shelley's attack on the establishment Wordsworth of the 1815 collected *Poems* is that Wordsworth (quite unlike Byron) actually believes what he has written about himself, identifies with his projected public image, and so conceitedly shirks the need for self-revision. The sonnet "To Wordsworth" written at the time of *Alastor* argues that Wordsworth's poetry of loss has overtaken the poet himself, who has forfeited his imagination without realizing it: "One loss is mine / Which thou too feel'st, yet I alone deplore" (S, p. 88). By *establishing* himself as a poet of loss, Wordsworth must necessarily "cease to be" one, for the imagination he extols is not a fixed and definite possession of the empirical author but something evermore about to be. Accordingly, although the Wordsworthian Narrator of *Alastor* believes he has outgrown the Poet, this delusion is seen to be merely the converse of the Poet's deluded desire not to outgrow the dream-maiden.

"Those who remain behind" (716) after the Poet's death therefore constitute not the Narrator but the audience itself. The assertion that "things . . . are not as they were" bespeaks one's own experience of the poem. In this sense, *Alastor* can be said to inaugurate the mature Shelley's attempt to legislate reform democratically by sublimating his assertive youthful polemicism in a poetics of consciousness-raising. Accordingly, his worst enemies are not outright antagonists but, as the preface makes clear, the "morally dead" who eschew intellectual struggle altogether. One such false consciousness is represented by the incomplete dialectics of the Wordsworthian Narrator. He sees readily enough that nature includes mind (the Poet), but neglects that nature is included in its turn by the self-conscious mind (the reader). Inasmuch as Shelley thus lays bare the fictiveness of *Alastor*'s narrative, the Poet's final disappearance signifies not the inevitable destruction of a moral paragon by a world not made for such passionate intensity, as the Narrator assumes, but an actual mental lapse in the audience, the failure of our mutable consciousness to maintain sight of the ideal. As the Shelleyan Julian asks in *Julian and Maddalo*, "Where is the love, beauty and truth we seek / But in our mind?" (S, p. 117). The apparent vanishing of these absolutes reflects not their illusoriness but our own inconstancy toward them.[27]

Shelley's critique of Wordsworth revises the dichotomy Abrams's influential *The Mirror and the Lamp* established between classical mimesis and Romantic expressivism. In the latter, heralded for Abrams by Wordsworth's preface to *Lyrical Ballads*, the artwork "ceases to be regarded as primarily a reflection of nature, actual or improved; the mirror held up to nature becomes transparent and yields the reader insights into the mind and heart of the poet himself."[28] *Alastor* deliberately subverts this pretense of an unmediated form of expression able to provide insight without need of interpretation. As we look into the mind of Shelley's Narrator, we see it presents still another mirror, one that Socratically reflects the limitations of our own minds as readers.

III

Hence *Alastor*'s constant, increasingly deliquescent repetition of image clusters, based on principles neither mimetic nor expressive but phenomenological. *Alastor* progresses through a series of distinctly different landscapes and journeys, from the familiar place-names of the Poet's relatively naturalistic search for arcane knowledge (67–271) to his strenuous allegorical voyage toward the dream-maiden's secret haunt, "Nature's cradle, and his sepulchre" (272–492), to his gentle fadeaway into the past through recursive recollections of childhood that finally efface all awareness of his immediate surroundings (492–671). Each of these subnarratives develops in parallel with the others, repeating previous scenes, objects, and events on a new stylistic level. The result is a gradual undermining of all mimesis, including that imitation of artless spontaneity by which Wordsworthian poetry achieves its expressivism. Take, for example, the poem's several spots of refuge. Despite the remoteness of the "loneliest dell" (146) where the Poet dreams of his maid, that dell still forms part of a sketchy pastoral world of cottagers and their impressionable flesh-and-blood daughters (254–71). In contrast, the "one darkest glen" (451) harboring the well-fountain contains only reflected images of reality. And yet the glen has this much in common with the dell: the images it presents are real phenomena. In contrast to both, the "one silent nook" (572) that the Poet discovers beside the abyss contains nothing at all, being merely the chamber of the winds. Through such metamorphoses, *Alastor*'s narrative is gradually cut loose from its moorings in an assumed reality "out there," enabling the reader to look *through* the dramatic action to its ground in his own reading mind.

This process commences with the sea change that follows the Poet's dream. Having arrived at "the lone Chorasmian shore . . . , a wide and melancholy waste" (272–73) that marks the extreme limit of his geographical travels, the Poet begins a voyage that evidently represents the continuation of his quest inside his mind. Thus the dream becomes recapitulated in thought. Upon his original awakening, we were told that "sleep, / Like a dark flood suspended in its course, / Rolled back its impulse on his vacant brain," raising the possibility he might recover the maiden in death: "This doubt with sudden tide flowed on his heart" (189–

200). Now, another "restless impulse" urges him to "meet lone Death" on the "black flood" of the storm-tossed sea (304–28). It appears the Poet has deliberately embarked on the same ebbing tide of sleep that earlier left him high and dry. His voyage of sexual introversion climaxes in a whirlpool that symbolizes his previous orgasmic dream.[29] Then, the dreamer "reared his shuddering limbs" and embraced the maiden just as "blackness veiled his dizzy eyes" (182–89); now, "the straining boat arose" with "dizzy swiftness" until it "paused shuddering" "on the verge" of an "overflow" (388–94). A different narrative style ensues with the shallop's escape from the whirlpool via a meandering stream (420–68). Havens's dismissal of this section as "pictures of nature for their own sake" (p. 1109) inadvertently hits the mark. Instead of indicating a return to nature, the preternatural abundance of images mirrored in the water is intended nonrepresentationally *as* imagery. The scenery's disembodied stillness shows the Poet beginning to suffer the self-estrangement inherent in the secluded Humean theater of the mind where perceptions "pass, re-pass, glide away and mingle" phantasmagorically. So, for instance, the soaring Chorasmian swan, which formerly appeared an inmate of this active universe (275–90)[30] and then reappeared as a floating "vagrant bird" (410), here reappears once more as a mere "painted bird" (465), an idle reflection. Its transformation only marks the growing vagrancy and unreality of the Poet himself.

Hence the subdued pathos of the scene at the well. The Poet having "kept mute conference with his still soul" upon waking from the dream (223–24) and then become "startled by his own thoughts" of the maiden whose increasing ubiquity makes her seem a "fair fiend" able to control his mind (296–98), he now objectifies the thoughts as conversation with an actual human presence. Gazing into the water, his peripheral vision coalesces the surrounding scenery into a Spirit of Solitude, an ironically companionable symbol of his isolation:

> A Spirit seemed
> To stand beside him—clothed in no bright robes
> Of shadowy silver or enshrining light,
> Borrowed from aught the visible world affords
> Of grace, or majesty, or mystery;—
> But, undulating woods, and silent well,
> And leaping rivulet, and evening gloom
> Now deepening the dark shades, for speech assuming
> Held commune with him, as if he and it
> Were all that was,—only . . . when his regard
> Was raised by intense pensiveness, . . . two eyes,
> Two starry eyes, hung in the gloom of thought.   [479–90]

Shelley deliberately portrays here the fabrication of what Frank Kermode has called "the Romantic Image."[31] By an act of narcissistic compensation, the love-starved Poet projects into human form his aesthetic appreciation of the unifying compositional tone—or in Wordsworth's phrase, the "sober colouring"—of the glen's various elements (woods, well, rivulet, and gloom). "In solitude, or in that deserted state" of unrequited sympathy, says the essay "On Love," we discover in nature "a secret correspondence with our heart. There is eloquence in the tongueless wind and a melody in the flowing of brooks and the rustling of the reeds beside them which . . . bring tears of mysterious tenderness to the eyes like . . . the voice of one beloved singing to you alone" (S, p. 474). Yet the Poet's self-solacing exacts a price. If the omphalos-like well represents the origin of necessity or "Power," the "secret springs" of causation (478; Hume uses the same phrase in *ICHU*, p. 34), then the Spirit observed there shows the impossibility of the mind's ever escaping itself so as to fathom those secrets, for "nothing exists but as it is perceived" (S, p. 477; CW 7:65). Evidently Shelley is an idealist insofar as he believes we half-create what we perceive, a skeptic insofar as he infers from this our inability to know the uncreated half of reality. The first attitude is reflected in the Spirit's loveliness, the second in its marginality.

At this stage of *Alastor*, then, the Poet's crossover from idealism to skepticism reaches its midpoint, a transient state in which the two viewpoints are epiphanically conjoined. Whereas the Narrator has like Wordsworth "at all times endeavored to look steadily at [his] subject" in writing,[32] the Poet gazes at himself in order to see out the corner of his eye. Like the Spirit of Intellectual Beauty Shelley would celebrate in his "Hymn" a year later, the Spirit of the Well is neither an enduring Wordsworthian *genius loci* wearing lineaments of "the visible world" nor a Plotinean visitor from the eternal Beyond, but an ideal form created by the mind in authentic Platonic fashion out of the provisional materials of experience in the world. Appropriately, what causes it to vanish is the Poet's self-conscious attempt to look at it directly. As his "intense pensiveness" turns "evening gloom" into an internalized "gloom of thought," he mistakes his own eyes actually reflected in the well for those of the dream-maiden. Thus the Spirit, deprived of immediate relation to the physical setting of which it is composed—forced, indeed, to supplant that setting, its own ground—hypostatizes into a mere hallucination.

Henceforth the Poet's quest is literally all downhill. His balanced glimpse of Intellectual Beauty collapses into a simpler, more dogmatic desire for a revelation independent of experience, a knowledge somehow beyond intellect. Having tracked to its apparent source the stream of consciousness or life (in Shelley's "intellectual philosophy," there is no real difference between the two),[33] exhaustedly he follows the diminishing rivulet onward from the well to its end in oblivion. However disembodied, the imagery of the journey toward the well remained particularized. By contrast, the trip downstream telescopes time and place impressionistically. The quest no longer persists "Day after day, a weary waste of hours" (245); instead, "fast years flow away" as the Poet yields without resistance to the "sightless speed" of Death (553, 610). Although the narrative continues to progress, it now depicts not the Poet traveling by great effort through nature but trains of recollected nature imagery traveling solipsistically through the inert, senile Poet.[34] In effect, *Alastor* has begun to turn inside out, exposing the unreality at its core.

At the edge of a precipice, the Poet's journey finally comes to a standstill. As his inner emptiness grows increasingly apparent, we begin to see past his preoccupying claustral quest to the expansive earthly realms that have evidently lain behind it all along:

> Lo! where the pass expands
> Its stony jaws, the abrupt mountain breaks,
> And seems, with its accumulated crags,
> To overhang the world: for wide expand
> Beneath the wan stars and descending moon
> Islanded seas, blue mountains, mighty streams,
> Dim tracts and vast, robed in the lustrous gloom
> Of leaden-coloured even, and fiery hills,
> Mingling their flames with twilight, on the verge
> Of the remote horizon. The near scene,
> In naked and severe simplicity,
> Made contrast with the universe.   [550–61]

The whiff of fresh air is unmistakable; it signifies the reader's liberation from the Poet's now obviously unnecessary and obsessive self-confinement. Throughout the poem's second half, his mounting solipsism is emphasized by a steady darkening of the narrative, from noon (420, 468) to evening (485, 526, 557) to moonlit night (602–07). Accordingly, the coincidence of his death with the setting moon's disappearance amid unhealthy "murky shades" that leave all "utterly black" (645–60), completely extinguishing the dramatic action, reveals the oppressiveness of his conviction that with his death, the whole world too must die. To return to the Narrator is to realize with relief that the darkest hour is just before dawn. Whereas the Poet's passing is first compared to a mist at nightfall— "a vapour fed with golden beams . . . ere the west / Eclipses it" (663– 67)—the epilogue reverses the image: "thou art fled / Like some frail exhalation; which *the dawn* / Robes in its golden beams" (686–88; italics mine). In the Poet's end is the Narrator's beginning.

IV

The Poet's spiraling descent into self-consciousness thus generates a saving countermovement in the mind of the reader.[35] For the Poet, his journey is a vicious regress from the original dream to thoughts of the dream, to thoughts of those thoughts, and so on.[36] The cycle depicts the skeptical epistemology of Hume's theater of the mind, where knowledge of external reality is limited to private perception: "Let us fix our attention out of ourselves as much as possible: Let us chace our imagination to the heavens, or to the utmost limits of the universe; we never really advance a step beyond ourselves, nor can conceive any kind of existence, but those perceptions, which have appear'd in that narrow compass" (*THN*, pp. 67–68). Accordingly, as the Poet leaves off traveling and the dramatic action peters out, the basically mental nature of his quest becomes increasingly apparent. *Alastor*'s repetitions cease to introduce literal objects from earlier in the narrative, and begin like mirrors to reflect the reader's thoughts of those objects. Hence the *Frankenstein*-like reversal by which the Poet, instead of pursuing and repossessing his dream-image, is pursued and controlled by it until finally it makes *him* into "an image, . . . a dream / Of youth . . . unremembered now" (661–71). Inasmuch as this is a poetic image, *Alastor* is explicitly shown to be a dangerous but necessary fiction. To identify directly with the Poet is, we see, to turn the poem into a narcissistic seduction fantasy no different from the Poet's identification with his dream-maiden. Once this is understood, however, the Poet can usefully represent "the invisible and unattainable point to which love tends," being "a miniature as it were of our entire self, yet deprived of all that we condemn or despise, the ideal prototype of every thing excellent or lovely that we are capable of conceiving as belonging to the nature of man" (S, pp. 473–74).

Thus the reader's subsumption of *Alastor*'s various personas, so far from annihilating all apprehension of difference, transfers that apprehension with renewed vividness from the fictional heterocosm to the concrete human realm where it properly belongs. *Alastor* works to eradicate what Shelley considers the passive sensationalist attitude toward the object-world embodied not only in the Narrator's view of nature but in our own initial acceptance of the poem as conventional descriptive narrative. Regardless of whether we judge such narrative to be mimetic or expressive, our expectations are grounded in an artificial distinction between "thought" and "the objects of thought": for if "we can think of nothing which we have not perceived, . . . [so] that beyond the limits of perception and of thought nothing can exist," then "*external* and *internal*, as applied to the establishment of this distinction, . . . is merely an affair of words" (*CW* 7:60, 65). This is not to say that actual different thoughts themselves are not distinct, only that their degree of externality or "outness" (as Coleridge terms it) is purely relative and therefore strictly of no metaphysical (as opposed to "ethical or oeconomical" [*CW* 7:60]) significance.

In this sense, the difference between poem and reader eventually disappears; not only is the dream-maiden a thought in the Poet's mind, but the Poet is himself seen to be a dimly remembered thought in the Narrator's mind, and all three are thoughts of the reader. At the same time, the example of the Poet serves to forestall any solipsistic tendencies inherent in this process. His fate illustrates nothing if not the warning of the "Speculations on Metaphysics": "If the inequalities, produced by what has been termed the operations of the external universe were levelled by the perception of our being, uniting, and filling up their interstices, motion and mensuration, and time, and space; the elements of the human mind being thus abstracted, sensation and imagination cease. Mind cannot be considered pure" (*CW* 7:61). Shelley undermines our assumption of the Poet and Narrator's difference from ourselves as well as from each other, not in order to deny difference, but on the contrary in order to reveal differentiation itself as a ground of knowledge. "Our evidence, with respect to the existence of other minds," claim the "Speculations," ". . . is undoubtedly, a periodical recurrence of masses of ideas, which our own voluntary determinations have, in one peculiar direction, no power to circumscribe or to arrest, and against the recurrence of which they can only imperfectly provide." By repossessing the speciously projected difference separating him from the Poet and Narrator, the reader becomes able to acknowledge the authentic otherness of the author himself, who, of course, is the one who arranged for the poem's systematic repetitions to elicit from the reader such "a periodical recurrence of masses of ideas" in the first place.

Since consciousness cannot get outside itself, we cannot say whether *Alastor* lifts the painted veil of life or lowers another. Nonetheless, the poem forcibly affirms our apprehension of *some* difference, however we construe it, to be the primary, unmediated truth of experience—unmediated because difference, reflecting the basic duality of subject-object relationships, is what makes possible the existence of distinct individual experiences at all. Even if the Poet does finally reunite with his dream-maiden, Shelley's point is that we cannot conceive such oneness except in terms of the same earthly dualities it would supersede.[37] The Poet's merely virtual reality as "an image" is that of the Hegelian "beautiful soul"; pictured as dying melodies and vanishing vapors, both characters illustrate, as Hegel says, "self-consciousness withdrawn into the inmost retreats of its being, with all externality, as such, gone and vanished from it—returned into the intuition of ego as altogether identical with ego."[38] Such idealists proceed as if direct wish fulfillment were still possible on earth and one could, like Keats's Adam, dream a demoiselle, awake and find it truth. "O, that the dream . . . were the true law / Of this so lovely world!" (681–86) laments the Narrator, thereby reminding us that it isn't, even as the suspiciously smug "so lovely" makes his tears seem crocodile. The mist of descriptive-narrative familiarity having faded by *Alastor's* end, leaving only vacancy—the Poet's blotted image and the Narrator's eviscerated rhetoric—we realize not only that things are "not as they were," but that paradoxically they never were as they were. Like Milton's Satan, "We know no time when we were not as now"—namely, changed, different, other.[39]

Alastor's evolution of style and narrative reflects Shelley's belief in the interdependence of thought with its objects. Since the poem passes through a variety of narrative styles, its ultimate unity arises only in retrospect through an act of unified perception by the reader. But if the reader thereby objectifies the poem, the poem also objectifies the reader; for what the reader perceives is, precisely, that *Alastor* was all along striving to expunge its putative hero and bring himself into focus. Such reversals, *A Defence of Poetry* explains, are of the very essence of poetry. Starting from the axiom that there exist "two classes of mental action, which are called reason and imagination," Shelley contrasts the mind as a passive wind harp productive of melodies with the mind as a musician able to transform melody into harmony by answering the breeze with "an internal adjustment" of its own (S, p. 480). He then applies this distinction to literature, contrasting the narrativity of "a story" with the symbiotic unity of "a poem": "a story is a catalogue of detached facts, which have no other bond of connexion than time, place, circumstance, cause and effect; the other is the creation of actions according to the unchangeable forms of human nature, as existing in the mind of the creator, which is itself the image of all other minds" (S, p. 485). On one hand, *Alastor* shows love is not, as the Poet supposes, an experience one can possess and know like a detached object without being oneself changed in the process. On the other hand, to see this is to glimpse beneath the poetic action one of the unchangeable forms of human nature—namely, the form of love embodied in our consciously "sympathetic" relationship to the author who is our hermeneutic "antitype," that portion of ourselves projected into the narrative and now become responsively other. In both cases, we see there is simply no need of a transcendence such as the Poet seeks. The process of self-realization at the heart of concrete human life, its insistence that we become progressively "more ourselves," offers a transcendence of its own.

Conclusion

The disintegration of *Alastor*'s Poet shows the crucial importance of temporality in supplying the ground of consciousness and personal identity. Unable to objectify repetition—unable, that is, to recognize repetition as such, to see how every successive event takes up elements of its predecessor and redirects them toward novel, incompletely determined ends, thereby grasping that they are not the same event but part of an ongoing pattern of repetitions-with-a-difference—Shelley's Poet loses the capacity to distinguish the present from the past. Blake emphasizes time's providential role in the "building up of Jerusalem" through works of imagination: "Time is the mercy of Eternity; without Times swiftness / Which is the swiftest of all things: all were eternal torment."[1] Without time, life would remain trapped in the State of Satan, an impossible condition of reified abstraction, meaningless repetition unrelieved by novelty. As *Milton* goes to show, Satanic sameness or eternal death, so far from pervading life, is paradoxically no more than the unreal exception that proves the rule that life is full of exceptions. The spiral form of the narratives we've examined, whereby they turn back upon themselves on levels of increasing self-consciousness, can be considered an analogue of the way we experience our identity as a function of our body's persisting sameness through all the differences of temporal existence. Blake's many statements to the effect that God is "the Real Man The Imagination which Liveth for Ever" (E, p. 783) aver that insofar as the artist expresses imagination, the total unified form of his artwork manifests "the Human Eternal Body in Every Man."[2] In contrast, Satan, the failure of articulation, is "this Body of Doubt that Seems but Is Not" (E, p. 253).

Yet the form of the narratives we've explored is merely virtual, a product of the interpretive act by which the reader apprehends in retrospect the unity of their different narrative styles. This merely virtual form corresponds to the body regarded as clothing for the soul; it reveals the pervasiveness of the soul or mind within the expressions of the body. Further, it shows that although the body does express the mind whether we want it to or not (even if my dissimulation doesn't expose itself by appearing excessively behavioral or unspontaneous, that in itself "says" something about my reptilian or schizoid character) nevertheless the expressions do not reveal their meaning without interpretation. By its ultimate act of self-destruction, the poem emphasizes the reader's role in translating its virtual form into a form of experience. Through the reader, the poem's words become flesh, as in reality the meanings of the soul become flesh through the expressions of the body.[3] Once we recognize that the various subnarratives all repeat the same basic plot line, each poem becomes an allegory of reading in which our retrospective realization of the plot's ideal unity itself supplies the climax. In completing the poem, then, the reader forfeits his infantile, largely escapist sense of being contained by it and assumes responsibility for embodying its meaning in his own life. In Hegel's terms, the self-conscious spirit having at long last repossessed its sundered portion, thus realizing its identity and achieving "absolute knowledge," is finally "at home with itself in its otherness as such."[4] But Hegel envisions this arrival home as futural and definitive, the paradisiacal end to history, whereas for the poets it possesses a positive human content precisely because of its irredeemable temporality—because, in other words, it has been proved upon our pulses, and so can last no longer than "a Moment, a Pulsation of the Artery" (E, p. 127), after which poet and reader must go their separate ways.

Put differently, one could say these poems' culminating act of self-destruction enables them to achieve the silence by which we know them to be other. Observes Georges Poulet of "the phenomenology of reading": "Whenever I read, I mentally pronounce an *I*, and yet the *I* which I pronounce is not myself. . . . I am thinking the thoughts of another. Of course, there would be no cause for astonishment if I were thinking it as the thought of another. But I am thinking it as my very own."[5] Through their symbiosis of style and narrative and resultant exploration of the cause-and-effect, subject-object relationships we ordinarily take for granted, *Milton*, *Christabel*, *Don Juan*, Canto II, and *Alastor* suspend the deductive Humean approach to personal identity where "myself" must be either "a distinct existence . . . different, and distinguishable, and separable from every other perception"[6] or else nothing at all. The poems offer what Blake terms a merciful "female space" of time wherein poet and reader, by recognizing their mutual dependence, are each enabled to objectify a provisional identity for the other. What distinguishes our Romantic narratives from the more conventional "Cartesian" narratives Poulet evidently has in mind (and Poulet admits his criticism "needs absolutely" the Cartesian cogito [p. 88]) is their progressively more explicit dramatization of their phenomenological premises, culminating in the reader's self-conscious confrontation of the authorial other he has internalized. The reason I finally experience the Romantic poet's thoughts as so *astonishingly* my own is my realization that they were previously portions of a mental world *not* my own, and hence demand thinking *about* now that they are mine. Each poem having constituted itself as a consciousness whose thoughts we are thinking becomes by its final silence a consciousness which now withholds assertion. Which is to say that it has made *us* into an other. By seeing that what the text says is precisely its silence or stillness, in which its self-identity or otherness reposes, we become able to ask what it is we *want* the text to know about itself. Asking this uncovers in turn our own desire to be known, revealing the fear of expressiveness that underlies the epistemological skeptic's reluctance to acknowledge otherness in the first place, his own above all.

All the poets acknowledge this silence, which is basically, in Stanley Cavell's phrase, "what the text knows about itself."[7] Where they differ is in their interpretation of what the silence means. For Blake it expresses the fullness of the Logos, the vision of which is at bottom a religious conversion, an experience of "self-annihilation" leading to rebirth and a new departure. In Coleridge's *Christabel*, no less Christian but considerably more bemused by guilt, the return to silence appears oppositely as a vicious circle reflecting man's cognitive impairment by original sin. In contrast to both, the pragmatic existentialist Byron sees the silence as filled not with good or evil but with myriad amoral possibilities forever cyclically recurring, the Promethean endurance of which defines man's moral voice, however faint. And for the skeptical idealist Shelley, the silence may not be full at all but void and inhuman; plainly it is a motive for metaphor, but whether the ensuing poetry images the truth or shrouds it can be determined only in relation to patently nonepistemological desiderata like hope and love.

Despite their great differences, all four poets aim to transform an originary silence which simply exists, alien and indifferent, the unspoken or unspeakable, not simply into a source of authority but more self-critically into a last resort from the coercive consolidation of authority—hence the constructive role they urge upon the reader, and hence their poems' striving for self-destruction as formal art objects. Such a prolifically decreative poetry is the Romantics' paradoxical solution to the usurping tendency of narrative, its proneness to appropriate reality rather than represent it. Culminating as they do in the reader's return to the concrete human immediacies left behind when his reading began, these poems show that although there are many narrative worlds, each inhabited by a more or less imperfect persona of the self, nevertheless there is only one World—what Wordsworth, whose conspicuous absence from this book perhaps entitles him to the last word, deems "the very world, which is the world / Of all of us,—the place where, in the end, / We find our happiness, or not at all!"[8]

Notes

Introduction

1 I use the word in the sense given it by Stanley Cavell in *The Claim of Reason: Wittgenstein, Skepticism, Morality, and Tragedy* (New York: Oxford Univ. Press, 1979); see esp. pp. 442–51.

2 Edward Said detected an underlying formalist aspect to the Derridean "endless refinement" of textual explication almost a decade ago, in "The Problem of Textuality: Two Exemplary Positions," in *Aesthetics Today*, ed. and rev. Morris Philipson and Paul J. Gudel (New York: New American Library, 1980), p. 87. For a conservative view of Derrida that emphasizes the traditionalism of his methods of reading while rejecting his antilogocentric stance, see M. H. Abrams, "Construing and Deconstructing," in *Romanticism and Contemporary Criticism*, ed. Morris Eaves and Michael Fischer (Ithaca: Cornell Univ. Press, 1986), esp. pp. 138–42. Consolidating such discontents, Frank Lentricchia has recently argued from a new-historicist Marxist perspective that deconstruction "may tell us how we deceive ourselves, but it has no positive content, no alternative textual work to offer to intellectuals. . . . Politically, deconstruction translates into that passive kind of conservatism called quietism; it thereby plays into the hands of established power" (*Criticism and Social Change* [Chicago: Univ. of Chicago Press, 1983], p. 51).

3 Elaine Scarry's frankly polemical *The Body in Pain: The Making and Unmaking of the World* (New York: Oxford Univ. Press, 1985) offers a wide-ranging discussion of the body's various acts and methods of self-representation via the physical world, although her sometimes rigid structuralism casts the argument at a high level of abstraction (rather inappropriately, considering her subject).

4 Jerome J. McGann, *The Romantic Ideology: A Critical Investigation* (Chicago: Univ. of Chicago Press, 1983), p. 71.

5 My position here is best summarized by the reconstructed deconstructionism of Tilottama Rajan in "Displacing Post-Structuralism: Romantic Studies after Paul de Man," *Studies in Romanticism* 24 (1985):451:

> What both post-structuralism and to a large extent deconstruction neglect is the role of the reader in the literary transaction. . . . [Hermeunetics] responds very differently, by calling on the reader to ground as emotional fact what is otherwise only linguistic intention. . . . For the legacy of both de Man and Derrida is that we

cannot now ignore the affinity between writing and other modes of relating to the world, like action, feeling, and reading, which try to escape the figurality of language. Yet even if there is a structural similarity between reading, writing, and feeling, there is also a qualitative difference between them. . . . While psychological and applicative reading are not simple processes, and do not ground the stability of the text any more than does rhetorical reading, they assume (or perhaps create) for literature the affective and referential functions that rhetorical reading suspends. [pp. 468–69]

6   Mary Jacobus, "The Art of Managing Books: Romantic Prose and the Writing of the Past," in *Romanticism and Language*, ed. Arden Reed (Ithaca: Cornell Univ. Press, 1984), p. 237.

7   *The Prelude*, XI, 142–44, in *Selected Poems and Prefaces of Wordsworth*, ed. Jack Stillinger (Boston: Houghton Mifflin Co., 1965), p. 333.

8   John J. Richetti, *Philosophical Writing: Locke, Berkeley, Hume* (Cambridge: Harvard Univ. Press, 1983), pp. 20–21.

Chapter 1

1   David Hume, *A Treatise of Human Nature*, ed. L. A. Selby-Bigge, rev. P. H. Nidditch (1739–40; Oxford: Clarendon Press, 1978), p. 67; henceforth cited as *THN*.

2   *Paradise Lost* IV, 75, in *John Milton: Complete Poems and Major Prose*, ed. Merritt Y. Hughes (New York: Odyssey, 1957), p. 279; henceforth cited as Hughes.

3   S. T. Coleridge, *Biographia Literaria*, ed. James Engell and W. Jackson Bate, 2 vols. (1817; Princeton: Princeton Univ. Press, 1983), 2:240; henceforth cited as *BL*. Also *Poetical Works of Coleridge*, ed. Ernest Hartley Coleridge (1912; London: Oxford Univ. Press, 1973), p. 487. All quotations of Coleridge's poetry are from this edition.

4   *The Triumph of Life*, in *Shelley's Poetry and Prose*, ed. Donald H. Reiman and Sharon B. Powers (New York: Norton, 1977), p. 466. All quotations of Shelley's poetry, as well as the essays "On Love," "On Life," and *The Defence of Poetry* are from this edition, henceforth cited as S. All other references to Shelley's prose are from *Complete Works*, ed. Roger Ingpen and Walter E. Peck (New York: Gordian Press, 1965), henceforth cited as *CW*.

5   A. D. Nuttall, *A Common Sky: Philosophy and the Literary Imagination* (London: Chatto & Windus, 1974), p. 106. See also Richard Kuhns, *Structures of Experience* (New York: Basic Books, 1970), pp. 104–08.

6   Norman Kemp Smith, *The Philosophy of David Hume* (New York: Macmillan, 1964).

7   To put it differently, Kemp Smith's implicit dichotomizing between reason and natural belief suggests that Hume renders the one utterly impotent and grants the other unbounded freedom to determine all the conditions of human experience. If reason is so passive and ineffectual a slave of the passions that reason might as well not exist, then it is easy to view Hume as anticipating the

worst excesses of Romantic irrationalism (although in fact Hume's phrase reflects the thoroughly conventional sentimentalism of his predecessors Shaftesbury and Hutcheson, as Kemp Smith himself would agree).

Richard Popkin's view of Hume as a modern Pyrrhonian, which develops from the naturalist interpretation, makes explicit this conflict in Kemp Smith's Hume; see his "David Hume: His Pyrrhonism and His Critique of Pyrrhonism," in *The High Road to Pyrrhonism*, ed. Richard Watson and James Force (San Diego: Austin Hill, 1980), pp. 103–32. In the writings of Sextus Empiricus, the Pyrrhonian is a philosopher who after much melancholic searching for truth finally concludes that he must suspend judgment; the irony is that after continuing this way for a while he finds himself to be enjoying the same calm of mind he had earlier thought to gain from the truth itself. According to Popkin, however, Hume discovers that feeling and custom make it simply impossible not to have beliefs about such things as causality, the existence of external objects, demonstrative reasoning, and probabilistic reasoning. Thus Hume's modern Pyrrhonism only leads back to the melancholy that suspension of judgment was supposed to have cured.

In contrast to Kemp Smith and Popkin, Donald W. Livingston has recently argued that the relation between reason and feeling in Hume is not polar but dialectical:

> The Pyrrhonian suspension of belief breaks the grip of all philosophical propositions, and the sheer primordial and inarticulate insistence of common life breaks the grip of the Pyrrhonian doubt. . . . The Pyrrhonian illumination shows that there is no Archimedean point outside common life as a whole from which it can be either certified or criticized. We have no alternative, then, but to *use* the prejudices and customs of common life as a framework for understanding the real. (*Hume's Philosophy of Common Life* [Chicago: Univ. of Chicago Press, 1984], pp. 26–31)

For Livingston, this "Pyrrhonian illumination" is reflected in the organization of the *Treatise* as an evolving narrative in which earlier assertions are progressively modified and refined. So, for example, he argues that Humean "perceptions" are not to be considered as ontological givens; rather, they turn out to be "acts of consciousness" meaningful only in the context of Hume's developing investigation into the a priori structure of ideas. And so Hume the phenomenalist yields to Hume the phenomenologist (pp. 48–58). Livingston's approach to the *Treatise* resembles in many respects my own approach to Romantic narrative poetry. This is not really surprising, since he virtually represents Hume as a Romantic manquè: he repeatedly invokes Hegel, tends to view the *Treatise* as a kind of quest-romance, and explicitly terms the concept of "common life" through which Hume's Pyrrhonian crisis is resolved "a transcendental concept."

8   See Richard H. Popkin, *The History of Scepticism from Erasmus to Spinoza* (Berkeley: Univ. of California Press, 1979), pp. 182–92.

9   See Hans Aarsleff, *From Locke to Saussure: Essays on the Study of Language and Intellectual History* (Minneapolis: Univ. of Minnesota Press, 1982), pp. 127–28.

10   John Locke, *An Essay Concerning Human Understanding*, 2 vols., ed. Alexander Campbell Fraser (1690; New York: Dover, 1959), 2:308–11.

11   Alfred North Whitehead, *Process and Reality: An Essay in Cosmology* (1929; New York: Free Press, 1978), p. 133. See his discussion of the above passage from Locke on p. 57ff.

12   Walter Jackson Bate, *From Classic to Romantic: Premises of Taste in Eighteenth Century England* (Boston: Harvard Univ. Press, 1946).

13   Abraham Tucker, *The Light of Nature Pursued*, 2 vols., 5th ed. (1760; London, 1840), 1:17.

14   William Godwin, *Enquiry Concerning Political Justice*, ed. Isaac Kramnick (1798; Baltimore: Penguin, 1976), p. 349.

15   *Areopagitica*, in Hughes, p. 733. Cf. *Paradise Lost* III, 109.

16   Compare Wordsworth's *Prelude*:

> Was it for this
> That one, the fairest of all rivers, loved
> To blend his murmurs with my nurse's song,
> And, from his alder shades and rocky falls,
> And from his fords and shallows, sent a voice
> That flowed along my dreams?   [I, 269–74]

17   G. W. F. Hegel, *On Art, Religion, Philosophy: Introductory Lectures to The Realm of Absolute Spirit*, trans. J. Glenn Gary (New York: Harper, 1970), pp. 57–58.

18   Robert Langbaum, *The Poetry of Experience: The Dramatic Monologue in Modern Literary Tradition* (New York: Norton, 1957), pp. 22–26.

19   Letter to George and Georgiana Keats of February 14–May 3, 1819, in *The Letters of John Keats*, 2 vols., ed. Hyder Edward Rollins (Cambridge: Harvard Univ. Press, 1956), 2:81.

20   Compare Keats's scheme with David Hartley's claim that "some degree of Spirituality is the necessary Consequence of passing through Life. The sensible Pleasures and Pains must be transferred by Association more and more every Day, upon things that afford neither sensible Pleasure nor sensible Pain, and so beget the intellectual Pleasures and Pains." It follows that this process "has a Tendency to reduce the State of those who have eaten of the Tree of knowledge of Good and Evil, back again to a paradisiacal one" (*Observations of Man: His Frame, His Duty, His Expectations* [1749; Gainesville, Fla.: Scholar's Facsimiles and Reprints, 1966], pp. 82–83).

21   Compare Hume's more irritable conclusion: "all the nice and subtile questions of personal identity can never possibly be decided, and are to be regarded rather as grammatical than as philosophical difficulties" (*THN*, p. 262). Cf. also Godwin: "in the emphatical and refined sense in which the word has sometimes been used, there is no such thing as action. Man is in no case, strictly speaking, the beginner of any event or series of events that takes place in the universe, but only the vehicle through which certain antecedents operate" (*Enquiry*, p. 169). Thus the antecedents to Shelley's pronouns—is it a, b, or c?—are always "all of the above": the verse rolls on in cumulative

fashion, like the Chariot of Life itself. Cf. John Ashbery on similar ambiguities in his poetry:

> The personal pronouns in my work very often seem to be like variables in an equation. "You" can be myself or it can be another person, someone whom I'm addressing, and so can "he" and "she" for that matter and "we." . . . my point is that it doesn't really matter very much, that we are somehow all aspects of a consciousness giving rise to the poem and the fact of addressing someone, myself or someone else, is what's the important thing at that particular moment rather than the particular person involved. (Janet Bloom and Robert Losada, "Craft Interview with John Ashbery," *New York Quarterly* 9 [1972]:224–25)

22   Earl R. Wasserman, *Shelley: A Critical Reading* (Baltimore: Johns Hopkins Univ. Press, 1971), p. 146. See Charles E. Robinson's detailed discussion of Shelley's concept of personal identity in *Shelley and Byron: The Snake and Eagle Wreathed in Fight* (Baltimore: Johns Hopkins Univ. Press, 1976), pp. 245–48.

23   Thomas Reid, *An Inquiry into the Human Mind on the Principles of Common Sense*, in *Works*, ed. William Hamilton, 2 vols., 8th ed. (1764; Edinburgh: James Thin, 1895), 1:129; henceforth cited as *CS*.

24   Friedrich Nietzsche, *Beyond Good and Evil*, trans. Walter Kaufmann (New York: Vintage, 1966), pp. 23–24.

25   Reid, *Essays on the Intellectual Powers of Man*, in *Works*, ed. William Hamilton, 2 vols., 8th ed. (1785; Edinburgh: James Thin, 1895), 1:233; henceforth cited as *IP*.

26   Cf. Lord Kames:

> The natural signs of emotion . . . being nearly the same in all men, form a universal language, which no distance of place, no difference of tribe, no diversity of tongue, can darken or render doubtful. . . . if these signs [physical gestures] were, like words, arbitrary and variable, the thoughts and volitions of strangers would be entirely hid from us; which would prove a great, or rather invincible, obstruction to the formation of societies: but, as matters are ordered, the external appearances of joy, grief, anger, fear, shame, and of the other passions, forming an universal language, open a direct avenue to the heart. (*Elements of Criticism* [1762; New York: Collins & Hannay, 1830], p. 195)

27   *The Friend*, ed. Barbara E. Rooke, 2 vols. (1818; Princeton: Princeton Univ. Press, 1969), 1: 509; henceforth cited as *Friend*.

28   Cf. S, p. 477 middle: the paragraph beginning "Let us recollect our sensations as children . . ."

29   The charged memories of Wordsworth's poetry are always subject to the caveat that they be "recollected in tranquillity"—that is, subordinated to the poet's present self, their potential uncanniness mastered and transformed into an egotistical sublime. The fragmenting self-fright generated in Shelley's dream catalog contrasts directly with the famous "Imagination!" apostrophe of *The Prelude* VI, 592–616, where it appears the process of writing about the past serves retrospectively to redeem its disappointments (see Geoffrey Hart-

man's account of the composition of this episode in *Wordsworth's Poetry 1787–1814* [New Haven: Yale Univ. Press, 1964], pp. 42–48; rpt. in *Romanticism and Consciousness*, ed. Harold Bloom [Norton: New York, 1970], pp. 290–95). Yet Wordsworth, too, has moments when writing merely produces self-alienation:

> . . . so wide appears
> The vacancy between me and those days
> Which yet have such self-presence in my mind,
> That, musing on them, often do I seem
> Two consciousnesses, conscious of myself
> And of some other being.   [*Prelude* II, 28–33]

Characteristically, this perturbed admission is prefaced by the stabilizing assurance that "A tranquillizing spirit presses now / On my corporeal frame" (27–28).

30   Somewhat similarly to Paul de Man, Mary Jacobus argues that framing mimesis within more mimesis, even to the point of endless regress, serves to prevent "the doubling whereby mimesis usurps on what it represents." Far from creating a sense of unreality or vertigo, such framing "maintains hierarchy, suspending the illegitimate aspect of representation." In this way the confusion of reality and representation, and the possibly uncanny return of the suppressed distinction between the two—a return liable to undermine our own ground by revealing that we've been living out representations rather than realities—is circumvented ("'That Great Stage Where Senators Perform': *Macbeth* and the Politics of Romantic Theater," *Studies in Romanticism* 22 [1983]: 378).

31   Boswell makes clear that Johnson did not, as is often supposed, merely kick the stone: "I shall never forget the alacrity with which Johnson answered, striking his foot with mighty force against a large stone, till he rebounded from it, 'I refute it thus'" (*Life of Johnson*, ed. George Birkbeck Hill and rev. L. F. Powell, 6 vols. [Oxford: Clarendon Press, 1934–1950] 1:471). Kicking the stone would have reflected the vulgar fallacy that our sensations of objects prove that the objects exist—an assertion hardly able to overturn the immaterialist argument that we can know nothing but those sensations. By contrast, Johnson's point is, as H. F. Hallett pointed out some time ago, that objects demonstrate their external existence by resisting and impeding us ("Dr. Johnson's Refutation of Bishop Berkeley," *Mind* 56 [1947]: 132).

32   Hume, *Letters*, ed. J. Y. T. Greig, 2 vols. (Oxford: Clarendon Press, 1931), 1:12–18. For the identification of Arbuthnot rather than George Cheyne as the intended recipient, see Ernest Mossner, "Hume's Epistle to Dr. Arbuthnot, 1734: The Biographical Significance," *HLQ* 7 (1943):135–52, also his *Life of David Hume*, 2nd ed. (Oxford: Clarendon Press, 1980), pp. 83–85.

33   The phrase echoes throughout the poem, at lines 243–44, 513–14, 597, and 704–05.

34   Hume, "An Abstract of *A Treatise of Human Nature*" (1740), in *THN*, p. 662.

35 For Hume's relationship with his audience, see John Sitter, *Literary Loneliness in Mid-Eighteenth-Century England* (Ithaca: Cornell Univ. Press, 1982), pp. 19–49.

36 Added to p. 97 in Hume's "Appendix," *THN*, p. 629.

37 Friedrich Schlegel, *"Lucinde" and the Fragments*, trans. Peter Firchow (Minneapolis: Univ. of Minnesota Press, 1971), p. 174.

38 Compare the later Heidegger's view that "man dwells in that he builds," and poetry, by "taking a measure for all measuring," gives "the authentic gauging of the dimension of dwelling" (*Poetry, Language, Thought*, trans. Albert Hofstadter [New York: Harper, 1971], p. 227).

39 Keats's "vale of Soul-making," where Heaven is discovered to be the repetition of our earthly pleasures "in a finer tone," builds on Raphael's hint to Adam that earth may be "but the shadow of Heav'n, and things therein / Each to other like, more than on earth is thought."

40 Newell B. Ford, *The Prefigurative Imagination of John Keats* (Stanford: Stanford Univ. Press, 1951), p. 23.

41 These epistemics are clarified by considering Stanley Cavell's recent suggestion that the problem of the hermeneutic circle—namely, that "you cannot understand a text before you know what the text says about itself; but obviously you cannot understand what the text says about itself before you understand the text"—is best reformulated according to the idea that "access to the text is provided not by the mechanism of projection but by that of transference," and "the goal of the encounter is not consummation but freedom" ("Politics as Opposed to What?" *Critical Inquiry* 9 [1982]:175–77).

Chapter 2

1 Anne Mellor, *English Romantic Irony* (Cambridge: Harvard Univ. Press, 1980), p. vii. A toughly critical discussion of Romantic irony, to which I am much indebted, is Peter L. Thorslev, Jr., *Romantic Contraries: Freedom versus Destiny* (New Haven: Yale Univ. Press, 1984), pp. 142–86. A more sympathetic account of Schlegel's relation to Kant, Fichte, and Schelling is Leonard P. Wessel, Jr., "The Antinomic Structure of Friedrich Schlegel's 'Romanticism,'" *Studies in Romanticism* 12 (1973):648.

2 David Simpson, *Irony and Authority in Romantic Poetry* (Totowa, N.J.: Rowman & Littlefield, 1979), pp. 190, 197.

3 Soren Kierkegaard, *The Concept of Irony with Constant Reference to Socrates*, trans. Lee M. Capel (1841; Bloomington: Univ. of Indiana Press, 1965), p. 294.

4 Friedrich Schlegel, *Athenaeum* no. 116, in *"Lucinde" and the Fragments*, trans. Peter Firchow (Minneapolis: Univ. of Minnesota Press, 1971), p. 174; henceforth cited as Firchow.

5 Paul de Man, "The Rhetoric of Temporality," in *Blindness and Insight* (Minneapolis: Univ. of Minnesota Press, 1983), p. 187. The best account of de Man's persistent existentialist metaphysics is, despite its hostility, Frank

Lentricchia, *After the New Criticism* (Chicago: Univ. of Chicago Press, 1980), pp. 283–317. I concur with Lentricchia's finding that de Man's concept of irony "is an empty kind of knowledge which looks suspiciously like cognitive impotence" (p. 296), and that "The Rhetoric of Temporality" looks toward an aesthetic formalism which would "place literary discourse in a realm where it can have no responsibility to historical life" (p. 310). But as my reading of de Man's essay will show, I cannot accept his further objection that de Man tacitly exempts himself from his thematics of blindness. Lentricchia wants to skewer de Man at both ends, condemning him for the severe purity of his formalism *and* for his "pride of historical place" (pp. 287, 290) which vitiates that formalism by producing renewed blindness when, says Lentricchia, de Man generalizes his insights as postmodern demystifications of criticism's Romantic errors.

6   It is perhaps fitting therefore that de Man's point is itself anticipated by the introduction to Hume's *Treatise of Human Nature*, ed. L. A. Selby-Bigge, rev. P. H. Nidditch (1739–40; Oxford: Clarendon Press, 1978), which observes that "those, who pretend to discover any thing new to the world in philosophy and the sciences" customarily "insinuate the praises of their own systems, by decrying all those, which have been advanced before them" (p. xiii). They thus pave the way for their own downfall, for though the predecessor is often enough guilty as charged, invariably the accuser's intemperant rhetorical posturing blinds him to the historically conditioned relationship between their systems. The very vehemence of his attack implies that his discovery is less a break with past ideas than a development and recapitulation of them; so that in the end "'tis not reason, which carries the prize, but eloquence" (p. xiv). Hume's point and de Man's central image are anticipated in their turn by Bacon, who in a famous passage attacks the Scholastics on much the same grounds: "their method . . . rests not so much upon evidence of truth proved by arguments, authorities, similitudes, examples, as upon particular confutations and solutions of every scruple, cavilation, and objection; breeding for the most part one question as fast it solveth another, even as . . . when you carry the light into one corner, you darken the rest" (*Of the Proficience and Advancement of Learning*, in *Works*, ed. James Spedding, 14 vols. [London: Longman's, 1857–74], 6:123). Clearly, de Man's ironic, "postmodern" awareness of how philosophic rationalism becomes subverted by its own rhetoric is powerfully present in the British empiricist tradition from the beginning.

7   For the reading of de Man's essay outlined in this and the subsequent paragraph, I am indebted to several discussions with James Ray Watkins of the University of Texas at Austin and to his M.A. thesis, "Irony Criticism Allegory: 'The Rhetoric of Temporality.'"

8   *The Complete Poetry and Prose of William Blake*, ed. and rev. David Erdman with commentary by Harold Bloom (Garden City, N.J.: Anchor, 1982), p. 3; henceforth cited as E.

9   *Prometheus Unbound* I, 449–51, in *Shelley's Poetry and Prose*, ed. Donald H.

Reiman and Sharon B. Powers (New York: Norton, 1977), p. 149; henceforth cited as S.

10 *Paradise Lost* X, 538–40, in *John Milton: Complete Poems and Major Prose*, ed. Merritt Y. Hughes (New York: Odyssey, 1957), p. 419; henceforth cited as Hughes.

11 John Locke, *An Essay Concerning Human Understanding*, 2 vols., ed. Alexander Campbell Fraser (1690; New York: Dover, 1959), 1:48–49.

12 Alfred North Whitehead, *Process and Reality*, ed. David Ray Griffin and Donald W. Sherburne (1929; New York: Free Press, 1978), pp. 51–60, 138–40; Hans Aarsleff, *The Study of Language in England, 1780–1860* (Minneapolis: Univ. of Minnesota Press, 1983), p. 31; see also his *From Locke to Saussure* (Minneapolis: Univ. of Minnesota Press, 1982), pp. 120–45.

13 Francis Bacon, *De Augmentis Scientiarum*, Book VI, Chap. 1; in *Works*, 4:438–39. Blake's "Proverbs of Hell and Memorable Fancies" recall Bacon's own proverbs and epigrams. Both men revert throughout their work to the myth of the defeated Titans buried under Mount Aetna as punishment for their rebellion but still capable of occasional eruption. For instance, plate 16 of *The Marriage*, which recounts how the insipid reasoning Devourers have used cunning to overthrow the stronger Prolific, recalls Bacon's assertion that "the affections do . . . make such secessions and raise such mutinies and seditions . . . that reason would become captive and servile, if eloquence of persuasions did not win the imagination from the affections' part, and contract a confederacy between the reason and imagination against them" (*Works*, 4:456–57). The difference, of course, is that Blake reads black where Bacon reads white.

14 Blake's intimate antipathy toward Locke can be seen, mutatis mutandis, in his relation to the senescent Wordsworth of the Immortality Ode. By adopting Plato's doctrine of the soul's preexistence, Wordsworth is led implicitly to accept the correlate Platonic doctrine of remembrance, and hence to express much the same skeptical attitude toward worldly knowledge as *The Marriage* does. While this may explain why in Crabb Robinson's report the ode moved Blake to tears, it also points up Blake's fundamental mistrust of Wordsworth. For Wordsworth's skepticism tends in the opposite direction from Blake's, toward a form of deterministic materialism that views the growing child as carried further and further from its vital prenatal source—contradictory adjectives, Blake would say, which show the source to be an impossible abstraction from reality. As an instance of the fallacy of misplaced concreteness, such an ethereal source is in Blake's eyes no more knowable or real than, ironically, matter itself is according to the Lockean epistemology: "what is Calld Corporeal Nobody Knows of its dwelling Place[.] it is in Fallacy & its Existence an Imposture[.] Where is the Existence Out of Mind or Thought[?] Where is it but in the Mind of a Fool" (E, p. 565). The ode begins by identifying the uncorrupted spiritual realm of infancy with a Plotinean "celestial light," but then proceeds to associate that light with the sun whose diurnal course is seen to image human life. Thus it gradually naturalizes and literalizes

its transcendental metaphor. Despite Wordsworth's statement early in the poem that "The Soul that rises with us, our life's Star, / Hath had elsewhere its setting, / And cometh from afar," the eternal Star fades in Shelleyan fashion into the temporal sun, becoming so closely identified with earthly human life that its setting conveys all the finality of death (whereas, strictly considered, the analogy suggests reincarnation, for the sun also rises—unless Wordsworth had in mind a *shooting* star, which would imply an even more drastic determinism). This process climaxes in the last stanza with a surprising but characteristic displacement. The vehicle of the poem's solar metaphor is now shifted onto the tenor, and the adult is shown to be a mere filter whose sole activity consists of tinting the light from the life-source from which he is now alienated: "The Clouds that gather round the setting sun / Do take a sober colouring from an eye / That hath kept watch o'er man's mortality." In contrast, for Blake "every Natural Effect has a Spiritual Cause, and Not / A Natural: for a Natural Cause only seems, it is a Delusion" (E, p. 124). If Wordsworth feels cut off as a result of aging from the divine source of inspiration, that is only because he has, in the words of The Marriage, "forgotten that all deities reside in the human breast."

15 Leopold Damrosch, Jr., *Symbol and Truth in Blake's Myth* (Princeton: Princeton Univ. Press, 1980), pp. 166, 181.

16 Mikhail Bakhtin, *Problems of Dostoevsky's Poetics*, ed. and trans. Caryl Emerson (Minneapolis: Univ. of Minnesota Press, 1984), p. 118.

17 This view of the Devil as liberating is supported by the fact that no chain is visible in copies A, B and C of *The Marriage*.

18 Joseph Antony Wittreich, Jr., *Blake: Angel of Apocalypse* (Madison: Univ. of Wisconsin Press, 1975), p. 205.

19 Wayne Booth, *A Rhetoric of Irony* (Chicago: Univ. of Chicago Press, 1974), p. 59n.

20 Cf. *The Marriage of Heaven and Hell*: "What is now proved was once, only imagin'd" (E, p. 36).

Chapter 3

1 *The Complete Poetry and Prose of William Blake*, ed. and rev. David V. Erdman, with commentary by Harold Bloom (Garden City, N.J.: Anchor, 1982), p. 40; henceforth cited as E.

2 Recent criticism emphasizes Blake's tendency to regard books as dangerous supplements of human form, which they work to bind and objectify. See, for example, Paul Mann, "*The Book of Urizen* and the Horizon of the Book," in *Unnam'd Forms: Blake and Textuality*, ed. Nelson Hilton and Thomas A. Vogler (Berkeley: Univ. of California, 1986), pp. 49–68; see also his discussion of *The Marriage* in "Apocalypse and Recuperation: Blake and the Maw of Commerce," *ELH* 52 (1985):1.

3 Cf. J. M. Murry on the first Memorable Fancy (plates 6–7): "the Devil whom Blake sees is Blake. The flat-sided steep . . . is the copper-plate on which he is writing at this very moment. He traces with corroding fires 'the sentence now

perceived by the minds of men, and read by them on earth.' Blake is simply describing what he is actually doing" (*William Blake* [1933; rpt. New York: McGraw Hill, 1964], pp. 67–68).

4 Cf. Nelson Hilton's remarks on the way words in Blake (Hilton's examples are from *The Marriage*) "strain to become pure graphic form." Although I do not share the premises of Hilton's discussion of polysemy in Blake, I can certainly agree with his conclusion that "The etched and engraved poem is the setting for the death of the reader, a death synonymous with imaginative transformation and rebirth, lamentation and morning" (pun intended) (*Literal Imagination: Blake's Vision of Words* [Berkeley: Univ. of California Press, 1983], pp. 1–27). In a related essay, W. J. T. Mitchell distinguishes between the "book" and the "scroll" in Blake's work: "the book is the symbol of modern rationalist writing and the cultural economy of mechanical reproduction, while the scroll is the emblem of ancient revealed wisdom, imagination, and the cultural economy of hand-crafted, individually expressive artifacts. . . . [Blake's] own texts, it seems clear, are both book and scroll—or neither" ("Visible Language: Blake's Wond'rous Art of Writing," in *Romanticism and Contemporary Criticism*, ed. Morris Eaves and Michael Fischer [Ithaca: Cornell Univ. Press, 1986], pp. 64, 82).

5 In view of Blake's constant attacks on Memory and Fancy, the term "Memorable Fancy" is evidently one of disparagement.

6 See David V. Erdman, *Prophet against Empire* (Princeton: Princeton Univ. Press, 1982), pp. 286–403 passim.

7 A. L. Morton, *The Everlasting Gospel: A Study in the Sources of William Blake* (London: Lawrence & Wishart, 1958), finds numerous parallels between Blake's imagery and that of Ranter and other seventeenth-century antinomian writings.

8 See Textual Notes, E, pp. 816–18. Cf. the letter to Hayley of October 23, 1804: "O the distress I have undergone, and my poor wife with me: incessantly labouring and incessantly spoiling what I had done well. Every one of my friends . . . knew my industry and abstinence from every pleasure for the sake of study, and yet—and yet—and yet there wanted the proofs of industry in my works" (E, pp. 756–57). Such misapplied industry precisely characterizes *The Four Zoas*.

9 Cf. Northrop Frye: "Gorgeous as it unquestionably is, one comes to wonder, in studying it, how far this Night Ninth is the real climax of the vision, and how far it has been added as an effort of will, perhaps almost of conscience" (*Fearful Symmetry* [Princeton: Princeton Univ. Press, 1947], p. 308). Bloom senses much the same thing in *Blake's Apocalypse* (Ithaca: Cornell Univ. Press, 1963), pp. 283–84. For a radically different assessment of the poem—based, however, on a view similar to the one I am proposing in this book for Romantic narrative generally, namely, that "narrative, text, and reader interconstitute one another ontologically"—see Donald Ault, "Re-Visioning *The Four Zoas*," in *Unnam'd Forms*, pp. 105–39, esp. 130–31.

10 See, e.g., "Auguries of Innocence:" "If the Sun & Moon should doubt / They'd immediately Go out." Or more ponderously, *Jerusalem*: "What seems

to Be: Is: To those to whom / It seems to Be, & is productive of the most dreadful / Consequences to those to whom it seems to Be: even of / Torments, Despair, Eternal Death" (32:51–54).

11   For *Milton*'s dates of composition, see E, p. 806. For the quarrel with Hayley, see Frye, pp. 327–32; also Margaret Storch's psychoanalytical examination, "The 'Spectrous Fiend' Cast Out: Blake's Crisis at Felpham," *Modern Language Quarterly* 44 (1983):115. The best factual account remains Mona Wilson, *The Life of Blake*, rev. ed. (1927; London: Oxford Univ. Press, 1971), pp. 145–79 passim.

12   Blake enforces his doctrinal point by making the speaker of these lines the Devil himself. Lucifer's essential human identity, reposing strengthless on its Death Couch in Eternity while the State of Satan prevails on Earth, still pronounces uncorrupted wisdom.

13   James Reiger, " 'The Hem of Their Garments': The Bard's Song in *Milton*," in *Blake's Sublime Allegory*, ed. Stuart Curran and J. A. Wittreich, Jr. (Madison: Univ. of Wisconsin Press, 1973), p. 277.

14   Susan Fox, *Poetic Form in Blake's "Milton"* (Princeton: Princeton Univ. Press, 1976), p. 24. Fox claims the two books of *Milton* are parallel in the manner of Milton's "l'Allegro" and "Il Penseroso." Yet Milton's poems are organized precisely to thwart our expectation that they will each describe complementary twenty-four-hour cycles. At the end of "Il Penseroso," in a passage that finds no counterpart in "l'Allegro" and which therefore disrupts their match-up by making "Il Penseroso" some twenty lines longer, Penseroso's daily routine prophetically opens out to encompass an entire lifetime and indeed a portion of eternity itself ("And bring all heaven before mine eyes"). It would thus appear that Allegro's worldly pleasures are subsumed and redeemed through Penseroso's moment of vision.

　　Fox's structuralist reading evidently follows from Northrop Frye's discussion of the relationship of theme to narrative: "Theme *is* narrative, but narrative seen as a simultaneous unity. At a certain point in the narrative, the point which Aristotle calls *anagnorisis* or recognition, the sense of linear continuity or participation in the action changes perspective, and what we now see is a total design or unifying structure in the narrative. . . . The elements of the narrative thereupon regroup themselves in a new way" ("The Road of Excess," in *Romanticism and Consciousness*, ed. Harold Bloom [New York: Norton, 1970], p. 123). But in emphasizing the simultaneity of *Milton*'s narrative action, Fox adopts the synchronic perspective of the visionary moment rather than the temporal perspective of the poet or reader. As a result, I believe she slights the importance of the poem's anagnorisis.

15   W. J. T. Mitchell, "Blake's Radical Comedy: Dramatic Structure as Meaning in *Milton*," in *Sublime Allegory*, p. 307. See also his "Style and Iconography in the Illustrations of Blake's *Milton*," *Blake Studies* 6 (1973):1.

16   *Friedrich Schlegel's "Lucinde" and the Fragments*, trans. Peter Firchow (Minneapolis: Univ. of Minnesota Press, 1971), p. 167.

17   S. Foster Damon, *William Blake: His Philosophy and Symbols* (1924; Gloucester, Mass.: Peter Smith, 1958), p. 175.

18   M. H. Abrams, "Structure and Style in the Greater Romantic Lyric," in *From*

Sensibility to Romanticism: Essays Presented to Frederick A. Pottle, ed. Frederick W. Hilles and Harold Bloom (New York: Oxford Univ. Press, 1965), p. 527. Rpt. in *Romanticism and Consciousness*, p. 201.

19 Joseph Antony Wittreich, Jr., "Opening the Seals: Blake's Epics and the Milton Tradition," in *Sublime Allegory*, p. 23. See also his *Blake: Angel of Apocalypse* (Madison: Univ. of Wisconsin Press, 1975), pp. 221–50, 167–70.

20 Cf. Harold Bloom, "The Internalization of Quest Romance," in *Romanticism and Consciousness*, p. 3.

21 The most dynamic analysis to date of *Milton*'s opening plates seems to me Christine Gallant's, although it is marred by Jungian terminology; see her *Blake and the Assimilation of Chaos* (Princeton: Princeton Univ. Press, 1978), pp. 119–23.

22 Friedrich Nietzsche, *Beyond Good and Evil*, trans. Walter Kaufmann (New York: Random House, 1966), pp. 25–26. For a similar but more Whiteheadian discussion of the visceral, "vector" quality of imaginative perception in Blake, see Donald D. Ault, *Visionary Physics: Blake's Response to Newton* (Chicago: Univ. of Chicago Press, 1974), esp. pp. 72–75, 96–97, 174–79, and 194–95.

23 The line appears at 2:25, 3:5, 4:20, 7:16, 9:7, and 11:31.

24 The different versions of *Milton* are explained in E, p. 806. It seems to me that modern editors cannot have the poem both ways without distorting it; they must bring themselves to choose between the preface and the additional plates.

25 While the episode of Satan and Leutha clearly revises Satan's encounter with Sin in *Paradise Lost* III, 745–65, Leutha's origins also seem distinctly Homeric. The letter to Butts of April 25, 1803, describes a poem which is evidently *Milton* and then mentions that it centers around "One Grand Theme Similar to Homers Iliad" (E, p. 728). The warfare at 8:38–41 is plainly modeled on the Homeric pattern whereby injured or overtasked heroes are rescued by a guardian deity. Leutha's story is a psychologized version of the Anger of Achilles, with herself as a Briseis usurped from Satan-Achilles by Palamabron-Agamemnon. Also as in Homer, Los convenes a Great Assembly to judge between the two warriors, and it wrongly condemns the enraged Satan, who then retaliates, like Achilles, by withdrawing from the other heroes, thereby weakening their forces.

26 *Paradise Lost* VII, 16–24, in *John Milton: Complete Poems and Major Prose*, ed. Merritt Y. Hughes (New York: Odyssey, 1957), p. 346; all Milton quotations are from this edition.

27 See Erdman, *Prophet against Empire*, pp. 294, 298.

28 The slogan also appears, again with reference to Hayley, in the letter to Butts of April 25, 1803.

29 See Stanley Fish, *Surprised by Sin: The Reader in "Paradise Lost"* (Berkeley: Univ. of California Press, 1971), chap. 4, "Standing Only: Christian Heroism," pp. 158–207.

30 Cf. Bloom, "Commentary," E, p. 918. Erdman similarly terms Ololon "history-as-it-should-have-been" in *Prophet against Empire*, p. 423.

31 Hence Milton does not defeat Urizen, the tyrant of law, until he embraces

Ololon and becomes Jesus. The letter to Butts of November 22, 1802, intimates that Blake's resolution of his personal crisis at the time of Felpham involved an Evangelical awakening: "Tho I have been very unhappy I am so no longer[.] I am again Emerged into the light of Day[.] I still & shall to Eternity Embrace Christianity and Adore him who is the Express image of God but I have traveld thro Perils & Darkness not unlike a Champion" (E, p. 720)—not unlike Milton, that is, or not unlike the Blake-poet of *Milton*.

32 Compare 31:12–27 with the Nativity Ode, sts. 21–22, and 31:46–64, with *Lycidas*, ll. 132–51.

33 *The Book of Thel* similarly shows a young virgin progressing through different states of being (lily, cloud, worm, clay) toward womanhood. But selfgrowth entails self-annihilation—Thel's path to maturity literally lies through the grave of her childhood—and this she cannot accept; recoiling from her death couch in Beulah, she flees back to the realms of innocence. Thel is the prototypical Daughter of Beulah, just as *The Book of Thel*, the earliest of the engraved Prophetic Books, represents Blake's first effort under supervision of the anxious Beulah muse. Thus when *Milton*'s Ololon returns to her death couch in "humiliation and sorrow" (35:33) and, unlike her virgin predecessor, bravely confronts "the Void Outside of Existence, which if enterd into / Becomes a Womb" (41:37–42:1), Blake is in a sense annihilating and reconceiving some fifteen years of mythologizing.

34 See Martha W. England, "Apprenticeship at the Haymarket?" in *Blake's Visionary Forms Dramatic*, ed. David V. Erdman and John E. Grant (Princeton: Princeton Univ. Press, 1970), p. 3.

35 As in the standard formula for the new dispensation, e.g., John 7.6: "My time is not come, your time is always ready."

36 The lines dramatize this fusion of the verbal and the physical through a revealed pun: "the Litteral Expression" is both "actual, nonallegorical" and "comprised of letters"—as well as "littoral," reflecting the fact that Blake's visions occur for the most part "upon mild Felpham shore" (38:13).

37 Morris Eaves, *William Blake's Theory of Art* (Princeton: Princeton Univ. Press, 1982), p. 183.

Chapter 4

1 David Hume, *A Treatise of Human Nature*, ed. L. A. Selby-Bigge, rev. P. H. Nidditch (1739–40; Oxford: Clarendon Press, 1978), p. 415; henceforth cited as *THN*.

2 William Godwin, *Enquiry concerning Political Justice*, ed. Isaac Kramnick (1798; Baltimore: Penguin, 1976), p. 364.

3 *Milton* 21:8–11, in *The Complete Poetry and Prose of William Blake*, ed. and rev. David V. Erdman with commentary by Harold Bloom (Garden City, N.J.: Anchor, 1982), p. 11; henceforth cited as E.

4 René Descartes, *Philosophical Works*, trans. Elizabeth Haldane and G. R. T. Ross, 2 vols. (1641; Cambridge: Cambridge Univ. Press, 1931), 1:150.

5 Coleridge, *Biographia Literaria*, ed. James Engell and W. Jackson Bate, 2

vols. (Princeton: Princeton Univ. Press, 1983), 1:285–86; cf. also 1:272–80 and editorial notes; henceforth cited as *BL*. Paul Valéry similarly regards the *cogito ergo sum* as "like a clarion sounded by Descartes to summon up the powers of his ego"—in other words, as simply a starting point for the mind's act of self-attention (*Masters and Friends*, trans. Martin Turnbull [Princeton: Princeton Univ. Press, 1968], p. 31).

6   Significantly, Blake supports this definition of imagination with a quotation from Bacon's *Advancement of Learning*: "Consider what Lord Bacon says[:] 'Sense sends over to Imagination before Reason have judged & Reason sends over to Imagination before the Decree can be acted.' "

7   *An Essay on Criticism*, II, 297–317, in *Poetical Works of Pope*, ed. Herbert Davis (London: Oxford Univ. Press, 1966), pp. 72–73.

8   Coleridge, "On Method," in *The Friend*, ed. Barbara E. Rooke, 2 vols (1818; Princeton: Princeton Univ. Press, 1969), 1:451–53.

9   Cf. Northrop Frye's influential distinction between an Augustan prose "literature of finished product" and a pre-Romantic literature of "poetic process," in "Towards Defining an Age of Sensibility," in *Eighteenth-Century English Literature: Modern Essays in Criticism*, ed. James L. Clifford (New York: Oxford Univ. Press, 1959), p. 311. Rpt. in Frye, *Fables of Identity: Studies in Poetic Mythology* (New York: Harcourt, 1963), p. 130.

10   Samuel Johnson, *Poems*, ed. David Nichol Smith and Edward L. McAdam (Oxford: Clarendon Press, 1974), p. 115.

11   F. R. Leavis, *Revaluation* (London: Chatto & Windus, 1936), pp. 111–12.

12   Samuel Johnson, "Life of Milton," in *Lives of the English Poets*, ed. John Wain (London: Dent, 1975), p. 101.

13   One glimpses such schizophrenia in the *Alastor* Poet's momentary panic that his suicidal thoughts have been put into his head by a demon (lines 290–98).

14   Cf. Steven Knapp, who argues that "the antithetical structure" of eighteenth-century personification anticipates a Kantian aesthetic of the sublime: "sublime personifications uniquely balance the conflicting criteria of power and distance required by the enlightened stance of urbane admiration. With its individuality utterly absorbed by the ideal it embodies, the personification is the perfect fanatic. It is both devoid of empirical consciousness and perfectly, formally conscious of itself. But the reassuring condition of such perfection is its sheer and obvious fictionality" (*Personification and the Sublime: Milton to Coleridge* [Cambridge: Harvard Univ. Press, 1985], p. 83). Arguing that much later eighteenth-century literature strives to present itself as, in Frye's terms, both "product" and "process," Fredric V. Bogel similarly finds that "Collins' moments of encounter are subtly pervaded by the ambiguity of presence and absence that resides in the structure of the invocation. The typical rhetorical situation of his poems is neither a pure confronting of absence nor a plenary experience of archaic powers but the calling into fuller being and substantiality of powers at once present and dim, or perceptible yet distant" (*Literature and Insubstantiality in Later Eighteenth-Century England* [Princeton: Princeton Univ. Press, 1984], p. 89).

15   *Poetical Works of Gray and Collins*, ed. Austin Poole (London: Oxford Univ.

Press, 1966), p. 321 (cited from the slightly different second edition of the poem).

16 A. S. P. Woodhouse, "The Poetry of Collins Reconsidered," in *From Sensibility to Romanticism: Essays Presented to Frederick A. Pottle*, ed. Frederick W. Hilles and Harold Bloom (New York: Oxford Univ. Press, 1965), pp. 91–98, 122–23. See also Earl Wasserman, "Collins's 'Ode on the Poetical Character,'" *ELH* 34 (1967), p. 98.

17 Paul H. Fry argues that Collins's efforts to recover originary power lead him to conflate a Platonic "blueprint" theory of creation, where the Creator "invokes the universe" in thought much like a poet, with the subsequent "weaving" and veiling whereby the actual phenomena are constituted in a process analogous to the actual writing of poetry. Consequently, "there can be no Crocean distinction between receiving and creating a stamp; that is, between impression and expression. Inspiration itself becomes chirographic, a sexless imprint upon Locke's sensorium that simultaneously enables and unmans Collins's ideal of chaste independence. As a result, Collins's experiments with the personified fusion of spirit and ground reduce all signification to a single plane; there is no difference between 'blueprint' and building, or between 'calling with thought' and weaving the birth of the universe" (*The Poet's Calling in the English Ode* [New Haven: Yale Univ. Press, 1980], pp. 127–28; see also pp. 106, 115–16). Hence the charged sensory vividness of Collins's personifications springs not from their intimacy with the concrete particulars of experience but from the poet's nervousness to suppress any such relationship. The numinous effect of:

> Long, Pity, let the Nations view
> Thy sky-worn Robes of tend'rest Blue
> And Eyes of dewy Light

or

> Vengeance in the lurid Air
> Lifts her red Arm, expos'd and bare

arises from the absence of any definite background against which to locate and focus these figures—hence their solipsistic evocativeness. Pity perhaps suggests the Virgin Mary, Vengeance Clytemnestra, but upon closer inspection each merely melts into the surrounding imagery. Pity's robes *are* the evening sky in which she walks forth, and the red arm of Vengeance *is* the lurid air in which Vengeance looms.

The metaphysical basis for this conflation is given in A. D. Nuttall's observation of a paradoxically Platonic strain within Locke: "in a way Locke out-Plato's Plato; for although Plato's forms inhabit their proper heaven they are less completely inaccessible than Locke's reality. . . . while Plato ascribed reality to the stable objects of knowledge and denied it to the fluctuating objects of sense, Locke denied reality to ideas and reserved it for a physical world which could never be observed" (*A Common Sky: Philosophy and the Literary Imagination* [London: Sussex Univ. Press, 1974], p. 19).

18 Wallace Jackson, *The Probable and the Marvellous: Blake, Wordsworth, and the Eighteenth-Century Critical Tradition* (Athens: Univ. of Georgia Press, 1978), p. 5.

19 Steven Knapp's emphasis on the deliberately theatrical, even farcical aspects of the "Ode to Fear" usefully corrects the assumption that the poem's occasionally hysterical tone anticipates the author's later madness (*Personification and the Sublime*, pp. 87–97).

20 Cf. Walter Jackson Bate: "Finally why, in our dissatisfactions, do we so strongly clutch at deterministic explanations that relieve us from the burden of deciding not only what we most want but what we can and should do about it? Could this not be the real 'burden' after all—not determinism, but the burden of choice?" (*The Burden of the Past and the English Poet* [New York: Norton, 1970], pp. 66–67).

21 Thomas Gray, *Poetical Works of Gray and Collins*, ed. Austin Poole (London: Oxford Univ. Press, 1937), pp. 33–34.

22 The balanced irony of the poem's concluding lines reflects the Pyrrhonian skeptic's suspension of judgment. Sextus Empiricus discusses the formula "No more" as signifying " 'One thing not more than another' . . . whereby because of the equal validity of the objects opposed we come in the end to a state of equilibrium. . . . By 'equilibrium' we mean an assent to neither. The formula 'No more,' for instance . . . we employ . . . in lieu of saying, 'I do not know to which alternative I ought to assent, and to which I ought not' " (*Selections from the Major Writings on Scepticism, Man, and God*, ed. Philip P. Hallie, trans. Sanford G. Etheridge [Indianapolis: Hackett, 1985], pp. 79–80).

23 Cf. Bertrand H. Bronson: the poet "has so long ceased to mention himself that we have been projecting into his lines our own identity, so that it is *our* voice which has been speaking our own train of thought all this while. It seems, therefore, perfectly natural to be addressing another as 'thee' " ("On a Special Decorum in Gray's *Elegy*," in *From Sensibility to Romanticism*, p. 176).

24 Similarly, the Eton College Ode asserts, "To each his suff'rings: all are men, / Condemn'd alike to groan," and suggests that those unselfish enough to surmount their own pain through sympathy with another's merely succumb to that other's pain as if it were their own.

25 "On Life," in *Shelley's Poetry and Prose*, ed. Donald H. Reiman and Sharon B. Powers (New York: Norton, 1977), pp. 477–78; henceforth cited as S.

26 Preface to *Lyrical Ballads*, 2nd ed. (1800), in *Selected Poems and Prefaces of Wordsworth*, ed. Jack Stillinger (Boston: Houghton Mifflin Co., 1965), p. 448.

27 Alfred North Whitehead, *Process and Reality: An Essay in Cosmology*, ed. and rev. David Ray Griffin and Donald W. Sherburne (1929; New York: Free Press, 1978), p. 211.

28 David Erdman has noted that "the momentary effects of dismay upon the Preface of *Jerusalem* remain even in the most brightly-coloured copy, remained perhaps in [Blake's] own will—for he could, after all, have made a new plate" ("The Suppressed and Altered Passages in Blake's *Jerusalem*,"

Studies in Bibliography 17 [1964]:10). Cf. David Simpson's suggestion that here and in the curious delete signs which Erdman recently found to be fitted to certain letters in *The Ghost of Abel*, "we can even see Blake writing *sous rature*, or under erasure" ("Reading Blake and Derrida: Our Caesars Neither Praised nor Buried," in *Unnam'd Forms: Blake and Textuality*, ed. Nelson Hilton and Thomas A. Vogler [Berkeley: Univ. of California, 1986], p. 14).

29   In this sense, *Jerusalem* returns to the fragmented organization of *The Marriage of Heaven and Hell*. Cf. Morris Eaves: "A missing God at the center of *The Marriage*, in fact, largely accounts for its odd structure, which is a series of apparently disconnected episodes tied less to each other than to the invisible God at the center" (*William Blake's Theory of Art* [Princeton: Princeton Univ. Press, 1982], p. 23).

30   Stanley Cavell, *The Claim of Reason: Wittgenstein, Skepticism, Morality, and Tragedy* (New York: Oxford Univ. Press, 1979), p. 369.

31   *Collected Letters of Coleridge*, ed. E. L. Griggs, 4 vols. (Oxford: Oxford Univ. Press, 1957–71), 4:836. Leopold Damrosch, Jr., also notes "the paradox of Blake's pictorial treatment of the body: whereas visible clothes are generally negative symbols (especially Vala's veil), the body itself is a form of clothing, so that although in visual terms nakedness is good, in philosophical terms the true spiritual existence is attained by taking off the garment of the body" (*Symbol and Truth in Blake's Myth* [Princeton: Princeton Univ. Press, 1980], p. 192).

32   *Don Juan* II, clxii, clxxxix, in *Poetical Works of Byron*, ed. Frederick Page, 3rd ed. (Oxford: Oxford Univ. Press, 1970), pp. 679, 682.

33   A somewhat similar reading of "Infant Joy" is adumbrated by Robert F. Gleckner in *Blake and Spenser* (Baltimore: Johns Hopkins Univ. Press, 1985), pp. 129–30.

34   Robert Nozick, *Philosophical Explanations* (Cambridge: Belknap, 1981), p. 220.

35   See Richard Rorty, *Philosophy and the Mirror of Nature* (Princeton: Princeton Univ. Press, 1979), esp. pp. 38–69.

36   Stuart Sperry, *Keats the Poet* (Princeton: Princeton Univ. Press, 1983), pp. 191–92.

37   *The Letters of John Keats*, ed. Hyder Edward Rollins, 2 vols. (Cambridge: Harvard Univ. Press, 1958), 1:369, 387.

38   See O. K. Bouwsma, "Descartes' Skepticism of the Senses," in *Philosophical Essays on Dreaming*, ed. Charles E. M. Dunlop (Ithaca: Cornell Univ. Press, 1977), p. 52.

39   *The Fall of Hyperion* I, 11–15, in *The Poems of John Keats*, ed. Jack Stillinger (Cambridge: Belknap, 1978), p. 478.

40   *Poetical Works of Coleridge*, ed. Ernest Hartley Coleridge (London: Oxford Univ. Press, 1973), p. 216.

41   Compare Freud's assertion of his "difference from a superstitious person: . . . I believe in external (real) chance, it is true, but not in internal (psychical) accidental events." Where the one sees "an omen, the finger of fate," Freud sees only "an accident without any further meaning." On the other hand, if he

should have the accident "while 'deep in thought,' or through 'absent-mind-edness,'" then he would regard it not "as an accident but as an action that had an unconscious aim and required interpretation" (*The Psychopathology of Everyday Life*, in *Standard Edition of the Complete Works of Freud*, trans. James Strachey, 24 vols. [London: Hogarth, 1960], 6:257–58). While agree-ing with Freud's conclusion that "a large part of the mythological view of the world . . . is nothing but psychology projected into the external world," the poets would perhaps point out that a psychological explanation does not *preclude* a supernatural one. It could be precisely *because* Christabel, Lycius, the *Alastor* Poet, and others are so self-absorbed that they become vulnerable to supernatural influence.

Chapter 5

1   G. Wilson Knight, *The Starlit Dome* (London: Oxford Univ. Press, 1941), p. 83.
2   *Poetical Works of Coleridge*, ed. Ernest Hartley Coleridge (London: Oxford Univ. Press, 1973), pp. 215–16. All quotations of Coleridge's poetry are from this edition. For the ensuing account of the mastiff bitch, I am heavily indebted to Edward Dramin, "'Amid the Jagged Shadows': Parody, Moral Realism, and Metaphysical Statements in Coleridge's Christabel" (Ph.D. Diss., Columbia Univ. 1972), a condensed version of which appeared as "'Amid the Jagged Shadows': *Christabel* and the Gothic Tradition," *Words-worth Circle* 13 (1982):221.
3   *Examiner*, June 2, 1816, pp. 348–49. Rpt. in *Coleridge: The Critical Heri-tage*, ed. J. R. de J. Jackson (New York: Barnes & Noble, 1970), p. 206; henceforth cited as *CH*.
4   William Roberts, *British Review*, viii, August 1816, 64–81; in *CH*, p. 225.
5   *Selected Poems and Prefaces by William Wordsworth*, ed. Jack Stillinger (Boston: Houghton Mifflin Co., 1965), p. 69; henceforth cited as *W*.
6   Jane Austen, *Northanger Abbey and Persuasion*, ed. John Davie (London: Oxford Univ. Press, 1971), p. 177.
7   Elsewhere Coleridge observes that "pretensions to the supernatural . . . one and all have this for their essential character, that the Spirit is made the immediate object of sense or sensation." This "absurdity" is "more or less offensive to the taste" (*Aids to Reflection*, 2nd ed., 1840 [1825; Port Wash-ington, N.Y.: Kennikat, 1971], p. 113).
8   Thomas Moore, *Edinburgh Review*, xxvii, September 1816, 58–67; in *CH*, pp. 229–30.
9   Humphrey House, *Coleridge: The Clark Lectures, 1951–52* (London: Hart-Davis, 1953), p. 124.
10 Cf. Mary Jacobus's description of Wordsworth's "The Idiot Boy" as a "bur-lesque of the supernatural ballad" in which "the reader is teased for wanting to be thrilled or scared" (*Tradition and Experiment in Wordsworth's "Lyri-cal Ballads" (1798)* [Oxford: Clarendon, 1976], pp. 251–52). Further, Carl Woodring notes that Wordsworth's "first stanza, beginning ' 'Tis eight o'clock,—a clear March night,' resembles the first stanza of *Christabel*. Of the

same date, each evokes by onomatopoeia the shout of an owl. Both poems, throughout, employ such devices of medieval ballads and romances as the rhetorical question" (*Wordsworth* [Cambridge: Harvard Univ. Press, 1968], p. 29). In the comic Part I, at least, *Christabel* is Coleridge's "Idiot Boy." Indeed, Coleridge's exuberant recitals of his poem while hiking the Harz Mountains in 1799 sound gleefully tongue-in-cheek; as the impervious Dr. Carlyon recalled, "At the conclusion of . . . the first stanza . . . he would perhaps comment at full length upon such a line as—'Tu-whit!—Tu-whoo!' that we might not fall into the mistake of supposing originality to be its sole merit[!!!]" (Clement Carlyon, *Early Years and Late Reflections* [London: 1836], p. 134). Coleridge's reported reaction to *Blackwood's* 1819 takeoff is revealing: "I laughed heartily . . . [but] it is in appearance, and in appearance only, a good imitation; I do not doubt but that it gave more pleasure, and to a greater number, than a continuation by myself in the spirit of the two first cantos" (*The Table Talk and Omniana of Samuel Taylor Coleridge*, ed. T. Ashe [London: George Bell, 1884], p. 314). The insinuation is evidently that the *Blackwood's* parody appears successful for precisely the reason that it is in reality a failure—namely, its ignorance that *Christabel* is *already* a parody.

11   *Critical Review*, August 1794, ii, 361–72; rpt. in Garland Greever, *A Wiltshire Parson and His Friends* (London: Constable, 1926), p. 169. Greever includes Coleridge's other reviews from the *Critical Review* of February 1797, 194–200; June 1798, 166–69; and August 1798, 442.

12   *Critical Review*, June 1798; and letter to Wordsworth of January 23, 1798, in *Collected Letters of Coleridge*, ed. E. L. Griggs, 4 vols. (Oxford: Oxford Univ. Press, 1956–71), 1:378; henceforth cited as *CL*.

13   See Thomas MacFarland, *Coleridge and the Pantheist Tradition* (Oxford: Oxford Univ. Press, 1956), pp. 1–52.

14   Arthur H. Nethercot, *The Road to Tryermaine* (New York: Russell, 1939), pp. 189, 198–201. Influential as it has been, Nethercot's argument directly contradicts the opening premise of Coleridge's review of *The Monk*: "The horrible and the preternatural . . . can never be required except by the torpor of an unawakened, or the languor of an exhausted, appetite" (Greever, p. 191).

15   Donald R. Tuttle, "*Christabel* Sources in Percy's *Reliques* and Gothic Romance," *PMLA* 53 (1938):445.

16   Matthew G. Lewis, *The Monk* (1794; New York: Grove, 1952), pp. 98–100.

17   Coleridge's speculations on this rumor appear in *CL*, 4:917–18.

18   *The Diary of William Polidori*, ed. W. Rossetti (1911), entry for June 18, 1816; cited in Richard Holmes, *Shelley: The Pursuit* (London: Chaucer Press, 1974), pp. 328–29.

19   Consider, for example, Lewis's note at the end of "The Cloud-King," a tale where the heroine overtasks the seemingly omnipotent Cloud-King and his demons by first commanding him to restore her lover, "the truest of lovers," and then commanding him to show her yet "a truer" one:

> Lest my readers should mistake the drift of the foregoing tale, and suppose its moral to rest upon the danger in which Romilda was involved by her insolence and

presumption, I think it necessary to explain, that my object in writing this story was to show young ladies that it might possibly, now and then, be of use to understand a little grammar; and it must be clear to every one, that my heroine would infallibly have been devoured by the demons, if she had not luckily understood the difference between the comparative and superlative degrees. (*Tales of Terror and Wonder*, intro. Henry Morley [London: Routledge & Sons, 1887], p. 167)

Furthermore, in Lewis's "Introductory Dialogue" to *Tales of Terror*, the Friend urges objections to the Author's excesses in exactly the same moralistic terms as Coleridge uses in his reviews:

These active pandars to perverted taste
Shall mar their purpose by too anxious haste.

. . .

The vicious taste, with such a rich supply
Quite surfeited, "will sicken, and so die." [p. 10]

For a valuable account of the phenomenal but short-lived success of William Bürger's "Lenore," its various English translations, and the sense of parody to which the poem soon gave rise, see Mary Jacobus, *Tradition and Experiment*, pp. 215–24.

20 William Empson, Introduction to *Coleridge's Verse: A Selection*, ed. Empson and David Pirie (New York: Schocken, 1972), p. 62; Leslie Brisman, "Coleridge and the Supernatural," *Studies in Romanticism* 21 (1982):159.

21 *Aids to Reflection*, 2nd ed., 1840 (1825; Port Washington, N.Y.: Kennikat, 1971), p. 113; henceforth cited as *AR*.

22 *The Notebooks of Samuel Taylor Coleridge*, ed. Kathleen Coburn, 3 vols. (New York: Pantheon, 1957), 2, entry 2509; henceforth cited as *N*.

23 Arguing that the hostile reactions of contemporary reviewers disclose their fear of being rendered passive and "feminized" by the poem's ability "to hold the reader as if it were his *own* dream or fantasy," Karen Swann demonstrates that despite their attempts to reduce the poem to "a derided genre (the Gothic) and gender (the feminine), . . . it is the poem which contains its critics, whose two responses to it—a spellbound accession to play and a petrified and petrifying refusal of exchange—are figured in the text" ("Literary Gentlemen and Lovely Ladies: The Debate on the Character of *Christabel*," *ELH* 52 (1985):406–07).

24 Arthur Lovejoy, "Coleridge and Kant's Two Worlds," in *Essays in the History of Ideas* (Baltimore: Johns Hopkins Univ. Press, 1948), pp. 254–55.

25 Edward E. Bostetter, *The Romantic Ventriloquists* (Seattle: Univ. of Washington Press, 1963), pp. 8, 118, 123.

26 *John Milton: Complete Poems and Major Prose*, ed. Merritt Y. Hughes (New York: Odyssey, 1957), p. 105. Martin Bidney's "*Christabel* as Dark Double of *Comus*," *Studies in Philology* 83 (1986):182, points out numerous comparisons between the two poems, concluding that "strong verbal echoes and parallels of imagery show that Coleridge wishes not only to emphasize elements of metaphysical dualism in Milton's poem, but to augment or intensify them whenever possible. . . . In *Christabel*, metaphysical pessimism

prevails" (p. 195). I concur with Bidney's observation but reject his assessment of it. Coleridge indeed emphasizes a dualistic, even "Gnostic" separation of good and evil—at least in Part I of *Christabel*—but only in order to demonstrate our need to interpret such metaphysical absolutes in moral and psychological terms. Metaphysical pessimism prevails only if one takes the poem's surface of irrational gothic supernaturalism as a literal portrayal of the moral conditions of earthly life.

27 Cf. *The Friend*, ed. Barbara E. Rooke, 2 vols. (1818; Princeton: Princeton Univ. Press, 1969), 1:103: "it be a truth, attested alike by common feeling and common sense, that the greater part of human misery depends directly on human vices and the remainder indirectly."

28 Cf. *N* 1, entry 1717: "My will & I seem perfect Synonimes—whatever does not apply to the first, I refuse to the latter / —Any thing strictly of outward Force I refuse to acknowledge, as done *by* me / it is done *with* me." Thus Coleridge notes of the alchemists: "The supposed exercise of magical power always involved some moral guilt, directly or indirectly" (*Literary Remains*, ed. Henry Nelson Coleridge, 4 vols. [1836; New York: AMS Press, 1967], 1:209; henceforth cited as *LR*. Coleridge's observations of his opium despondency closely describe Christabel, who like him is "in a moral *marasmus* from negatives—from misdemeanours of Omission, and from Weakness & moral cowardice of moral Pain" (*CL* 3:48). Empson's Introduction to *Coleridge's Verse* likewise considers the spell cast by the dead sailors upon the Ancient Mariner to be a function of "neurotic guilt." Cf. also Coleridge's letter of March 12, 1811: "Moral obligation is to me so very strong a Stimulant, that in 9 cases out of ten it acts as a Narcotic. The Blow that should rouse, *stuns* me" (*CL* 3:307).

29 *Biographia Literaria*, ed. James Engell and W. Jackson Bate, 2 vols. (1817; Princeton, Princeton Univ. Press, 1983), 2:6.

30 For an examination of the poem's many parallels with *Paradise Lost*, see my unpublished article, "From Stereotypes to Truth: Christabel as Ironic Miltonic Eve."

31 Carl Woodring, "Christabel of Cumberland," *Review of English Studies* 7 (1966): 43.

32 Compare the opening lines of William Bürger's celebrated "Lenore" (first translated by William Taylor in March 1796; this is Matthew Lewis's rendering in *Tales of Terror and Wonder*, p. 273):

> At break of day, with frightful dreams
>   Lenora struggled sore:
> "My William, art thou slaine," said she,
>   Or dost thou love no more?"

33 A similar glimpse of nature red in tooth and claw comes toward the end of *The Rime of the Ancient Mariner*: the ghost ship's sails remind the Hermit of dead leaves in winter, when "the owlet whoops to the wolf below, / That eats the she-wolf's young" (536–37; the rough-hewn syntax even suggests cannibalism). Like the passage from *Christabel*, this one works to undercut the

simplistic piety of the Mariner's closing moral of love for all things great and small.

34   I'm conflating a passage from Coleridge's original lecture on the slave trade with the slightly revised version appearing in his published essay on the subject (*Lectures 1795 On Politics and Religion*, ed. Lewis Patton and Peter Mann [Princeton: Princeton Univ. Press, 1971], p. 249; *The Watchman*, ed. Lewis Patton [Princeton: Princeton Univ. Press, 1970], p. 139).

35   Edward Dramin, " 'Amid the Jagged Shadows': Parody, Moral Realism, and Metaphysical Statements in Coleridge's *Christabel*" (Ph.D. Diss., Columbia Univ., 1972).

36   Compare Coleridge's comment on Robespierre in the letter to Thelwall of December 17, 1796: "the ardor of undisciplined Benevolence seduces us into malignity." Hence the equally dangerous-sounding quietism expressed in the letter to his brother George of March 10, 1798, where Coleridge plans "to destroy the bad passions not by combating them, but by keeping them in inaction," thereby "preventing the passions from turning reason into a hired advocate."

37   Thus Coleridge canceled the line giving Geraldine the withered side and bosom of the traditional witch: "lean and old and foul of hue." Evidently he realized it was too unambiguously supernatural to leave anything to the imagination and thence to imply something about the perceiver. The reaction of Hazlitt, who having seen the passage in manuscript considered it "absolutely necessary to the understanding the whole story," which he proceeded to interpret as a conventional, if basically "disgusting" (*CH*, pp. 206–07) tale of supernatural seduction, shows that Coleridge's intuitions in this matter were correct.

38   James Gillman, *The Life of Samuel Taylor Coleridge* (London, 1838), p. 283. See also Derwent Coleridge's edition of the *Poems* (London: Moxon, 1870), p. xlii.

39   A canceled passage of the poem insinuated this point more plainly. The dreams that have led Christabel to her demon-lover seem orgasmically Teresan: "Dreams that made her moan and leap / As on her bed she lay in sleep." Significantly, Coleridge notes that Teresa was "in the habit of privately . . . reading books of chivalry . . . all night to herself" (*LR* 4:68).

40   See, e.g., Anne of Swansea (Mrs. Julia Anne Curtis), "The Unknown! or the Knight of the Blood-Red Plume," rpt. in *Gothic Tales of Terror*, ed. Peter Haining (Baltimore: Penguin, 1972), p. 230. In contrast, see Matthew Lewis, "Courteous King Jamie," in *Tales of Wonder*, p. 261—a tale one expects to end in disaster, given Lewis's propensities for the macabre, but which closes with the traditional happy ending.

41   Laurence S. Lockridge, *Coleridge the Moralist* (Ithaca: Cornell Univ. Press, 1977), p. 53. Cf. Coleridge's letter to Josiah Wedgwood of January 5, 1798, written at the climax of his struggle whether or not to accept a Unitarian ministry:

> If a man considered himself as acting in opposition to his principles *then only* when he gave his example or support to actions and institutions, the existence of which

produces *unmingled* evil, he might perhaps with a safe conscience perpetrate any crime. . . . If on the other hand a man should make it *his principle* to abstain from all modes of conduct, the general practice of which was not permanently useful, or at least absolutely harmless, he must live, an isolated Being: his furniture, his servants, his very cloathes are intimately connected with Vice and Misery.

Starting from the assertion that "the nature of absolute evil is the insidious and inevitable corruption of good *into* evil, a corruption that is successful precisely in proportion to the real purity of the good," Walter H. Evert makes much the same argument about the Beatrice of Shelley's *Cenci* as I am making about Christabel. See his "Coadjutors of Oppression: A Romantic and Modern Theory of Evil," in *Romantic and Modern: Revaluations of Literary Tradition*, ed. George Bornstein (Pittsburgh: Univ. of Pittsburgh Press, 1977), p. 29. The Count's prediction that "what [Beatrice] most abhors / Shall have a fascination to entrap / Her loathing will" (IV, i, 85–87), distinctly echoes Christabel's "forced unconscious sympathy" with Geraldine.

42 Similarly, Edward Duffy sees parody in Sir Leoline's bombastic self-importance, which he calls "a literary caricature . . . [of] a specific kind of inadequate vision," namely gothic romance ("The Cunning Spontaneities of Romanticism," *Wordsworth Circle* 3 [1972]:237–40).

43 "There is one criterion by which we may always distinguish benevolence from mere sensibility—Benevolence impels to action, and is accompanied by self-denial" (*Watchman*, 140).

44 *The Friend*, ed. Barbara E. Rooke, 2 vols. (1818; Princeton: Princeton Univ. Press. 1969), 1:314.

45 James Hogg, *The Private Memoirs and Confessions of a Justified Sinner* (1824; New York: Norton, 1970).

46 Cf. Coleridge's frighteningly casual observation of Wordsworth during the Highlands tour of summer 1803: "My words & actions imaged on his mind, distorted & snaky as the Boatman's Oar reflected in the Lake" (*N* 1, entry 1473).

47 In reporting his visionary dream, Bracy stresses that the Christabel-dove appeared "Among the green herbs in the forest alone. / . . . / For nothing near it could I see, / Save the grass and green herbs underneath the old tree" (536–40); and hence in the dream Christabel is the one "uttering fearful moan"—not Geraldine, as the poem's opening scene leads one to believe. Bracy thus implies that the "bright green snake" coiled about Christabel, "Swelling its neck as she swelled hers" (549–54), is her own green envy and pride.

48 For further discussion of Coleridge's concept of the "phantom image," see Lockridge, pp. 154–56.

49 David Hartley, *Observations on Man: His Frame, His Duty, and His Expectations* (1749; Gainesville, Fla.: Scholar's Facsimiles and Reprints, 1966), pp. 82–83.

50 Compare *N* 1, entries 1185 and 1392.

51 See, e.g., Constance Hunting, "Another Look at 'The Conclusion to Part II' of *Christabel*," *English Language Notes* 12 (1975):171.

52   Compare Adam Smith's Humean discussion of the disutile aspects of "wonder" arising from a person's failure to "fill up the gap" or "interval" felt to exist between two events or objects not customarily connected together: "a person of the soundest judgment, who had grown up to maturity, and whose imagination had acquired those habits, and that mold, which the constitution of things in this world necessarily impress upon it . . . would soon feel the same confusion and giddiness begin to come upon him, which would at last end . . . in lunacy and distraction" ("The History of Astronomy," in *Essays on Philosophical Subjects*, ed. W. P. D. Wightman [1790; Indianapolis: Oxford Univ. Press, 1980], pp. 41–44).

    The Ancient Mariner's shooting of the albatross can likewise be seen as a reaction against its disturbingly unworldly perfection. Cf. Stanley Cavell: "It seems to me that the focus of the search for motive should be on the statement in the poem that 'the bird . . . loved the man / Who shot him with his bow.' Then the idea may be that the killing is to be understood as the denial of some claim upon him. . . . He may only have wanted at once to silence the bird's claim upon him and to establish a connection with it closer, as it were, than his caring for it: a connection beyond the force of his human responsibilities" ("In Quest of the Ordinary: Texts of Recovery," in *Romanticism and Contemporary Criticism*, ed. Morris Eaves and Michael Fischer [Ithaca: Cornell Univ. Press, 1986], pp. 193, 197).

53   Cf. "Fears in Solitude":

> Oh! blasphemous! the Book of Life is made
> A superstitious instrument, on which
> We gabble o'er the oaths we mean to break;
>
> . . .
>
> All, all make up one scheme of perjury,
> That faith doth reel; the very name of God
> Sounds like a juggler's charm.   [70–80]

54   Cf. *N* 2, entry 2207: "Vivid flashes in mid day, the terror without the beauty.—A ghost by day time / Geraldine."

55   Compare Wordsworth:

>   . . . the soul,
> Remembering how she felt, but what she felt
> Remembering not, retains an obscure sense
> Of possible sublimity, whereto
> With growing faculties she doth aspire,
> With faculties still growing, feeling still
> That whatsoever point they gain, they yet
> Have something to pursue.   [*Prelude* II, 334–41]

56   Cf. George Levine: "Thus parody as a form always seems simpler and less serious than it is likely to become. . . . The texture of parody is normally comic, while the object of parody is normally a literature allowing too easy triumphs for hero or heroine, that is, literature in a comic form. The logic of

rejection would often entail (as in *Northanger Abbey* itself) an unhappy ending. But a comic texture tends to imply a comic form so that to be true to its content, parody would likely be untrue to its form" (*The Realistic Imagination: English Fiction from Frankenstein to Lady Chatterley* [Chicago: Univ. of Chicago Press, 1981], p. 72). In a different context, Lockridge sees Coleridge as torn between his Lutheran-Calvinist doctrine of man's depraved will and his liberal humanist belief in individual self-realization (p. 218). Evidently the first of these strains appears in *Christabel*'s incomplete narrative, the second in the reader's need to unify the poem's different narrative styles by grasping and mastering their implication of original sin.

Chapter 6

1   See Freud's remarks on "criminals from a sense of guilt":

> Such deeds were done principally because they were forbidden, and because their execution was accompanied by mental relief for their doer. He was suffering from an oppressive feeling of guilt, of which he did not know the origin, and after he had committed a misdeed this oppression was mitigated. His sense of guilt was at least attached to something.
>
> Paradoxical as it may sound, I must maintain that the sense of guilt was present before the misdeed, that it did not arise from it, but conversely—the misdeed arose from the sense of guilt. ("Some Characters Met With in Psycho-Analytic Work," in *Works*, Standard ed., ed. James Strachey, 24 vols. [London: Hogarth, 1957], 14:332)

See also Nietzsche's rather more lurid account of "the pale criminal," who because he does "not want to be ashamed of his madness" rationalizes his "thirst after the bliss of the knife" by robbing his murder victim (*Thus Spake Zarathustra*, in *The Portable Nietzsche*, ed. Walter Kaufmann [New York: Viking, 1968], pp. 150–51). Probably referring to Wordsworth and himself, Coleridge writes how "[A] did a real injury & a very great one to B. in order to make his Hatred more natural, less daemonish" (*Notebooks*, ed. Kathleen Coburn, 3 vols. [New York: Pantheon, 1957], 1, entry 1481).

2   William Empson, Introduction to *Coleridge's Verse: A Selection*, ed. Empson and David Pirie (London: Faber, 1972), pp. 27–40, 75–78; Edward E. Bostetter, "The Nightmare World of *The Ancient Mariner*," *Studies in Romanticism* 1 (1962):241.

3   Robert Penn Warren, "A Poem of Pure Imagination: An Experiment in Reading," in *Selected Essays* (New York: Vintage, 1966), p. 198; see esp. pp. 226–50.

4   *The Statesman's Manual*, in *Lay Sermons*, ed. R. J. White (Princeton: Princeton Univ. Press, 1972), p. 30.

5   See *The Friend*, ed. Barbara E. Rooke, 2 vols. (Princeton: Princeton Univ. Press, 1969), 1:313–25.

6   An important discussion of motivation and casuality in the poem is Frances Ferguson, "Coleridge and the Deluded Reader: *The Rime of the Ancient*

Mariner," *Georgia Review* 31 (1977):617. A valuable recent account of how
the poem anticipates traditional epistemological readings based on the sub-
ject/object dialectic is Arden Reed's bleakly deconstructionist "The Mariner
Rimed," in *Romanticism and Language,* ed. Arden Reed (Ithaca: Cornell
Univ. Press, 1984), p. 168, and esp. pp. 192–201.

7 *Milton* 26:44–46, in *The Complete Poetry and Prose of William Blake,* ed.
and rev. David V. Erdman, with commentary by Harold Bloom (Garden City,
N.J.: Anchor, 1982), p. 124.

8 I cannot agree with Katherine Wheeler's optimistic view that "the Wedding
Guest, in his final stunned state, . . . seems to have undergone a genuine
transformation of his ordinary view of human experience and its possibilities," and is thus "the model of an audience" for the poem (*The Creative
Mind in Coleridge's Poetry* [London: Heinemann, 1981], p. 64). In fairness,
though, I should mention that the present study's approach to Romantic
narrative poetry in general does resemble Wheeler's approach to *The Rime*:

> In 'The Ancient Mariner,' the distance achieved by the glossing technique makes it
> possible to reflect the primary observer in art: the reader. . . . By destabilizing real-
> ity in this way, that is, by setting up a rival reality within the context of aesthetic il-
> lusion that so closely resembles the reality of the observer's situation as to shatter
> the boundary between the two, the formal distinctions between mind and nature,
> external and internal, thought and thing, are questioned as real or illusory. Indeed,
> they are exposed as absolute distinctions characteristic only of an illusory reality.
> (p. 42; see also p. 155)

Yet this seems a better account of Coleridge's idealist intentions than of the
darkly ambiguous *Rime* itself. Because the poem's time frames are not organized on the principle of repetition-with-a-difference, they fail to elicit a
retrospective unifying insight from the reader, so that the Mariner is forced to
shoulder the burden of repetition alone by continually retelling his tale. So far
from yielding a dialectical synthesis of subject and object, the progression
formed by the time frames is a sequential one stretching from the Mariner's
voyage before 1530 (his ship was, he says, "the first" to discover the Pacific,
circumnavigated by Magellan in 1530; additionally, his various Catholic
expostulations imply that the Reformation hasn't yet occurred), through his
subsequent tale and the comments made by the glossator evidently some time
in the seventeenth century (as the style of the gloss, and the general area of
Coleridge's own prose readings, would suggest), down to the poem's publication in its final version in 1816. The effect of this series is to link the first two
events, which are fictitious, with the last one, which is an actual fact, so that
the poem thrusts forward to include present-day readers as well. Indeed, the
poem could hardly do otherwise, since the Mariner is presumably still alive-
in-death. Thus it might appear that the reader who grasps the Mariner's
evangelical message in both its ironical and literal senses transforms him into
a sort of holy fool, redeeming his tale from guilt and incompleteness. 'Tis a
consummation devoutly to be wished—and yet, regardless of whether the
Mariner's burning heart (585) emblemizes Catholic love or hellish, self-

preoccupied guilt, whether he be a joyous proselytizer or a dejected exile, whether the Wedding Guest is stunned with new awareness or with sheer incomprehension, the Mariner himself evidently remains quite ignorant of any relationship with the *contemporary* reader. Such a reading may redeem the Mariner in *our* eyes, but that's small comfort to him.

9   *The Rime of the Ancient Mariner,* 601–09, in *Poetical Works of Coleridge,* ed. Ernest Hartley Coleridge (London: Oxford Univ. Press, 1973), p. 208.

10   For a crucial discussion of the poem's ongoing historicism and its deliberately mediated relationship with the reader, see Jerome McGann, "The Meaning of *The Ancient Mariner,*" *Critical Inquiry* 8 (1981):35. McGann argues that the reader is deliberately invited to revise the poem's indeterminate meaning, but only within the hermeneutic parameters of Christian community and tradition.

11   See, e.g., Max Schulz, *The Poetic Voices of Coleridge* (Detroit: Wayne State Univ. Press, 1964), pp. 86, 120; and James Boulger, "Imagination and Speculation in Coleridge's Conversation Poems," *Journal of English and Germanic Philology* 64 (1965):691. "Overgrown" is how Milton's Eve describes the herbs and flowers of Eden when she argues Adam into letting her tend them by herself; when Satan finds her, she is supporting various drooping flowers "with Myrtle band" (*Paradise Lost,* IX, 209–19, 424–33, in *John Milton: Complete Poems and Major Prose,* ed. Merritt Y. Hughes [New York: Odyssey, 1957], pp. 383–84, 388). Like Eve, the poet of "The Eolian Harp" experiences nature's tendency to wildness as a moral temptation.

12   Paul Magnuson similarly notes that "the five lines on the 'intellectual Breeze,' which form a separate verse paragraph after 1797, are not separate from the surrounding context in 1796 [when the poem was first published as "Effusion xxxv"]; they form one verse paragraph with the preceding description of 'idle flitting phantasies' and Sara's caution which follows. The *And* in the phrase 'And what if' that introduces them suggests 'for example' rather than 'in addition' as it does when it introduces a separate verse paragraph" (" 'The Eolian Harp' in Context," *Studies in Romanticism* 24 [1985]:8).

13   Letter to Murray of February 16, 1821: "I meant . . . to have displayed him gradually gaté and blasé as he grew older—as is natural" (*Letters and Journals of Byron,* ed. Leslie A. Marchand, 12 vols. [Cambridge: Belknap, 1978], 8:78; henceforth cited as *L&J*).

14   *Byron: Poetical Works,* ed. Frederick Page, 3rd ed. (London: Oxford Univ. Press, 1970), pp. 341–42. All quotations of Byron's poetry are from this edition.

15   William H. Marshall, *The Structure of Byron's Major Poems* (Philadelphia: Univ. of Pennsylvania Press, 1962), pp. 120–24.

16   Comparison of *Mazeppa,* 417–22 ("For time at last sets all things even . . ."), with the letter to Lady Byron of March 5, 1817, suggests Byron identified his own position after the separation from his wife with that of Mazeppa:

> For myself I have a confidence in my Fortune which will yet bear me through—
> ["Chance is more just than we are"]—the reverses which have occurred—were
> what I should have expected . . .—However I shall live to have to pity you all . . .

time & Nemesis will do that which I would not—even were it in my power remote
or immediate.—You will smile at this piece of prophecy—do so—but recollect
it.—it is justified by all human experience—no one was ever even the involuntary
cause of great evils to others—without a requital—I have paid and am paying for
mine—so will you. [*L&J*, 5:181]

See also the letter to Lady Byron of November 18, 1818.

17   See Jerome McGann, *"Don Juan" in Context* (Chicago: Univ. of Chicago
Press, 1976), pp. 59–61. I am much indebted to McGann's book. The fullest
account of the composition of *Don Juan* is Truman Guy Steffan, *The Making
of a Masterpiece: Byron's "Don Juan"*, vol. 1 of *Byron's "Don Juan": A
Variorum Edition*, 2nd ed. (Austin: Univ. of Texas Press, 1971); see esp. pp.
362, 365–67.
18   Alvin Kernan, *The Plot of Satire* (New Haven: Yale Univ. Press, 1965), pp.
176–79.
19   Edward E. Bostetter, Introduction to *Twentieth Century Interpretations of
"Don Juan"*, ed. Bostetter (Englewood Cliffs, N.J.: Prentice-Hall, 1969), p.
14.
20   George Ridenour, *The Style of "Don Juan"* (New Haven: Yale Univ. Press,
1960).
21   Peter J. Manning, *Byron and His Fictions* (Detroit: Wayne State Univ. Press,
1978), p. 260. See also Jerome McGann, pp. 156–65 passim. The reader's
cyclical experience of *Don Juan*'s stanzas resembles William James's account
of the process of truth verification: "Truths emerge from facts; but they dip
forward into facts again and add to them; which facts again create or reveal
new truth, and so on indefinitely. The facts themselves are not *true*. They
simply *are*. Truth is the function of the *beliefs* that start and terminate among
them" (*Pragmatism: A New Name for Some Old Ways of Thinking* [1907;
Cambridge: Harvard Univ. Press, 1975], p. 108).
22   Andrew Rutherford, *Byron: A Critical Study* (Stanford: Stanford Univ. Press,
1961), p. 172.
23   "Remarks on Don Juan," *Blackwood's Magazine* 5 (August 1819):512. Rpt.
in *Byron: The Critical Heritage*, ed. Andrew Rutherford (New York: Barnes
& Noble, 1970), pp. 166–72; henceforth cited as *CH*.
24   Letter of Shelley to Byron of October 21, 1821, in *CH*, p. 197. Compare
Byron's letter to Murray of February 1, 1819: "I maintain it is the most moral
of poems—but if people won't discover the moral that is their fault not mine"
(*L&J* 6:99).
25   *Childe Harold's Pilgrimage* IV, 97; cited in Jerome McGann, pp. 146–47.
26   Pedrillo's death is a comment on the earlier assertion that "the desire of life /
Prolongs it":

> . . . this is obvious to physicians,
> When patients, neither plagued with friends nor wife,
>   Survive through very desperate conditions,
> Because they still can hope, nor shines the knife
>   Nor shears of Atropos before their visions:

> Despair of all recovery spoils lengevity,
> And makes men's miseries of alarming brevity.   [II, lxiv]

For Pedrillo, it wasn't the knife of Atropos that shone before his vision, but the surgeon's scalpel: the men have tried to take fate into their own hands. It is hard to know what McGann means when he claims of this stanza that "even in the doctor/patient context one is forced to concede the virtues of despair. As Byron suggests, it 'makes men's miseries of alarming brevity. . . .' In Byron's view, if anything is human—like hope and despair, for example—it will serve human ends, sometimes well, sometimes equivocally, sometimes badly" (pp. 164–65). Surely, something that serves human ends badly doesn't really serve human ends at all. Thus for the cannibals the virtues of despair are nonvirtues. Far from simply offering the men relief from an agonizing existence, the cannibalism gives them the worst of both worlds: *more* suffering—despair, insanity, and convulsions rolled into one—and death as well. However brief, such misery is "alarming" indeed.

27 E. R. Dodds, *The Greeks and the Irrational* (Berkeley: Univ. of California Press, 1951), p. 36.

Chapter 7

1 Coleridge, *The Friend*, ed. Barbara E. Rooke, 2 vols. (1818; Princeton: Princeton Univ. Press, 1969), 1:455–57.

2 G. W. F. Hegel, *Hegel's Science of Logic*, trans. A. V. Miller (New York: Allen & Unwin and Humanities Press, 1969), p. 841.

3 *Poetical Works of Coleridge*, ed. Ernest Hartley Coleridge (London: Oxford Univ. Press, 1973), p. 178. The letter to Southey of July 1797 provides a closer glimpse of this domestic mishap: "dear Sara accidentally emptied a skillet of boiling milk on my foot." If dear Sara thereby ensured that her husband would have to stay home with her, Coleridge's oxymoron, "accidentally emptied"—rather than "spilled"—suggests he well recognized her resentment of his preference for the company of his friends.

4 Cf. Karl Kroeber on the Romantic "spot" in nature, in "Coleridge's 'Fears': Problems in Patriotic Poetry," *CLIO* 7 (1978):359, esp. 363–66.

5 *The Complete Poetry and Prose of William Blake*, ed. David Erdman with commentary by Harold Bloom (Garden City, N.J.: Anchor, 1982), p. 136.

6 Coleridge, *Biographia Literaria*, ed. James Engell and W. Jackson Bate, 2 vols. (1817; Princeton: Princeton Univ. Press, 1983), 2:244; henceforth cited as *BL*.

7 *A Defence of Poetry*, in *Shelley's Poetry and Prose*, ed. Donald H. Reiman and Sharon B. Powers (New York: Norton, 1977), p. 491; henceforth cited as S.

8 See William Keach, *Shelley's Style* (New York: Methuen, 1984), pp. 79–117.

9 Shelley, "Speculations on Metaphysics," in *Complete Works*, ed. Roger Ingpen and Walter E. Peck, 10 vols. (New York: Gordian Press, 1965), 7:65; henceforth cited as *CW*.

10 Friedrich Schlegel, *"Lucinde" and the Fragments*, trans. Peter Firchow (Minneapolis: Univ. of Minnesota Press, 1971), p. 195.

11 Seymour Chatman, "What Novels Can Do That Films Can't (and Vice Versa)," in *On Narrative*, ed. W. J. T. Mitchell (Chicago: Univ. of Chicago Press, 1981), p. 118.

12 See, for example, Roger Murray, *Wordsworth's Style: Figures and Themes in the Lyrical Ballads of 1800* (Lincoln: Univ. of Nebraska Press, 1967), pp. 25–80 passim.

13 Cf. Basil Willey's speculation that Wordsworth's poetic decline might be attributable to an ultimately hostile determinism implicit in the associationist principles behind his whole program of making poetry out of his recollections of childhood ("Postscript: On Wordsworth and the Locke Tradition," in *The Seventeenth-Century Background: Studies in the Thought of the Age in Relation to Poetry and Religion* [Garden City, N.Y.: Doubleday, 1953]; rpt. in *The English Romantic Poets*, ed. M. H. Abrams [New York: Oxford Univ. Press, 1975], p. 112). For Hartley as for Hume, the "ideas" or "reflections" of memory are derived from intenser, more vivid "impressions" or "sensations," so that the older Wordsworth gets—or to put it more paradoxically, the more Wordsworth matures as a poet—the more likely he is to lose touch with his sources of imaginative power. Most of the major poems of 1802–05 suggest such a reading, as does at least one well-known passage from *The Prelude*: ". . . the hiding places of man's power / Open; I would approach them, but they close. / I see by glimpses now; when age comes on, / May scarcely see at all" (XII, 277–86).

14 *Collected Letters of Samuel Taylor Coleridge*, ed. E. L. Griggs, 4 vols. (Oxford: Oxford Univ. Press, 1956–71), 4:496. It is often pointed out that Coleridge's organicism involves a tacit denial of man's radical existential freedom to create his own moral character. Unlike an acorn, which is biologically determined to become an oak, the existence of "Andrew Cooper" is predicated on his own conscious choices, ideals, and failures. For a useful recent summary of problems with the Romantic application of organicist doctrine to the self, see Peter L. Thorslev, Jr., *Romantic Contraries: Freedom versus Destiny* (New Haven: Yale Univ. Press, 1984), pp. 84–125. Wordsworth also recognizes the potential duplicity of an imagination that, as Coleridge says, "dissolves, diffuses, dissipates, in order to re-create" (*BL* 1:304). The danger is that there will be no re-creation but only the "uncreating Word" of Pope's Dulness:

> If words be not . . . an incarnation of the thought, but only a clothing for it, then surely they will prove an ill gift; such a one as those poisoned vestments, read of in the stories of superstitious times, which had power to consume and to alienate from his right mind the victim who put them on. Language, if it do not uphold, and feed, and leave in quiet, like the power of gravitation or the air we breathe, is a counter-spirit, unremittingly and noiselessly at work to derange, to subvert, to lay waste, to vitiate, and to dissolve. (*Prose Works*, ed. W. J. B. Owen and Jane Worthington Smyther, 3 vols. [Oxford: Clarendon Press, 1974], 2:85)

A language that fails to nourish conciliating affections for nature leads to madness and primordial chaos, for it has disavowed its Logos-like power to give nature intelligible form. See Frances Ferguson's discussion of the issues this passage raises in *Wordsworth: Language as Counter-Spirit* (New Haven: Yale Univ. Press, 1977), pp. 1–34.

15   See, e.g., Geoffrey Hartman, *Wordsworth's Poetry, 1787–1814* (New Haven: Yale Univ. Press, 1964), passim; see also Richard J. Onorato's equally skeptical, psychoanalytical-biographical account of Wordsworth's efforts to repress his doubts toward the imagination in *The Character of the Poet: Wordsworth in "The Prelude"* (Princeton: Princeton Univ. Press, 1971), esp. pp. 29–87 and 152–63.

16   Wordsworth, *Selected Poems and Prefaces*, ed. Jack Stillinger (Boston: Houghton Mifflin Co., 1965), p. 185; henceforth cited as W.

17   Cf. James K. Chandler's remarks on the factitiousness of the ostensibly spontaneous, meditative form of Wordsworth's and Coleridge's "conversation" poems, in "Romantic Allusiveness," *Critical Inquiry* 8 (1982):461.

18   Onorato, *The Character of the Poet*, pp. 45–47. See also L. J. Swingle, "Wordsworth's 'Picture of the Mind,'" in *Images of Romanticism: Verbal and Visual Affinities*, ed. Karl Kroeber and William Walling (New Haven: Yale Univ. Press, 1978), pp. 86–88.

19   Coleridge, "Anima Poetae," from *The Portable Coleridge*, ed. I. A. Richards (New York: Viking, 1950), pp. 314–15.

20   Coleridge, *Notebooks*, ed. Kathleen Coburn, 3 vols. (New York: Pantheon, 1957), 2, entry 2370.

21   John Ashbery, "The Skaters," in *Rivers and Mountains* (New York: Ecco Press, 1966), pp. 35–36.

22   The repeated image in "The Skaters" of "the human brain, with its tray of images" (36) harks back to Hume's theater of the mind by way of Keats's admission, "I am sometimes so very sceptical as to think Poetry itself a mere Jack a lanthern to amuse whoever may chance to be struck with its brilliance" (*Letters* 1:242).

23   John Keats, letter of October 27, 1818, in *The Letters of John Keats*, ed. Hyder Edward Rollins, 2 vols. (Cambridge: Harvard Univ. Press, 1958), 2:387.

24   *The Poems of Keats*, ed. Jack Stillinger (Cambridge: Belknap, 1978), p. 371. Although I reject his Neoplatonism, I am following in broad outline the reading of Earl R. Wasserman in *The Finer Tone: Keats' Major Poems* (Baltimore: Johns Hopkins Univ. Press, 1967), pp. 178–223.

25   Cf. Walter Jackson Bate, *John Keats* (Cambridge: Harvard Univ. Press, 1963), pp. 580–85. For a reading of "To Autumn" that likewise begins with Keats's awareness that subjectivity is "the carrier of reality, the transparent medium of its presence," but that proceeds to draw very different conclusions from Bate, see Richard Macksey, " 'To Autumn' and the Music of Mortality: 'Pure Rhetoric of a Language without Words,'" in *Romanticism and Language* (Ithaca: Cornell Univ. Press, 1984), pp. 263–308, esp. pp. 298ff. Macksey argues that the poem "is not about the tumescent plenitude of reality only; it is also about its constituting polar opposite—emptiness"; and he goes on to

claim that the poem's ironic recognition of mortality and belatedness is "a recognition for the reader of the essential negativity of all linguistic constructs and the permanence of the repetitive cycles that they can never successfully enclose."

Chapter 8

1   Raymond D. Havens, "Shelley's *Alastor*," *PMLA* 45 (1930):1109.
2   All quotations of Shelley's poetry, as well as "On Love," "On Life," and *A Defence of Poetry*, are from *Shelley's Poetry and Prose*, ed. Donald H. Reiman and Sharon B. Powers (New York: Norton, 1977); henceforth cited as S. All other citations of Shelley's prose are from the *Complete Works*, ed. Roger Ingpen and Walter E. Peck (New York: Gordian Press, 1965); henceforth cited as *CW*.
3   Albert S. Gérard, *English Romantic Poetry: Ethos, Structure, and Symbol in Coleridge, Wordsworth, Shelley, and Keats* (Berkeley: Univ. of California Press, 1968), pp. 144–49 esp.
4   Earl R. Wasserman, *Shelley: A Critical Reading* (Baltimore: Johns Hopkins Univ. Press, 1971), pp. 3–41. A good, not yet dated synopsis of what more theoretical criticism has been doing with or to Shelley is Jonathan Arac, "To Regress from the Rigor of Shelley: Figures of History in American Deconstructive Criticism," *boundary* 2 8 (1980):241.
5   David Hume, *A Treatise of Human Nature*, ed. L. A. Selby-Bigge, rev. P. H. Nidditch (1739–40; Oxford: Oxford Univ. Press, 1978), p. 252; henceforth cited as *THN*.
6   *Collected Poetry of W. B. Yeats* (London: Macmillan, 1961), p. 333.
7   See Roy R. Male, Jr., "Shelley and the Doctrine of Sympathy," *Univ. of Texas Studies in English* 29 (1950):183. I am in agreement with Male, but find that the doctrine has epistemological considerations that he does not treat. Another useful discussion is James Engell, *The Creative Imagination* (Cambridge: Harvard Univ. Press, 1981), pp. 143–60.
8   Adam Smith, *The Theory of Moral Sentiments* (1759; New York: Augustus Kelly, 1966), pp. 194, 216; see also pp. 162–63.
9   David Marshall, "Adam Smith and the Theatricality of Moral Sentiments," *Critical Inquiry* 10 (1984):610, 601.
10   Robert Cumming, *Human Nature and History: A Study of the Development of Liberal Political Thought*, 2 vols. (Chicago: Univ. of Chicago Press, 1969), 2:218.
11   Cf. Smith's description of the murderer whose remorse shows not guilt per se so much as his horrified realization that he has forfeited the "fellow-feeling" of his spectators, real and imagined. Attempting to enter into *their* feelings, he discovers that they are utterly unable to enter into *his*: "Everything seems hostile, and he would be glad to fly to some inhospitable desert, where he might never more behold the face of a human creature, nor read in the countenance of mankind the condemnation of his crimes" (*Theory of Moral Sentiments*, p. 84).

12   Begun about a year later in 1816, Mary Shelley's *Frankenstein* echoes a number of *Alastor*'s themes and images, as well as their apparent sources in Hume, who in the above-cited passage from the *Treatise* actually calls himself a "strange uncouth monster." The *Frankenstein* monster's bewilderment on awakening to life—"Who was I? What was I? Whence did I come? What was my destination? These questions continually recurred, but I was unable to solve them" (ed. M. K. Joseph [London: Oxford Univ. Press, 1969], p. 128)—recalls Shelley's questions in the essay "On Life"—"What is Life? . . . what are we? Whence do we come, and whither do we go? Is birth the commencement, is death the conclusion of our being?" (S, pp. 475–76). Hume's demolition of cause and effect similarly undermines his confidence in possessing a knowable past: "Where am I, or what? From what causes do I derive my existence, and to what condition shall I return? . . . What beings surround me? . . . I am confounded with all these questions" (*THN*, p. 269).

       Frankenstein's paradoxical relationship to his creation directly parallels that of the *Alastor* Poet to his dream-maiden. In a similar reversal of the master-slave relationship, Frankenstein's rejection of his creature ultimately renders him the slave of its will (pp. 153, 167): he comes to shun society no less than the monster eventually does, and he is just as obsessed with revenge; that he should feel this way is, indeed, the *monster's* ultimate revenge on *him* (pp. 201–02). Thus as he concludes his tale by undertaking to pursue his pursuer, he implicitly admits that his pursuit has no meaning because he has effectively become that which he seeks: "I pursued my path towards the destruction of the demon more as a task enjoined by heaven, as the mechanical impulse of some power of which I was unconscious, than as the ardent desire of my soul" (p. 204). Such precisely is the fate of the *Alastor* Poet. For both characters, the consequence of this passivity is a most naive superstitiousness. Although raised a child of the Enlightenment, Frankenstein comes quite unscientifically to believe his arctic quest is overseen by a providential "guiding spirit" (pp. 203–05), the irony being that this is the monster himself, Frankenstein's alienated double, who is deliberately assisting Frankenstein's quest in order to prolong his sufferings. One sees the same emotionally paralyzing ambivalence in Shelley's Poet, for whom the dream-maiden is both nemesis and savior.

13   *Paradise Lost* IV, 180–81, in *John Milton: Complete Poems and Major Prose*, ed. Merritt Y. Hughes (New York: Odyssey, 1957), p. 282; cf. also Book IV, 582–85.

14   Luther Scales, "The Poet as Miltonic Adam in *Alastor*," *Keats-Shelley Journal* 22–23 (1972–73):126.

15   See William Keach, *Shelley's Style* (New York: Methuen, 1984), pp. 79–117.

16   *Childe Harold's Pilgrimage* III, iii, in *Byron's Poetical Works*, ed. Frederick Page, 3rd ed. (Oxford: Oxford Univ. Press, 1970), p. 209. While it appears *Alastor* was influenced generally by the first two cantos of Byron's poem, the third canto, composed at Geneva in company of the Shelleys three months after *Alastor*'s publication, was influenced in turn by Shelley's poem. Like the Poet, Harold doesn't actually die; he just fades away. As Jerome McGann remarks, the Rhine Valley sequence of Canto III reveals "the dangers that a

life of self-subsistent imaginative solitude holds out. . . . [Harold] presents a wistful and deeply pathetic image . . . , for his impulses carry him far into another world of tender and soothing childlike fantasies. He is not spiritually wasted, but his whole being is so ingrown that his communion is now only with the absent and the dead" (*Fiery Dust: Byron's Poetic Development* [Chicago: Univ. of Chicago Press, 1968], pp. 85–86). McGann's description exactly fits Shelley's Poet as well. Similarly, it is interesting that *Prometheus Unbound*, a poem about the patience to endure wrongs without avenging them, was conceived about the same time as Byron's separation from Lady Byron, when he wrote *Mazeppa*, a tale of vengeance, and was struggling, as his letters show, to master his desire to retaliate against her.

17 David Hume, *An Inquiry Concerning Human Understanding*, ed. Charles W. Hendel (1748; Indianapolis: Bobbs-Merrill, 1977), p. 68; henceforth cited as *ICHU*. As Reiman notes, "If we understand the Poet to embark on the Aral Sea, his shallop . . . would be carried by a supernatural impulse up the Oxus to its headwaters in the Hindu Kush Mountains" (S, p. 76).

18 Alfred North Whitehead, *Adventures of Ideas* (New York: Free Press, 1961), p. 181.

19 Cf. "On Life": "Man is a being . . . existing but in the future and in the past, being, not what he is, but what he has been, and shall be" (S, p. 476). Shelley's comparison of thought to "one in dread who speeds through the recesses of some haunted pile, and dares not look behind" makes metaphysical the similarly gothic picture in "Tintern Abbey" of the young Wordsworth as following "Wherever nature led: more like a man / Flying from something that he dreads, than one / Who sought the thing he loved" (*Selected Poems and Prefaces of Wordsworth*, ed. Jack Stillinger [Boston: Houghton Mifflin Co., 1965], p. 109).

20 C. E. Pulos, *The Deep Truth: A Study of Shelley's Scepticism* (Lincoln: Univ. of Nebraska Press, 1962), p. 41.

21 The Narrator's closing reference to the Wandering Jew, so far from showing his inability to conceive the ideal, as Wasserman says, attests his belief that the balm of immortality does indeed exist—not physically, but in poetry and myth. What the Narrator wishes is that man would retract his groundless belief in a literal afterlife, the superstitious search for which inevitably becomes a "blighting curse" (679) upon imagination, the sole actual basis for such hopes. In his view, the delusive Christian God, "profuse of poisons" (676), not only fails to bestow immortality as a gift but actively keeps us from achieving it for ourselves through creative struggle. The Promethean-sounding Ahasuerus argues much the same point in *Queen Mab* VII.

22 Compare the less paradoxical Dugald Stewart: "The connexion between the Desire of Society and the Desire of Knowledge is very remarkable. The last of these principles is always accompanied with a wish to impart our information to others;—inasmuch, that it has been doubted, if any man's curiosity would be sufficient to engage him in a course of persevering study, if he were entirely cut off from the prospect of social intercourse" (*Outlines of Moral Philosophy* [Edinburgh, 1801], pp. 87–88).

23   Cf. Hegel's account of how Stoicism, in its striving after "freedom of thought," "takes only pure thought as its truth, and thus lacks the concrete filling of life. It is, therefore, merely the notion of freedom, not living freedom itself" because its thought lacks "a content to supply the sphere of the ego." Stoicism thus conduces to the "essential negativity" of skepticism, which "is the realisation of that of which Stoicism is merely the notion, and is the actual experience of what freedom of thought is." In other words, skepticism raises into painful self-consciousness the basic emptiness at the core of Stoic idealism (*The Phenomenology of Mind*, trans. J. B. Baillie, 2nd ed. [1807; New York: Harper Torchbooks, 1967], pp. 245–46).

24   See, e.g., Norman Thurston, "Author, Narrator, and Hero in Shelley's *Alastor*," *Studies in Romanticism* 14 (1975):119.

25   M. H. Abrams, "Style and Structure in the Greater Romantic Lyric," in *From Sensibility to Romanticism: Essays Presented to Frederick A. Pottle*, ed. Frederick W. Hilles and Harold Bloom (New York: Oxford Univ. Press, 1967), p. 527. Rpt. in *Romanticism and Consciousness*, ed. Harold Bloom (New York: Norton, 1970), p. 201.

26   For a useful discussion of this problem, see James K. Chandler, "Romantic Allusiveness," *Critical Inquiry* 8 (1982):461; see also Hazard Adams, *The Interests of Criticism: An Introduction to Literary Theory* (New York: Harcourt Brace, 1969), pp. 73–80. Keats's view of Wordsworth is strikingly similar to Shelley's:

> It may be said that . . . Wordsworth &c should have their due from us. but for the sake of a few fine imaginative or domestic passages, are we to be bullied into a certain Philosophy engendered in the whims of an Egotist—Every man has his speculations, but every man does not brood and peacock over them till he makes a false coinage and deceives himself. (*The Letters of John Keats*, ed. Hyder Edward Rollins, 2 vols. [Cambridge: Harvard Univ. Press, 1958], 1:223)

27   Compare *The Sensitive-Plant*, which ends by claiming that the ruined Edenic garden and dead Lady "In truth have never past away— / 'Tis we, 'tis ours are changed—not they" (Conc., 19–20), or the similar assertion in *Adonais* that the hero is not dead but " 'Tis we . . . We decay Like corpses" (345–49). Accordingly, the "modest creed" with which *The Sensitive-Plant* concludes— namely, that "in this life . . . Where nothing is—but all things seem," it is "Pleasant . . . To own that death itself must be, Like all the rest,—a mockery" (Conc., 9–16)—recalls Plato's urbane skepticism toward the close of the *Phaedo*:

> Of course, no reasonable man ought to insist that the facts are exactly as I have described them. But that either this or something very like it is a true account of our souls and their future habitations . . . is both a reasonable contention and a belief worth risking, for the risk is a noble one. We should use such accounts to inspire ourselves with confidence. (*Collected Dialogues of Plato*, ed. Edith Hamilton and Huntington Cairns, trans. Hugh Tredennick [Princeton: Princeton Univ. Press, 1963], 114d, pp. 94–95)

28 M. H. Abrams, *The Mirror and the Lamp: Romantic Theory and the Critical Tradition* (New York: Oxford Univ. Press, 1953), p. 23.

29 John C. Bean considers this episode to be "an allegory of sexual orgasm, or more properly, of that visionary moment, ecstatic, self-obliterating, transcendent, that mystic poets have frequently described as orgasm" ("The Poet Borne Darkly: The Dream-Voyage Allegory in Shelley's *Alastor*," *Keats-Shelley Journal* 23 [1974]:68). Bean was right the first time, if indeed less "proper": the whirlpool allegorizes the Poet's previous wet dream.

30 The source of the Poet's apostrophe on the swan is evidently Plato's *Phaedo* 84e–85b, where Socrates claims the song of the dying swan expresses not grief at leaving the world but rather the soul's joy at the prospect of returning home to the divine master to which it has remained faithful. Inasmuch as the Poet concludes by asking, "And what am I that I should linger here, / With voice far sweeter . . . / . . . / . . . wasting these surpassing powers / In the deaf air, to the blind earth" (285–89), the allusion reemphasizes his inability to create through love, in Byronic fashion, a terrestrial paradise of his own. Plato's passage also underlies Coleridge's long gloss in *The Rime of the Ancient Mariner* on the homeward-returning stars (lines 263–71), and Ololon's springtime descent to earth in Blake's *Milton*; in these cases, too, the tenor of the image is reversed, ironically insinuating that the protagonists' otherworldliness is a mask for their destructive guilt and anxiety.

31 Frank Kermode, *Romantic Image* (New York: Vintage, 1964), esp. pp. 5–12. Cf. Paul de Man's discussion of the "shape all light" that appears under similar circumstances in *The Triumph of Life*, in "Shelley Disfigured," in *Deconstructionism and Criticism*, ed. Geoffrey Hartman (New York: Seabury Press, 1979), esp. pp. 53–60.

32 Preface to *Lyrical Ballads*, 2nd ed., in *Selected Poems and Prefaces of Wordsworth*, ed. Jack Stillinger (Boston: Houghton Mifflin Co., 1965), p. 450.

33 Cf. "On Life": "The difference is merely nominal between those two classes of thought which are vulgarly distinguished by the names of ideas and external objects" (S, p. 477).

34 This development reflects much the same "warping, or modification, of vehicle by tenor" that W. K. Wimsatt, Jr., sees to characterize Romantic nature imagery in general. Analyzing Coleridge's sonnet "To the River Otter," Wimsatt argues that "both tenor and vehicle . . . are wrought in a parallel process out of the same material. The river landscape . . . is both the occasion of reminiscence and the source of the metaphors by which reminiscence is described" ("The Structure of Romantic Nature Imagery," in *Romanticism and Consciousness*, p. 82). To put it differently, the physical stream that the poet is writing about eventually flows inward to become a stream of associative thought, thereby literalizing its latent metaphoric status as the stream of the poet's life.

35 See Frances Ferguson on "Mont Blanc": "Shelley here focuses on a central paradox of the sublime—that we should take pleasure in the contemplation of anything that presents a threat to our tendency toward self-preservation. . . . 'Mont Blanc' creates an image of sublimity that continually hyposta-

tizes an eternity of human consciousness. Because even the ideas of the destructiveness of nature and the annihilation of mankind require human consciousness to give them their force, they thus are testimony to the necessity of the continuation of the human" ("Shelley's 'Mont Blanc': What the Mountain Said," in *Romanticism and Language*, ed. Arden Reed [Ithaca: Cornell Univ. Press, 1984], p. 210).

36 See Lisa Steinman, "Shelley's Skepticism: Allegory in *Alastor*," *ELH* 45 (1978), 255. *Alastor*'s use of repetition can be seen to reverse the "binding-down" and detouring of narrative desire that Peter Brooks finds to be characteristic of plot generally. In Brooks's reading of Freud's *Beyond the Pleasure Principle* as a "dynamic-energetic model of narrative plot," repetition serves to create a "postponement in the discharge" (sexual gratification or literary catharsis) that leads back to the quiescence in which the plot, like life itself, originates.

> Narrative . . . must ever present itself as a repetition of events that have already happened, and within this postulate of a generalized repetition it must make use of specific, perceptible repetitions in order to create plot, that is, to show us a significant interconnection of events. An event gains meaning by its repetition, which is both the recall of an earlier moment and a variation of it: the concept of repetition hovers ambiguously between the idea of reproduction and that of change, forward and backward movement. . . . We cannot say whether this return is a return *to* or a return *of*: for instance, a return to origins or a return of the repressed. (*Reading for the Plot: Design and Intention in Narrative* [New York: Random House, 1984], pp. 99–100)

The plot of *Alastor*, on the other hand, is not *developed* by means of repetitions; it *is* those repetitions and little else. The poem deploys repetition in reflexive fashion not to create a (representational) narrative but to undermine the possibility of one, thus explicitly dramatizing the dangerously uncanny nature of the Poet's attempted return to his transcendent origins.

Shelley's "reflexive" phrasings of the Poet's quest—"His wandering step Obedient to high thoughts" (106–07) leads him across "the wide pathless desart of dim sleep" (210) where, having "kept mute conference With his still soul" (223–24) and become at one point "Startled by his own thoughts . . . in his own deep mind" (297–99), he continues "Obedient to the light That shone within his soul" (492–93)—blasphemously echo the description of Jesus wandering into the desert in *Paradise Regained*, with the dream-maiden playing the role of Holy Spirit. Jesus, says Milton,

> One day walk'd forth alone, the Spirit leading,
> And his own deep thoughts, the better to converse
> With solitude, till far from the track of men,
> Thought following thought, and step by step led on,
> He enter'd now the bordering Desert wild,
> And with dark shades and rocks environ'd round,
> His holy Meditations thus pursu'd.   [I, 189–95]

It is generally accepted that such passages give grounds for regarding the dramatic action of *Paradise Regained* as largely internal to the hero. Shelley intended the Poet's quest to be taken the same way.

37 Cf. the essay "On a Future State," which argues that although one cannot logically refute the assertion of an afterlife, "it is enough that such assertions should be either contrary to the known laws of nature, or exceed the limits of our understanding, that their fallacy or irrelevancy to our consideration be demonstrated" (*CW*, 6:206).

38 G. W. F. Hegel, *The Phenomenology of Mind*, trans. J. B. Baillie, 2nd ed. (1807; New York: Harper Torchbooks, 1967), pp. 665–67. A more immediate prototype of the Poet's self-consuming subjectivity is the boy of Wordsworth's "Nutting." Compare Wordsworth's account of his voluptuous reverie amid a murmuring streamside bower not unlike the scene of the Poet's dream—"of its heart secure, / The heart luxuriates with indifferent things, / Wasting its kindliness on stocks and stones, / And on the vacant air" (40–43)—with the *Alastor* Poet's address to the departing swan: ". . . what am I that I should linger here, / With voice far sweeter than thy dying notes, / . . . / . . . wasting these surpassing powers / In the deaf air, to the blind earth . . .?" (285–89). But whereas the *Alastor* Poet moves ever deeper into this state of pure subjectivity, the boy Wordsworth reacts against it by tearing the bower apart, thus reaffirming the subject-object dialectic that Wordsworth, like Hegel, sees to be necessary to the growth of a poet's mind.

39 Thus the Narrator's closing remark that the Poet leaves "Those who remain behind, not sobs or groans, / The passionate tumult of a clinging hope, / But pale despair and cold tranquillity" (716–18) echoes the catharsis Milton prescribes at the close of *Samson Agonistes*: "His servants he [Samson] with new acquist / Of true experience from this great event / With peace and consolation hath dismist, / And calm of mind, all passion spent" (1755–58). Similarly, the Narrator's quotation of Wordsworth's phrase about woe "too deep for tears" recalls Manoa's repeated "Nothing is here for tears" (1721). Considering the deliberate bewilderment of Shelley's conclusion, however, these allusions only underscore how fully he rejects the return to the status quo ante implicit in Aristotelian catharsis.

Conclusion

1 *The Complete Poetry and Prose of William Blake*, ed. and rev. David V. Erdman, with commentary by Harold Bloom (Garden City, N.J.: Anchor, 1982), pp. 232, 121; henceforth cited as E.

2 Art thus replaces the church as the living body of Christ-Albion: "All things acted on Earth are seen in the bright Sculptures of / Los's Halls & every Age renews its powers from these Works," which represent "every little act, / Word, work, & wish, that has existed" (E, pp. 161, 157–58). This museum of intellectual beauty—better, call it the eternal artist's workshop, since its continual activity resists institutionalization—is for Blake the dwelling place

of basic human value. Cf. Morris Eaves, *William Blake's Theory of Art* (Princeton: Princeton Univ. Press, 1982), esp. pp. 56, 194–95.

Even Thomas Reid has to admit the existence of a principle akin to what Blake calls "the Poetical Genius," since he asserts that "language and all the fine arts" are grounded in an innate "natural knowledge of the connexion between these signs ['the features of the face, the modulations of the voice, and the motion and attitude of the body'], and the things signified by them ['the thoughts, purposes, and dispositions of the mind']" (*An Inquiry into the Human Mind on the Principles of Common Sense*, ed. William Hamilton, 2 vols., 8th ed. [1764; Edinburgh: James Thin, 1895], 1:121).

3 The organized form the reader finally constructs from the several different styles of the Romantic narrative poem can be seen to make up what Roland Barthes calls "our body of bliss . . . utterly distinct from . . . the text of grammarians, critics, commentators, philologists (the pheno-text)":

> Does the text have a human form, is it a figure, an anagram of the body? Yes, but of our erotic body. The pleasure of the text is irreducible to physiological need. . . . The pleasure of the text is that moment when my body pursues its own ideas—for my body does not have the same ideas I do. (*The Pleasure of the Text*, trans. Richard Miller [New York: Hill & Wang, 1975], pp. 16–17)

In Blake's terms, the pleasure of the text is that moment when we embrace the exhortation of Albion-Jesus to recompose the eternal human form divine: "wake! expand! / I am in you and you in me, mutual in love divine" (E, p. 146).

4 G. W. F. Hegel, *The Phenomenology of Mind*, trans. J. B. Baillie (1807; New York: Harper, 1967), p. 790.

5 Georges Poulet, "Criticism and the Experience of Interiority," in *The Structuralist Controversy*, ed. Richard Macksey and Eugenio Donato (Baltimore: Johns Hopkins Univ. Press, 1972), pp. 59–60. Like Poulet, the Romantics often describe poetry in reader-response terms as, in the words of Shelley's *Defence of Poetry*, "a going out of our own nature, and an identification of ourselves with the beautiful which exists in thought, action, or person, not our own." In Poulet's essentially Cartesian view of introspection, however, the author's consciousness is predominant:

> The consciousness inherent in the work is active and potent; it occupies the foreground; it is clearly related to its *own* world, to objects which are *its* objects. In opposition, I myself, although conscious of whatever it may be conscious of, play a much more humble role content to record passively all that is going on in me. A lag takes place, a sort of schizoid distinction between what I feel and what the other feels; a confused awareness of delay, so that the work seems first to think by itself, and then to inform me what it has thought. [p. 63]

For the Romantics, the aim is to relinquish such authorial predominance precisely because it is confined to "its *own* world."

6   David Hume, *A Treatise of Human Nature*, ed. L. A. Selby-Bigge, rev. P. H. Nidditch (1739–40; Oxford: Clarendon Univ. Press, 1978), p. 259.
7   Stanley Cavell, "Politics as Opposed to What?" *Critical Inquiry* 9 (1982):175–77.
8   *The Prelude* XI, 142–44, in *Selected Poems and Prefaces of Wordsworth*, ed. Jack Stillinger (Boston: Houghton Mifflin Co., 1965), p. 333.

Index

INDEXED IN: _Eng. Lit. Index_